D1190466

Risk and Response

Risk and Response

Management and Social Change in the American Insurance Industry

James E. Post
Boston University

Lexington Books
D.C. Heath and Company
Lexington, Massachusetts
Toronto

Library of Congress Cataloging in Publication Data

Post, James E.
Risk and response.

Bibliography: p.
Includes index.
1. Insurance–United States. 2. Insurance–Social aspects–United States. 3. Aetna Life & Casualty. I. Title.
HG8531.P67 658'.91'368973 76-3870
ISBN 0-669-00645-9

Published simultaneously in Canada.

Printed in the United States of America.

International Standard Book Number: 0-669-00645-9

Library of Congress Catalog Card Number: 76-3870

To Jeannette, Christopher,
and Margaret

Contents

List of Figures

List of Tables

Preface

The social environment, and particularly the way that environment changes, is becoming a central concern of modern management. It is unmistakable that postindustrial business environments are creating pressures that are not alleviated by, and therefore demand something other than, traditional responses to change. This book is concerned with social change and the way in which it has influenced and been influenced by the American insurance industry. Major themes in the industry's development have been identified and updated to the 1970s; the manner in which the industry and one of its leading firms have responded to several of the crucial issues of the past decade have been analyzed; an interpretation is given of the current relationship between the insurance industry and the changing goals of American society, and an assessment is made of what that changing relationship may mean in the years ahead.

Several lines of continuing research have been brought together in this book. For a number of years, the author has been analyzing the effect of change on specific private carriers, industry trade associations, and the life and nonlife segments of the insurance business. Secondly, a major concern with public policy as an expression of changing social values, and law as a means of implementing policy, has served to shape the analysis undertaken in this book. Finally, a growing interest in the strategies that managements of private sector and public sector organizations can develop in coping with various forms of social, political, and economic change has been directly served by this research.

The research underlying this book has been accomplished with the significant assistance of many executives, lawyers, and operating managers in the insurance industry, and from staff members at a number of state insurance departments and commissions. They have provided valuable information and have shared insights that have clarified and sharpened the focus of the research. Anonymity having been promised, I can only thank them and add that they know who they are.

Valuable comments and reviews have been received from Lee E. Preston, Carlos Kruytbosch, Robert Chatov, and Mark Van deVall, all of the State University of New York at Buffalo; from Dow Votaw of the University of California at Berkeley; Glenda Copes Reed of the Aetna Life and Casualty Company; and Hop Holmberg of Boston University. I am grateful to each of them for the time that was given and the thoughtful criticisms and suggestions they made. Dean Peter P. Gabriel and Associate Dean David Furer also offered encouragement throughout the writing process and I am grateful to them. Mary Byron and Lysa Loberfeld typed the major versions of the study and deserve a special note of thanks for their endurance and unfailing good humor. David Chidekel proved an able and talented research assistant whose assistance is much valued.

Institutionally, I am indebted to the Travelers Insurance Companies, which sponsored a research fellowship program in which I participated in 1972; to the Aetna Life and Casualty Company, which made available its library resources and provided the opportunity to research the manner in which corporate responses develop to multiple issues; to the General Electric Foundation, which provided financial support during the research phase of the project; and to the School of Management at Boston University, which provided assistance in the final preparation of the manuscript. The conclusions of the study, however, are the sole responsibility of the author, and not of the above named organizations.

1 Insurance and Social Change

Change and the Insurance Environment

In July 1741 the *Diligence* of Whitehaven, England returned from the James River area of Virginia in the North American colonies with a large cargo of tobacco. The sponsors of the voyage, including Daniel Dixon whose 5/16 ownership made him the leading financeer in the venture, had invested heavily in outfitting the ship, paying the crew, and purchasing provisions. Happily for them, the tobacco sold at high prices and yielded a dividend of more than 20 percent. In neither the year before nor the year after, however, did the cargos of the *Diligence* produce dividends for investors. In 1740 the supply of tobacco was plentiful when the ship arrived, and the price was depressed; in 1742 the *Diligence* required costly midvoyage repairs.

The risks of depressed markets and damaged vessels were only a few of the many risks encountered in the maritime trades in the eighteenth and nineteenth centuries. Storms, piracy, foreign seizure, and even mutiny were common risks of the day. In an age of limited communications, moreover, it was difficult for merchants to assess the nature of the risks that threatened their investments. Rather than let entire fortunes ride on the return of a ship whose status they couldn't possibly know for months, they often sought to minimize risks by inducing others to share in the voyage. As in the case of the *Diligence*, shares were sold to a group of investors. Later, a fee-for-service system arose where other merchants assumed an indemnification responsibility for a fraction of a cargo's worth. If the ship was lost, they would reimburse investors; if it returned safely, they would make a profit by keeping the fee. Such a syndicate to underwrite risk was the forerunner of the American insurance company. And the manner in which risk prompted innovative responses by the risk-bearers—first through fractional ownership, then through the insurance syndicate—foreshadowed a continuing pattern of industry development.

Organizations frequently arise as the creative response to a set of environmental circumstances and conditions. Once created, however, neither the organization nor the environment remain static. External conditions change, organizational goals and objectives change, and management is faced with the need for finding ways to effectively respond.

Change that has implications for the managers of organizations also has great consequence for society. Societies as well as individuals seek to use organizations as means to ends; and these societal ends and purposes also change.

Thus the manner in which organizations respond to social change is of concern to more than those persons and groups directly associated with the entity. Because organizations are a central fact of modern life, they become engulfed in the tension between our purposes as individuals and our collective purposes as members of social communities.[1] These purposes, with all of their inconsistencies, contradictions, and lack of logic are not readily reconciled. It is nevertheless important that both men and organizations make the attempt.

No organization, whether in the private or public sector, is immune to the effects of change. Even the social dominance some people ascribe to the modern corporations[2] does not mitigate the fact that they too, like governments or universities, must respond to a variety of social constraints, uncertainties, and environmental forces.

The ideological proposition that only economic change, or the economic effects of change, ought to be considered by managers in selecting a response must be specifically rejected.[3] Because social change affects organizations in ways that are not always, or ever, reflected in the marketplace alone, the long interlude that sometimes occurs between the first expression of a public concern and a change in the "rules of the game" which govern all organizations is a critical period for both management and society. Often it is during this period of new social expectations that the opportunity for adjustment of the gap between expectations and organization performance is greatest. Hence it is important to managers and the public that responses occur during this interim between the rising of a new social concern and a legislative or legal change.

The relations between an organization and its environment are neither inherently stable and harmonious nor necessarily conflicting or volatile. The relationship between most organizations and society includes elements of both harmony and conflict, and, of course, a particular organization's behavior can have both positive and negative consequences for society. Few conventional models of the organization-society relationship accommodate the reality of both harmonious and conflicting social relationships between a firm and the public. Yet it is this very interplay of conflict and harmony that characterizes reality and seems basic to an understanding of actual organization-environment interaction.[a]

As the relationship between an organization and its environment evolves over time, the simultaneous existence and interplay of conflict and harmony becomes increasingly conspicuous, continuously raising new issues. Two brief examples from the insurance industry illustrate the point and suggest the complexity of the evolution that occurs.

[a]These models are described in the next section of this chapter. Also discussed is the "interpenetrating systems" model, based on the work of Talcott Parsons. It departs from the other models and specifically recognizes the inherent existence of conflict and harmony in the relationship between the firm and society.

Example 1. The Union Fire Company was founded in 1735 as a fraternal organization whose members were pledged to fight fires. After fifteen years of operation, the members began to pool their money, thereby establishing a "mutual fund" to insure their own homes. Two years later, in 1752, they founded the Philadelphia Contributorship for Insurance of Houses from Loss by Fire, the first American fire insurance company. The sale of fire insurance spread widely in the United States, and before the twentieth century was several decades old, fire insurance coverage was required on mortgaged buildings as a protection for lenders. The great fires that occurred in Boston, Chicago, and San Francisco in the late 1800s and early 1900s resulted in the bankruptcy of some insurers but also reinforced the public's awareness of the need for insurance protection. The fire insurance industry has grown steadily throughout the twentieth century and fire insurance has become a virtual necessity for property owners.

Insurer assessments of the fire insurance business have changed however, and by the 1960s many insurers were seeking to limit the fire insurance coverage available to some sections of urban areas on the basis of large underwriting losses. Following the civil disorders that occurred during the summer of 1967, a number of insurers threatened refusal to write any insurance in the cities. The only alternative to such abandonment, according to the companies, was a government-sponsored reinsurance program that would protect the insurers against unanticipated riot-occasioned losses. In return, insurers would voluntarily attempt to provide inner city property owners access to additional fire insurance. Amid accusations that insurers were blackmailing the public, Congress enacted such a reinsurance plan in 1968.

Example 2. Unlike fire insurance, life insurance generally has not been considered a necessity by American families. Consequently, the growth of the American life insurance industry depended on salesmanship aimed at convincing the public of the need for life insurance protection. The archetype of life insurance salesmanship, and a major force in the industry's development, was Henry B. Hyde. As president of the Equitable, Hyde successfully combined aggressive selling, advertising, and a religious endorsement or two with a tontine life insurance policy that held out both the promise of security and speculative returns if one could outlive one's neighbors. Hyde's success occurred in the late 1800s, but the aggressive sales approach survived and propelled the industry to a point where, by 1969, total life insurance in force in the United States exceeded $1 trillion. New life insurance purchases in the same year had a face value exceeding $159 billion; among adults and families, 86 percent of the men and 74 percent of the women had some form of life insurance coverage. Annual life insurer income from policies in force amounted to more than $20 billion in 1969; investment income to life insurers amounted to $9.4 billion in the same year, based on assets of more than $197 billion.[4] Amid this apparent success, however, potentially serious change was occurring. Inflation was eroding the real value of life insurance and prompting a customer movement toward other forms of financial protection. At the same time, legislation that would compel insurers to invest reserves in specified geographic areas was being actively promoted in a number of states and discussed in Congress, In addition, consumer pressure was building for pricing disclosures and the simplification of policy terms.

These two brief examples illustrate the manner in which harmony becomes conflict and stable environments become unstable. Moreover, they suggest the great importance to management of anticipating, understanding, and responding to social change. Certainly, the issue of how, or whether, fire insurance can be provided to all properties exposed to fire risks is an important issue to insurers and society alike. Similarly, the flow of personal investor savings, the manner in which corporate investment decisions are made, and the degree of disclosure required in insurance transactions are issues of importance to both the industry and the public. Further, all these are issues about which the firms and segments of the public may take conflicting stands. How these issues are resolved and the implications that the process of resolution has for organizations and society make the topic of management and social change an important one.

Key Concepts

Perspectives on the relationship between management and society have been drawn from numerous areas of study, including law, economics, history, organization theory, sociology, political science, and moral philosophy, among others.[5] Agreements about the nature of the relationship, appropriate micro unit behavior, or both are infrequent. Given the great breadth of this background and the potential for semantic confusion that inevitably results from so many different perspectives, the principal terms that will be used in this study are identified and discussed in the remainder of this chapter.

Organizations as Systems

A *system* consists of two or more components, or subsystems, that interact with each other and are separated from other systems and their external environment by a boundary. Boundaries are not impenetrable, however, and organizations that interact with their environments are generally said to be *open systems.* An open system not only engages in interchanges with the environment but is one in which such interchange is an essential factor underlying the system's continuing viability and its ability to change.[6] In the context of systems theory, the social environment, or society, is generally described as a *suprasystem.* This suprasystem is relatively larger than any single organizational system and contains within it many such systems as well as other elements. The suprasystem thus constitutes the environment with which any individual organization exists and interacts. In these terms, the study of management-society relations is focused on the interactions that occur between individual organizational systems and the suprasystem that is their host environment.

Not all systems interact with all parts of the environment, nor to the same extent, nor in the same ways. Even within a single class of organizations, some are more open to environmental interaction than others; and within a single organization, openness may vary with hierarchical level or the type of activity involved.[7] Business enterprises are certainly open systems, highly dependent on interaction with the suprasystem for their existence and continuing operation. Yet even among firms in the same industry, considerable diversity exists in terms of their receptiveness and response to environmental stimuli.

Organizations differ in their responses to social change because of differing perceptions of that change or differing assessments of the implications of that change for the entity, or because of differing conclusions about a preferred future environment. In each case, it is the determination of management that shapes the eventual action of the organization. Thus it is important to recognize the internal organizational conditions that govern what form the response to change will take.

Management structures exist and managerial functions are performed in order to coordinate the activities of a number of people to achieve a common purpose or goal. An organization involves internal specialization and a hierarchy of authority and responsibility through which the specialized activities are coordinated and focused toward a common purpose.[8] The interest in and concern with the hierarchy of authority in organizations has contributed to the development of a general theory of bureaucracy. But that development, as Parsons points out, may have obscured the significance of the unique qualitative breaks attributable to specialization that occur within an organization.[9] These breaks are reflected in the three main internal subsystems of every organization: the technical, managerial, and institutional.[10]

Every organization has a technical core of activities that defines the special competencies of the enterprise. The *technical subsystem* involves those activities which are at the heart of the organization's existence. In the case of insurance companies (Table 1-1), the technical core consists of *underwriting*, wherein risk selections are made, and *investment*, wherein premium reserves are invested for the purpose of meeting future policy liabilities.

These two technical performances depend upon a set of input-output relations with the environment that include acquiring needed resources (applicants) and disposing of output (investment funds). These two sets of activities thereby constitute the technical core of the organization and require an overall capability for the coordination of resource procurement and output distribution.

Table 1-1
Subsystems of an Insurance Company

Technical Subsystem:

Underwriting, involving the selection of insurable risks and the calculation of rates.

Investment of insurance premiums in permissible investment options, such as land, municipal and industrial bonds, and common stocks.

Managerial Subsystem:

Coordination of underwriting and investment activities.

Sales activities designed to secure resources (candidates and premiums) for the underwriting and investment departments.

Settlement of claims that involve distribution of insurance reserve funds to legitimate claimants under insurance policies.

Institutional Subsystem:

Legal activities directed toward preserving the insurance fund for legitimate claimants.

Public relations activities directed at providing information and cultivating understanding of insurance activities.

Community and public affairs wherein the insurer's relationship with the local, state, and national communities in which it operates is preserved and cultivated (includes lobbying).

This coordination function is performed by the organization's *managerial subsystem.* In insurance companies (Table 1-1), the managerial subsystem particularly involves the *sale* of insurance policies and the *adjustment* of claims. Unlike the technical subsystem, which is concerned with internal relations among operating components, the managerial subsystem is especially concerned with the "markets" for the firm's product and the distribution of its output. These associations are vital to the performance of the technical subsystem, and intensive activity is needed to coordinate and maintain these lateral relations.

Parsons has argued that each of the organization's subsystems performs a unique function, distinct from, yet vital to, each of the others. Higher levels cannot command the lower levels to perform because the functions of each are qualitatively different.[11] In this context, the unique function of an organization's *institutional subsystem* is to secure social legitimacy for the organization and its activities. This is a function that is not performed through routine technical and managerial activities, for acquiring and maintaining social legitimacy involves a constant reassurance to society that the organization is performing the social role that is contemplated for it. Of course, society is neither monolithic nor represented by a single spokesman. Thus the institutional subsystem of the firm must constantly identify those elements of the suprasystem to which it must account in order to maintain its legitimacy.[b]

[b]This approach specifically acknowledges that power and influence are important features of the environment, but also that the holders of power and influence do change at times.

This discussion of organizational subsystems gives rise to several important questions about their development. Specifically, does the development of the technical subsystem precede that of the managerial and institutional subsystems? Also, what factors contribute to the particular pattern of development? At the level of the industry, another type of question arises: Is there a parallel pattern of technical, managerial, and institutional issues, interests, and concerns for the industry? If so, has the relative importance of these issues changed as the industry has developed? What factors account for the preeminence of one type of concern during a particular period of time? The growth of the insurance industry provides some tentative answers to these questions.

The history of the insurance industry indicates that the pattern of technical, managerial, and institutional development differed between the life and nonlife sectors of the industry. In the nonlife sector, the development of underwriting and investment knowledge (technical core) accompanied the significant development of such managerial aspects of the business as sales and claims settlement. In the life sector, actuarial principles (technical) predated most important sales and administration concepts (managerial). In both sectors, questions of legitimacy (institutional) arose with the industry's emergence and have been of continuing importance. In the mid-twentieth century, however, such questions have sparked broad public debates and have become a major problem for the industry. Thus, in both sectors of the industry, social change has impacted on the technical, managerial, and institutional aspects of the business.

The development of one insurer's internal subsystems is discussed at length in Chapter 8 and shows that technical, managerial, and institutional components have existed since the company's founding, although the structural and chronological development of the organizational subsystems varied with the pressures and demands of the times.

Relevant Publics

As an organization develops, the subsystems within it continue to interact with a variety of other organizations and groups in the environment. For insurance companies, the technical subsystem develops close associations with actuarial associations and groups concerned with professional underwriting standards. The managerial subsystem, being primarily concerned with premium levels, claims, and the maintenance of overall profitability, is primarily involved with current policyholders, potential clients, and competitors. The institutional subsystem, represented by legal staffs and political affairs specialists, pays particular attention to legislative bodies, state insurance departments, and the effect of political criticism on industry-related legislation.

The selective interaction of each of the subsystems with the environment is inherent in the concept of *relevant publics.* Not all segments of society are related to or affected by an organization; and those that are related to it are not related in the same way. Thus the composition of those segments of the suprasystem with which the organization interacts are likely to vary and change with time. One task of management is to continuously identify those segments of society that are relevant to the entity.[c] Attempts to describe the environment of the firm as consisting of a set of "constituencies" fail because they do not recognize that publics that are relevant at one point in time are not always relevant, nor are they relevant in the same way.

The subsystems of the organization also differ in the number of relevant publics with which they interact. The technical subsystem's contribution to the success of the organization involves dealing with relatively few external relevant publics. The managerial subsystem, responsible for resource procurement and output disposition, has a noticeably larger set of relevant publics with which it must be concerned; and the institutional subsystem, with its interest in preserving social legitimacy and negating public criticism, has a virtually unlimited number of relevant publics with which to be concerned. This arrangement of interests and interactions with the environment has serious implications for an organization. For example, although the insurer is an open system with many relevant publics, it is clear that the technical subsystem is the least open to external influence and the institutional is the most open. The perception of change and the assessment of its implications differ among subsystems, and the determination of alternative types of response reflect these differing interests. This, in turn, has a direct effect on how policy is made within the organization.

Organization Status[12]

The selective interaction that occurs between an organization and its relevant publics can be restated in terms of management's continuing efforts to maintain a hospitable environment. These attempts to create and maintain an atmosphere receptive to the organization's activities are actions taken to stabilize the environment and reduce uncertainty.[13] In fact, what these actions indicate is the organization's intention of interacting with its relevant publics in a way that will preserve its position, i.e., its *status.* In a sense, an organization's status refers to its place "in the scheme of things." Judgments about the scheme and the organization's place in it are continuously being made by relevant publics and the organization's management; those judgments variously result in criticism of,

[c]Definitions of society that are intent on capturing the concept of the whole are of limited usefulness in the analysis of the management-society relationship. See Gross [63]. Rather than rely on such definitions, the term *relevant public* suggests both a segment of the whole and one that has a special meaningfulness for the organization involved. Should management fail to identify a public that is in fact relevant to the organization, it can be anticipated that action will be initiated by that public to make management aware of its existence.

or support for, the organization. Thus the organization's status is the concern that is at the hub of a set of actions taken by management and relevant publics to adjust, amend, maintain, or change the organization and its environment.

The view that an organization is created for the purpose of accomplishing some socially endorsed task and that the organization has only to follow the "rules of the game" as defined by the suprasystem in performing its task underlies a *legal model* of the status of the organization. That is, the suprasystem defines the status of the organization when it grants the original charter of the organization's existence. Subsequently, that place "in the scheme of things" is altered as the suprasystem changes the rules of the game.

Whereas the legal model is grounded in political theory, a conceptually close economic model is the *market model*, which holds that the organization and society are collateral social systems, distinct and apart from one another, interacting solely through a process of exchange. That exchange occurs exclusively in the marketplace, thereby identifying both the framework for the exchange and the process through which it occurs. An alternative economic model that also assumes that the organization and society are collateral systems is the *exploitation model.* Here too the systems interact through the market, exchanging performances one for the other. The principal difference, of course, is that the exchange described in the exploitation model is overwhelmingly unidirectional in its outcome. An exchange of sorts occurs, to be sure, but it is always the organizational system that extracts a larger measure from society (surplus value) than it returns in exchange.

Both the market and the exploitation models assume that the only interaction occurring between the systems is exchange through the market process. The *technostructure model*, by contrast, recognizes that managers of organizations (or "technocrats," if one follows Galbraith) influence the basic social choices of other organizations, including government, and ultimately, the goals of society itself.[14] It is in its ultimate influence on the setting of social goals that the technostructure enjoys its greatest triumph, for in so doing, it ensures that the environment and the organization are harmonized in their purpose and social direction. See Table 1-2.

Organizational Action

Organizational action can be viewed as behavior undertaken to preserve status and/or to move the organization to a more preferred status (e.g., to move from number 2 in market share to number 1 by "trying harder"). The status models do not specifically identify the forms of organizational action that must occur within the framework of the model. Indeed, analyses of organizational action have often proceeded without reference to the underlying nature of the relationship between the organization and the environment. Two main directions

Table 1-2
Models of Organizational Status

Legal Model:

Microorganization has its charter from the suprasystem and its status involves the pursuit of its charter grant. Organization looks to such relevant publics as courts, legislature, and administrative agencies to identify rules of the game and changes therein.

Market Model:

Microorganization exchanges performances with relevant publics in the marketplace. Its activity is confined to the market process; it adheres to rules of the game as defined by suprasystem.

Exploitation Model:

Microorganization exchanges performances with relevant publics in the suprasystem through the market process. In each exchange, the microorganization extracts from the relevant public an extra measure–surplus value.

Technostructure Model:

Microorganization(s) dominate the values and goals of the suprasystem. Relevant publics include other members of technostructure in private sector and those in public sector. Unity of values develops among all technocrats.

have been taken in characterizing organizational action. One, following in the tradition of Cyert and March,[15] has concentrated on action that indicates the organization's efforts to adapt to its environment. The second view is a composite of many studies, some of which have an affiliation with the muckraker image of organizational action as being manipulative in nature. Organizational action, in this context, is an attempt to shape an environment that is more conducive and receptive to the organization's purposes. The contrast between the adaptive and manipulative models is stark, but also useful. Like the status models, behavior models are simple and abstract for the purpose of drawing critical differences. In fact, many specific actions taken by organizations are compatible with one or another of the models, and some actions can be interpreted as being of either type. Nevertheless, the two types of action models can be drawn in terms of critical components. These elements are summarized in Figure 1-1.

The *adaptive model* begins with the assumption that there are various "states" of organization-environment relations in which the organization can operate. Some states are surely more preferred than others by management. When an external disturbance occurs, change is introduced into the relationship between the organization and its environment. The disturbance prompts management to respond in a way that moves the organization to the most preferred available state. This is accomplished by management's assessment and evaluation of the change, its consideration of internal decision variables, and the application of known and previously used decision rules (e.g., never bargain with protesters on the first day). The external shocks and their influence on the internal decision variables of the organization serve to change the actual state of the organizational system's relations with the environment. Whether the new state is a more preferred or less preferred state determines the likelihood that the decision rule will be used again in the future.[16]

The manipulative model also begins with the assumption that there are preferred states, or sets of conditions, in which the organization can operate. Managerial dissatisfaction with present conditions or a desire to improve conditions can prompt initiative taking by the organization to create change. The *manipulative action model* holds that an organization acts to change the environment before external shocks occur. Management continuously analyzes its internal decision variables (synonymous with "interests") and applies previously successful decision rules in an effort to change the environment and achieve a state of external conditions that are most preferred for the organization's operations. Actions taken to influence the environment and create the preferred state include cooptation, bargaining, lobbying, representation, and the socialization of relevant publics. In principle, management can authorize any action that will incrementally improve the opportunities for the achievement of organizational goals.[17] As in the adaptive model, decision rules and actions that successfully lead to a preferred state are likely to be used again in the future; those that fail will not; thus the organization's management undergoes a learning process whether its behavior is adaptive or manipulative in nature.

The adaptive and manipulative models of organizational action apply to all of the status models discussed above. Even though one type of behavior may be more theoretically consistent with a particular status model, the other mode of action may also occur, if only as a deviant case. In Figure 1-2 the status and action models are linked together, and examples of adaptive and manipulative action are identified for each combination.

Interpenetrating Systems

The existence of distinct subsystems within an organization, each interacting with a set of relevant publics, points to the great number of individual interchanges between the organization and society. Presumably, much conflict as well as harmony is involved as the organization and society interact over time. Hence, as the relationship lengthens, the number of interactions increases and the complexity of the organization-environment relationship grows in two distinct ways.

First, more complex means develop within the organization for dealing with external forces. As open systems become more complex, increasingly complex mediating processes are developed for the purpose of intervening between external forces and the organization.[18] Secondly, the systems each acquire some power to influence the other. The organization develops a capacity to affect the environment, a condition that allows efforts to shape the environment for the organization's purposes. Management can initiate action designed to stimulate or alter the behavior of other actors who are relevant publics for the organization.[19]

The emergence of these two developments–more complex means within the organization for mediating external forces and the ability of the organization to shape the environment as well as respond to it–make it inappropriate to discuss the relationship between a firm and the suprasystem solely in terms of market

A. *Adaptive Model*

Characteristics

1. Preferred "states" of organization-environment relations
2. External disturbances or shocks
3. Internal decision variables and decision rules
4. External shocks and decision variables change the state of the system
5. Decision rules that lead to the preferred state are likely to be used again; those which lead to a nonpreferred state are less likely to be used in the future.

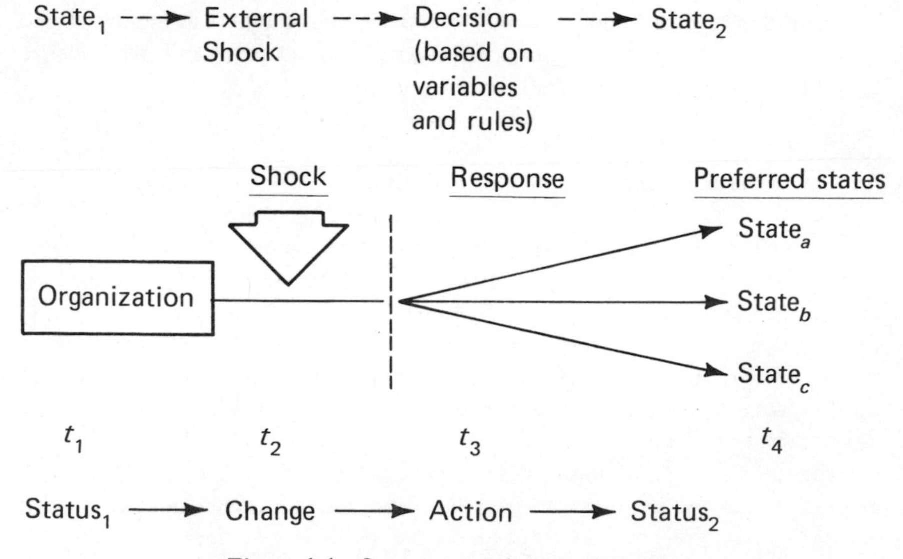

Figure 1-1. Organizational Action Models.

B. *Manipulative Model*

Characteristics

1. Preferred states of organization-environment relations
2. Internal decision variables and decision rules
3. Application of decision rules to change the state of the environment through:
   (a) Cooptation, as through sharing responsibility or sharing power;
   (b) Bargaining, as through attempts to cooperate and achieve accommodation;
   (c) Lobbying, as to influence decisions of other relevant publics;
   (d) Representation, as to develop networks and associations of relevant publics;
   (e) Socialization, as by convincing other relevant publics of organizational values.

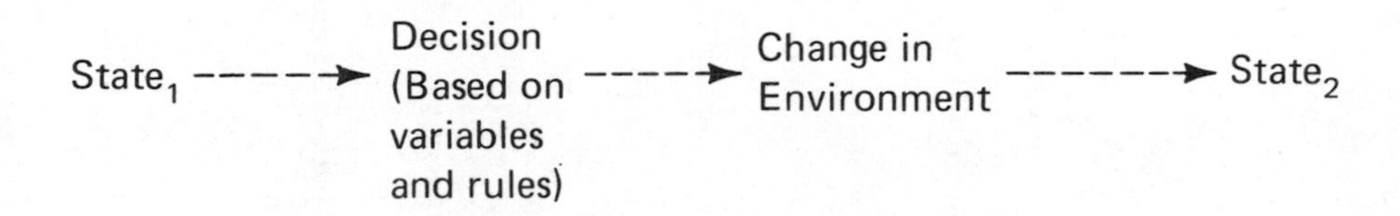

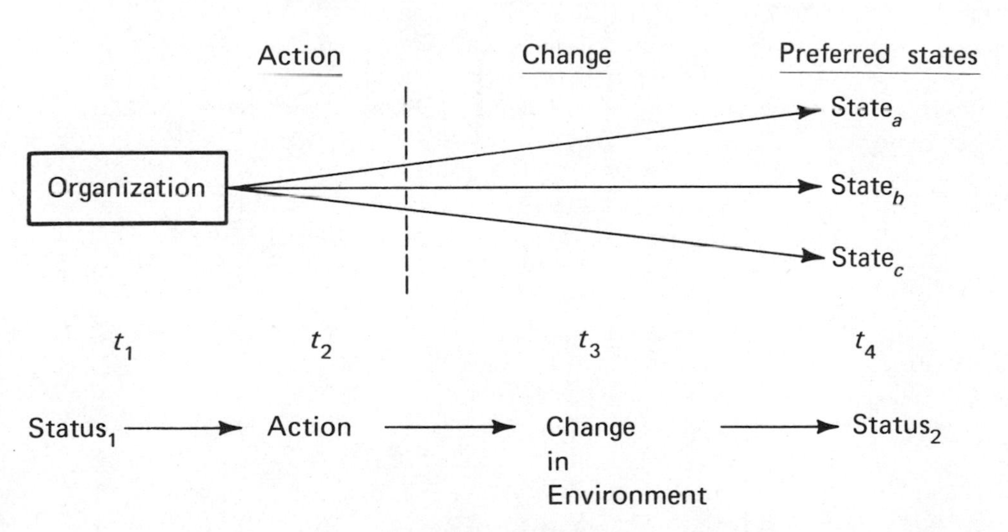

Figure 1-1. (continued)

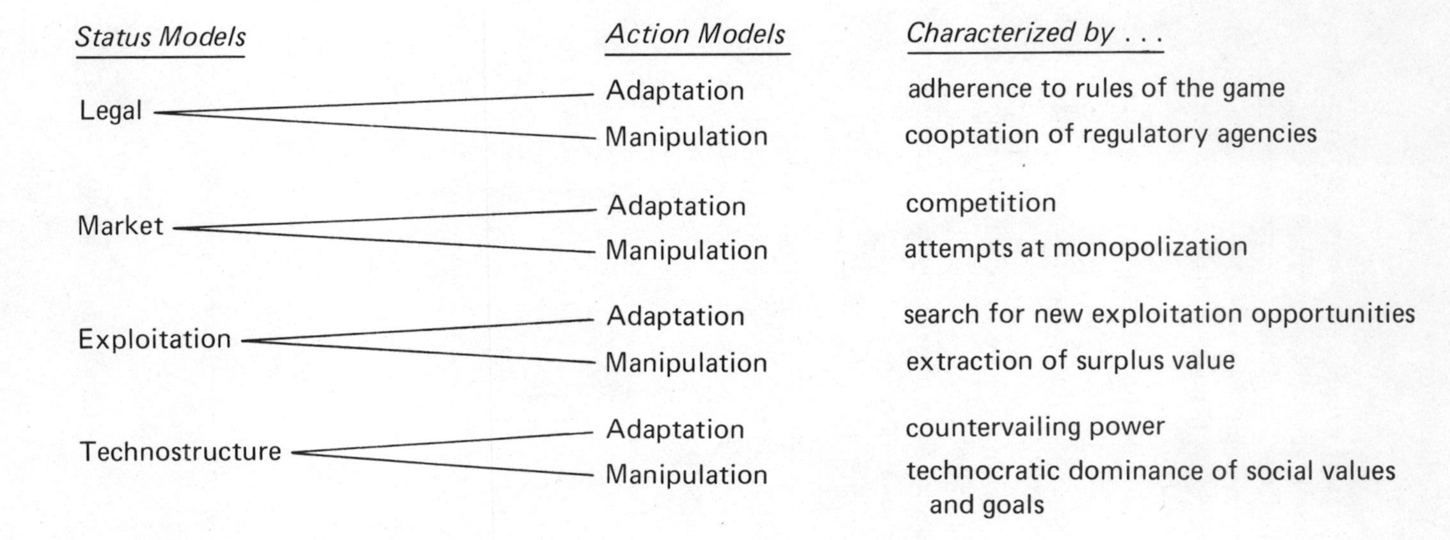

Figure 1-2. Organizational Status and Action: A Typology.

actions (including exploitive ones) or legal status. The firm and society are not collateral social systems, and they do not interact in only one way. Indeed, a key shortcoming of the conventional market and legal models is their inability to explain management action that obviously occurs on a regular basis but that is outside the market process. The technostructure model, as described in Galbraith's writings, is founded on that very shortcoming. It is Galbraith's attempt to explain activities that are inconsistent with conventional legal and economic notions of the relationship between the firm and society that led him to conclude that the basic relationship itself differed from that assumed in the conventional models.

Of course, the technostructure model also assumes that the organization (via the technocrats) will inevitably come to dominate the relationship with the environment. As a description of reality, that conclusion seems faulted. Even granting that some integration of organization and suprasystem values may occur, it still seems clear that society, in the form of relevant publics, influences the values of the organization. It is this continuing ability of each system to influence the other, as well as to be influenced, that suggests that the technocratic model is not yet an accurate description of social reality. An alternative view, and one that specifically recognizes the continuing ability of each social system to influence the other, is that which treats the organization-environment relationship as one involving *interpenetrating systems.*

According to Talcott Parsons, when two or more analytically distinguishable relational systems constitute partial determinants of process in a concrete empirical system, the systems are interpenetrating in nature.[20] The interpenetrating systems model[21] of the organization-environment relationship assumes that the organization and suprasystem are more than collateral systems engaged only in exchange. Yet the organization is neither dominated by the suprasystem, as the legal model assumes, nor capable of dominating the suprasystem, as the technostructure model describes. The interpenetrating systems model emphasizes that the systems are related and that they interact in a variety of ways and through processes that the systems themselves shape. In this context, the interpenetrating systems model is the broadest of the status models in terms of potential processes of interaction between the firm and society; it is also the least rigid in terms of the patterns of legitimate action that can occur within the framework of the model.

As discussed above, each of the status models assumes that only an adaptive or manipulative pattern of action will be consistent with the organization's status in society. Yet other types of action occur, thereby raising the issue of deviant organizational behavior. The difficulty that exists for the student of organization-environment relations is that analysis of actual organizational behavior shows that both adaptive and manipulative actions occur and, more importantly, that both are legitimate within the framework of the American political economy. Equating adaptive and manipulative action with permissible and deviant behavior is acceptable if one begins with, and adheres to, a single status model. If the starting point for analysis is observation or the recognition that none of the models entirely explains reality, however, the acceptability of the equation breaks down.

The interpenetrating systems model avoids this intellectual problem by permitting one to begin with a factual framework, namely, the American political economy. Recognizing that conflict and harmony between organizations and individuals are inherent in this setting and that organizations will act to change the environment as well as react to it, the interpenetrating systems model allows the discussion of the management-society relationship to focus on the processes through which interchange occurs, the manner in which the parties affect these processes, and the effect of this interchange on the organization and society over time. In this way, it becomes plausible to consider the possibility of modes of organizational behavior other than the adaptive and manipulative and to search for structural features in the interpenetrating relationship that might account for specific patterns of organizational action (Table 1-3).

There are a number of variables related to the interpenetration between specific organizations and society that require brief clarification. First, the *scope* of the interpenetration reflects the extensiveness of the overall relationship between an organization and society, and differs considerably among organizations. The range of activities in which the firm engages, the number of communities in which it operates, and the size of its employment, purchasing, and charitable contributions budgets all help to define the scope of its interpenetration.

A second variable is the degree of *salience* perceived by either the organization or society with regard to a particular issue. Some matters are extremely important to the organization, others less so; the same is true with respect to the relevant publics. Hence in discussing salience we must distinguish between an issue's salience to the organization (internal salience) and its salience to society (external salience). To illustrate, job safety is a matter of general

Table 1-3
Interpenetrating Systems

Definition:

Microorganization and suprasystem are related through a number of interaction processes that *both* systems influence and shape. Relevant publics are constantly changing, both in number and composition; organization interacts through market and public policy processes and has other unstructured contacts.

Relevant Action Modes:

1. Adaptation
2. Manipulation
3. Other Action Modes
4. Inaction

social concern. But it is a matter of less concern in a clerical work setting (low internal salience) than in an automobile assembly plant (high internal salience). Salience may also be reflected in the intensity of relevant public's responses. General employment layoffs are sure to produce some discontent in a community (external salience), but the layoff of affirmative action participants is likely to provoke a more intense and concentrated response. The latter has a very high external salience to at least one relevant public, the affirmative action employees.

A third factor with which interpenetration varies is the *continuity* of the relationship. That is, to what extent are the contacts between the organization and specific elements in society temporary and transient as opposed to permanent and lasting? A firm with only a transient connection to a local community—an out-of-state mail order firm, for example—has a significantly different relationship than a large employer or a firm involved in a twenty-year industrial development lease requiring municipal improvements. The actual or contemplated continuity of the relationship differs greatly between the situations and identifies important dimensions of the relationship between the firm and society.

Purpose and Organization of this Study

It was several years ago that Lee Preston and I initially sought to analyze and categorize various approaches to the study of the relationship between managed organizations and society. We found in the social systems literature a rich source of concepts and a lexicon of terminology that facilitated the comparative analysis of other approaches to the subject and suggested a new model of the management-society relationship. It was in the course of this work that the interpenetrating systems model was conceived.

The publication of *Private Management and Public Policy* [136] marked the initial application of our systems concepts to the practical problems of the business firm's relations with society. As we saw it at the time, those problems tended to revolve about two central questions: (1) What is the scope of the responsibility of the firm for its effects and consequences on society? (2) By what criteria should the firm be judged in assessing whether or not it has met its responsibilities? In the course of responding to these questions, our argument raised other questions and issues that could not be resolved without additional research. *Risk and Response* is the product of one phase of that research and is an attempt to deal forthrightly with a number of those previously unanswered questions.

Risk and Response attempts to accomplish three objectives. First, an effort has been made to articulate and amplify some of the relatively new concepts and intellectual tools provided by the systems literature and to relate them to the manner in which managed organizations interact with society over time. The interpenetrating systems approach is specifically employed as a device for sharpening our understanding of how one important industry has influenced, and been influenced, in its continuing relationship with the American public.

The American insurance industry is a complex amalgam of private and public sectors and interests whose roots are deep in the nation's history. Traditional analyses of the industry have favored an historical interpretation that emphasizes a changing public interest and industry responsiveness to that interest. There is considerable evidence, however, that more prurient interests governed insurer behavior at various times. Such behavior also had an important effect on shaping the industry's relation with the American public, but conventional analyses seemed strangely unable to integrate such effects within their guiding theses. On the other hand, analyses that emphasize the chauvinistic interest of insurers generally fail to acknowledge the public interests that have genuinely been served by a mature American insurance industry. Because of the shortcomings of previous analyses, this study also attempts to analyze anew the emergence of the American insurance industry. The use of a systems framework has shed light on important elements in the industry's development that have not been analyzed elsewhere, and at the same time, this study has served to sharpen our own understanding of the limits and strengths of the interpenetrating systems model.

The third purpose of the study was to focus on the question of how an individual organization simultaneously faced with many issues of change developed the policy and action responses for coping with the issues. Many studies in the management-society area focus on how an individual firm or industry responds to one issue (e.g., pollution or minority affairs) over a period of time. These studies highlight intraindustry differences and result in hypotheses as to why one firm differs from another in its response. But these studies do not approach the question of how the management of one firm copes with a variety of issues over time. Hence issues of management policy formation, internal dissonance and dissent, and organizational learning are avoided. These are some of the central issues in the dynamics of dealing with change, and they are not well developed in the management literature. Therefore this study was designed to deal with the multiple issue and organizational policy questions mentioned above. The opportunity to examine a single firm's responses to a variety of issues affords the researcher an opportunity to learn much about internal processes and, ultimately, about patterns of response to change.

It was pointed out in the preceding section of this chapter that interpenetration between a firm and society can be expected to vary with such factors as the scope or extent of the involvements between the firm and the public, the salience to each of current issues, and the continuity of the relationship between the actors. Not surprisingly, the remainder of this book is organized in a way that affords a more detailed examination of each of these dimensions.

The broad scope of the relationship between the American insurance industry and American society is discussed in Chapters 2 and 3. Since insurance is an item of commerce founded on an idea rather than a consumable product, it is required that we look at the underlying ideas of risk, insurance as a risk treatment, and the public interest as important factors in an industry based on, as Louis Brandeis once noted, "other people's money." Chapter 2 concentrates on these ideas and the ideologies that have emerged around them. Chapter 3, in turn, deals with the factual history associated with the creation of insurance markets in the United States and the means by which insurers influenced and responded to those markets. The material discussed in Chapters 2 and 3 is the basic information upon which various critical interpretations have also been based. The conventional interpretations of this history are reviewed in Chapter 4, and a basis is prepared for distinguishing conventional analyses from that developed in this study.

The history of the relationship between the insurance industry and American society is often expressed in the pressures for the invocation of public policy. In Part II (Chapters 5 and 6), the salience of a constantly changing agenda of public issues involving the insurance industry is discussed. The manner in which public policy has evolved, including the specific history of insurance regulation in the United States, highlights the changing importance of various issues associated with the sale of insurance, its promotion to the public, and the behavior of those who propose to sell it. Important in an historical sense, this evolution is also germane to the understanding of how society articulates new expectations and brings them to the attention of an entire industry. The continuing importance of the public policy process, therefore, is fundamental to an understanding of more recent trends and changes in the environment of the insurance industry.

Part III of the study concentrates on the insurer-society relationship since the 1960s. Chapter 7 includes a discussion of the changing public issues agenda for the industry during the 1960s and 1970s. The rapid growth in the number of issues and the areas of changing public expectations underscores the complexity of the environment in which insurers now operate. As a prelude to understanding how a particular firm develops patterns of response to change, a brief review of the history and business strategy of Aetna Life and Casualty is presented in Chapter 8. Aetna's status as an industry leader in sales, competitive behavior, and in response to social change make it an interesting case study in management policy formation. A discussion of the Aetna's specific responses to several important areas of social change is presented in Chapter 9. Overall, Part III emphasizes the individual firm's ability to respond to change and the importance that the continuity of the relationship between the firm and its relevant publics has in guiding management responses to social change.

Having analyzed the variables affecting the existing interpenetration between the industry and society in Parts I, II, and III, an effort is made in Part IV to synthesize the results of two hundred years of management-society interaction and to suggest something of the direction this relationship may take in the next quarter century. These ideas are presented in Chapter 10, and the argument is made that the ideology of insurance has found its foremost expression in the emergence of the "insurance state."

In conclusion, this study is an analysis of the continuing relationship between a particular industry and society; moreover, it is a broader study of the internal and external processes associated with managed organizations and social change.

Notes

1. See Lawrence and Lorsch [92] p. 99.

2. Galbraith [57].

3. The argument is most readily associated with such economists as Milton Friedman [55] and Frederick Hayek [69]; an argument founded in political considerations is presented in McConnell [104].

4. All data derived from Institute of Life Insurance [76].

5. See Preston [134] for a review.

6. See Buckley [20], p. 50, for a discussion.

7. Maurer [101] notes that every organization is open to environmental influence, but some are more open than others. A business or political organization is more open than a monastery or prison.

8. See Schein [141] chapter 2.

9. Parsons [123] chapter 2.

10. Parsons [123] p. 60.

11. Parsons [123] p. 66.

12. A more complete discussion of these models is contained in Preston and Post [136].

13. In this regard see Thompson [156] and Lawrence and Lorsch [91].

14. On the making of basic social choices in underdeveloped as well as industrialized nations, see Robinson [139]. The frequent presence of technical advisors from industrialized nations makes the technostructure argument germane in underdeveloped as well as developed nations.

15. Cyert and March [36].

16. The elements of this model are most clearly presented in Cyert and March [36].

17. The manipulative model is not generally identified as such, but Hellriegel and Slocum [70] do discuss elements of the model and provide a

useful introduction. Hall [66] discusses elements of the model in the context of changing organizational goals; and Thompson [156] and Cyert and March [36] describe organizational action that is consistent with such a model.

18. See Buckley [20] p. 58.
19. Cohen and Cyert [32] p. 352.
20. Parsons [122] p. 649.
21. See Preston and Post [136] chapter 2.

Part I
Interpenetration and the American Insurance Industry

2 The Ideologies of Insurance

Insurance and Social Values

It was pointed out in Chapter 1 that the interpenetration that exists between a firm, or industry, and society depends upon a number of variables including the scope or breadth of the systems' involvement over time. In analyzing the interpenetration that has evolved between the insurance industry and the American public it is readily apparent that more than the numerical indicia of jobs, products, and gross sales have influenced the relationship. To an extent that is not true in most manufacturing industries, there is a necessary symmetry of social values between insurers and the public. This symmetry, in turn, has had a crucial effect on the development of the industry and the behavior of insurers. In this chapter we briefly introduce risk as the underlying concept upon which insurance is based and the public policy process as the forum in which many new social expectations have been communicated to the industry. Each of these matters is amplified in succeeding chapters.

The bulk of this chapter is devoted to a consideration of the way in which social values and insurer values have affected the interpenetration that has developed during the nineteenth and twentieth centuries. These values, or *ideologies* as we shall refer to them, help to explain the motivations that have guided insurer behavior in America and comprise an important factor in prediciting insurers' responses to new issues of social change.

Risk and Insurance

There is a virtual consensus among insurance historians that risk is the essential problem to which insurance provides an answer. Human beings readily recognize the existence of certain kinds of risks, or risk situations, and also demonstrate an anxiety for finding a way of protecting against the losses those risks can produce. It is important to note that risk exists only in the perception of an observer—that is, what otherwise exists as a natural condition becomes a risk when someone observes that condition and perceives it to be of danger to a person or property. This is a point not often stressed by professors of insurance, but it is fundamental to understanding how changes in social values affect the insurance industry.

The dangers of an untimely death, storms at sea, and fire have been recognized for centuries as risks for which protective steps might be taken. Among those steps have been the development of life insurance, marine insurance, and fire insurance. Of more recent vintage is the public awareness of the risk inherent in old age, poor health, unemployment, and defective products. For these matters too, protective steps have been taken to minimize the adverse effects. The characterization of risk as a basic human problem, and of insurance as a means for minimizing the seriousness of the problem, is as applicable to the range of major insurance problems in the 1970s as in the past. Hence problems such as health care, crime, legal services, floods and natural disasters, automobiles, boats, snowmobiles, and even overseas investment risks are all within the purview of modern insurance practice. The agenda of important social and personal problems changes with time. The existence of the insurance principle and the knowledge of its repeated and diverse use in the past render it a fundamental social tool in coping with these problems. It is not only a matter of convenience, it is the result of a societal acceptance of insurance as a basic means (and perhaps *the* basic means) of dealing with risk.

Risks are not of equal magnitude, nor are they of equal importance to the risk bearers.[1] The risk bearer may not recognize the risks accompanying a given course of conduct; and for those that are recognized, a judgment may be made to ignore them or allow them to take a "normal" course. The latter situation is one in which the risk-bearer in effect calculates that the cost of inaction (possible loss multipled by the liklihood of occurrence) is less than the cost of acting to safeguard against the loss.

Safeguards are positive treatments of risk and are of three types: those that eliminate the risk, those that reduce it, and those that negate or minimize the effect of the risk event.[2] Insurance is a means of effecting the latter approach, although modern insurance practice often includes advisement as to the means for eliminating or reducing risks.[a]

The fundamental principle upon which insurance practice has been based for several centuries is a simple one: pooling of risk. When a group of persons that are all subject in general to the same foreseeable event (e.g., fire) pool a sum of funds, it becomes possible for those who actually do suffer the event to recover from the "risk pool." Those who do not suffer the event within the calculated time period have, in effect, purchased a conditional promise of protection, the condition being the occurrence of the event. Such a principle extends to virtually all forms of insurance other than life insurance. For life insurance, the unpredictable risk event is the *time* of death, not death itself. Thus participants in a life insurance pool receive protection against an *untimely* (or premature) death.[3]

The circumstances and public attitudes regarding risk have changed dramatically over the course of several hundred years. Religious doctrines that once

[a]Many property and casualty companies have created engineering departments for this purpose.

viewed insurance as violating the expressed will of the Lord have given way to ministerial endorsement of specific insurance plans and, in the extreme case, specific companies;[4] growing commercial needs have stimulated the development of marine, fire, and assorted casualty coverages; and large-scale demographic and attitudinal changes have contributed changing conceptions of the private-public balance in the provision of insurance. These ideas about risk and the appropriate ways of dealing with it have directly changed insurance practice in many ways. More importantly, they have often served to reinforce—and occasionally inhibit—trends that had developed within the industry itself. Where conflicts developed, or where various legal and nonlegal barriers existed to inhibit change, ideas were worked out in the public policy process.

Public Interests and Public Policy

Throughout its history insurance has been a subject of public policy consideration and action. In one respect, this reflects an awareness of the broad interests of the public in an activity that promises to protect them from the effects of risk in return for payments that are supposed to form a fund from which claims can be paid. In another way, public policy relating to insurance is a manifestation of a larger history of public concern about the organization of industry in the United States. Traditionally, three broad alternatives have dominated public choice about how to organize economic activity: the activity may be left to the development of market forces, the state may undertake to perform the activity on its own as a public enterprise, or the state may regulate, to some greater or lesser extent, the development of market forces. In the United States, insurance has almost never been treated as a matter suitable for market regulation alone, and state regulations have long governed both the creation of insurers and their legitimate activities. In part, this reflected English experience with insurance regulation; but it also reflected special American concerns with concentration of government, as well as economic power, and a distaste for government enterprise. The result was a state, not federal, system of insurer regulation that has been frequently questioned in terms of its effectiveness but that has also generally prevailed.

In the twentieth century another major public policy change has occurred, as a number of public, government-sponsored insurance programs have been devised and implemented. Since the mid-twentieth century, the result has been a modern insurance industry that is an amalgam of market forces, regulatory restrictions on insurer status and operations, and public insurance programs. Within this framework, American society has developed a set of expectations about insurer performance that identifies and defines the industry's status. At the level of the firm, these are the social expectations of a company's relevant publics. Since many expectations are reflected in the market actions of relevant publics, the market is one process insurers observe carefully. Because expectations are also manifested through the public policy process, this too is a process that insurers must observe closely. Thus, in addition to being a device for adjusting interests, the public policy process is a means of communication, a device through which relevant publics can convey their approval, disapproval, expectations, and anticipations of insurer actions.

Responses to Risk: The Ideology of Insurance[5]

Ideas about risk and the need to create means for minimizing its adverse economic and social consequences have changed continuously and have been instrumental in the industry's development. For convenience, we distinguish between general social thought about insurance (*societal ideology*) and views held within the industry (*insurer ideology*). Though there has been considerable overlap between the two ideologies, there have also existed areas of conflict, many of which have been resolved through the use of the public policy process. In the remainder of this chapter we concentrate on the general themes of ideological development in the United States. Three general time periods are involved: the *preindustrial* period, including colonial America; the *industrial* period, from the early 1800s to the mid-1900s; and the *postindustrial* period, ranging from the mid-twentieth century to the present.

The Preindustrial Period

The preindustrial period was characterized by long-standing social attitudes supporting mutual assistance to community members. The social view of risk and the need for risk-reducing associations were expressed in the kinds of social organizations that people formed. Among the earliest forms of human social organization was the tribal association, which was a pooling of resources for community purposes, ultimately organized on a principle of consensual membership. As the tribe gave way to the extended family association, the new organizing principle was patrimonial authority, although the purpose of mutual assistance to each group's members remained.

The societal ideology favoring mutual assistance continued during the ascendancy of the village system and its outcome, feudalism, though greater faith was increasingly placed in the specialized provider of security, the landlord. Where mutual assistance was exchanged for group membership alone in earlier forms, feudalism demanded loyalty to the landlord, as well as group membership, in exchange for security.

With the rise of the town, the need for new organizations to provide security increased. The tribal association had been unified by consent, the family by patrimonial affiliation, and the feudal village by the land. None of these organizing principles were inherent in the town. The social response to this need for security was the formation of such new organizations as the guild. The restrictiveness of guild membership created a new demand however: the need to justify the limiting of security to a restricted few. The guild represented a refusal to aid all members of a social community equally and, hence, was a repudiation of the mutual assistance principle. To reinforce the commitments of guild members and legitimate their social power, ideologies developed that linked craftsmanship, apprentice training, and the welfare of the craftsman and the townspeople to the guilds.

The Church offered an alternative to this particularization of security by assisting the unprivileged but was unable to significantly influence an evolving societal ideology that favored commercial development. As commercial development occurred, greater faith was placed in competitive efforts and risk-taking in pursuit of private gain. Nevertheless, wealthy and successful merchants were reluctant to risk their entire fortunes on such single ventures as sea voyages. The rise of marine insurance evolved from this desire to profit, but not at the risk of losing all. In England commercial underwriters performed the insurance service; in colonial America this need gave rise to coalitions of merchants who underwrote shares of each other's voyages, thereby spreading the risk of loss among them. Thus amid an incipient commercialism, the principle of mutual aid—albeit, in a highly particularized form—also became a part of the American insurance tradition.

In summary, the preindustrial period witnessed a social recognition of the need to provide security against risk and the formation of a variety of means to satisfy that end. Beginning with cohesive and embracing social arrangements and extending to the development of specialized organizations, mutual assistance began to break down as commercialism and social individualism ascended. Insurance had become a commercial venture, subordinating the principle of mutual assistance to that of private profit.

Industrialization

In granting an organization the power to sell insurance, gather public funds, and become a repository of the public's security, a fear arose in some quarters that too much power was being vested in these commercial ventures. Thus, even in the colonial period, the charters establishing insurance companies granted only limited powers. Perhaps reflecting the bitter British experience with insurance company failures and swindles during the early 1700s, it seemed that such companies were to be endorsed only where other social forms of security were insufficient. Thus, at the outset, the insurance market was less a positive creation of public policy than an accommodation to the inability of other social units to provide security from risk.

Given the public animosity and skepticism that attended the founding of American insurers, it is not surprising that the early insurance companies found it important to develop a redeeming social ideology, a set of ideas and views that would legitimate their existence. Insurers faced a dual problem: first, there was the need to convince the public that commercial companies, organized for the profit of their owners, were desirable means of supplying insurance protection; and second, the public must be convinced of the necessity for these companies to operate in an unfettered manner in the course of supplying these services to the market. These needs gave rise to what Reinhard Bendix identifies as "entrepreneurial ideologies," ideas espoused by those who exercise authority in economic enterprises that seek to explain or justify that authority.[6] The insurer ideology was therefore composed of ideas that both justified the grants of power made to the companies by state legislatures and identified the emerging commercial nature, as opposed to the mutual assistance ethic, of insurance.

Once insurance was accepted as a legitimate item of sale, the market for it expanded. Commercial growth and westward expansion opened new markets; risks increased in number and were more diverse in character, conditions that stimulated the expansion and diversification of lines of coverage. The service nature of insurance meant, however, that its status as a necessity depended upon its appeal to the public's mind. In that respect, insurance was inexorably linked to current social thought.

Three important tenets of social thought in the nineteenth century constituted the intellectual foundation upon which the insurance industry was built. The first was the notion of *private*. Specifically, it was the *privatization of risk* that enabled the insurance industry to develop. By the 1800s, risk was no longer perceived as a community matter. Privateness also extended to property, and the current of thought that supported the protection and preservation of one's own property provided latent support for the use of insurance to meet that end.

A second important theme in American social thought was that of *individualism*. Individualism, in the sense that it suggested self-reliance and independence, was a much proclaimed virtue in the nineteenth century.[7] As applied to insurance, individualism took an important twist. Since insurance involved reliance on the promised protection of a third-party insurer, it was not entirely harmonious with the idea of independence. However, insurance indemnity payments negated the need to depend on one's neighbors, relatives, or the community, and thereby reinforced one's independence.

Self-reliance was reinforced by a third intellectual theme, the *idealization of self-interest*. Self-interest has been the intellectual justification for competition and competitive behavior in American society for several hundred years. As an ethic it has justified the promotion of most American products and services, including insurance. The purchase of insurance, according to the sales pitch, is a purchase of protection that will safeguard one's property, further business independence and freedom from creditors and lendors in times of need, and promote personal welfare. If one cannot afford the loss, one cannot afford to be without insurance!

This triune of intellectual themes—privatization, individualism, and self-interest—proved to be powerful among businessmen. The search for security from risk ranged far beyond marine and fire insurance and stimulated the development of many new liability and casualty lines of coverage. Salesmen found interested and responsive buyers throughout the nation.

A fourth element of social thought in the nineteenth century was *family responsibility*. While this theme had relatively little influence in nonlife areas, it was an important element in the evolution of life insurance. The responsibility that one owed to a family, in death as in life, was a theme traceable to ancient times when membership in burial societies enabled a man to create an estate for his survivors. Yet the idea of family responsibility was not sufficient, by itself, to spark the great growth of the American life insurance industry. Too many alternatives existed for those who wished to leave an estate, especially real property (land). For the life insurance industry to grow, the product needed to appeal to chords of American life other than responsibility.

What life insurance needed was a product that appealed to the other dominant aspects of prevailing social thought: private gain, individualism, and self-interest. By the 1860s, Henry Hyde's speculative tontine plan was as attractive an investment as stocks, securities, or land. Ostensibly, it provided the security of life insurance with the chance to realize an additional speculative gain. The plan touched base with the personalized ends symbolized in the privateness, individualism, and self-interest themes, as well as the altruistic purposes inherent in the family responsibility theme. In this respect, life insurance in the late 1800s was a remarkably well-marketed product.

Currents of social thought were also reflected in the ideologies of the insurers of the period. Nonlife companies stressed their financial solvency and ability to withstand catastrophe;[8] these reinforced the client's sense of wellbeing and gave assurance that he too would be capable of withstanding catastrophe.[9] Within the companies, emphasis was placed on prompt payment of legitimate claims, a refusal to pay spurious claims, protection of the insurance fund, and the prudent management of reserves. Technical competence, including underwriting and financial administration, was stressed as the means of preserving the company's good name and good will.

In a way, life insurers also reflected the responsibility themes that made them viable. As discussed in Chapter 3, the early life companies tended neither to advertise nor to solicit great numbers of new members; a tradition of fiduciary responsibility to policyholders and beneficiaries developed.[b] Public

[b]Interestingly, the first American life insurers were church-related and guildlike in their operation. The Presbyterian Ministers Fund was founded in 1715 and the Episcopal Corporation in 1769. Neither sold insurance to the public, but they were established for the purpose of providing security for ministers and their families, that is, a public service was rendered to a chosen membership.

service, limited to a select group of relevant publics, was felt to be the basis for survival.

As the large mutuals began to enjoy success in the late 1840s and 1850s, the private interests of managers became more apparent. Dividends were paid out without being justified by earnings, perquisites for top managers increased in opulence and number, and company investments and managers' personal investments often became entangled. The speculative fervor that accompanied the tontine plans was later reflected in the increasingly speculative investments of the life insurers and their entanglements during the "high finance" era between 1890 and 1920. Public responsibility and fiduciary trust were not irrelevant ideas at the time, simply inconvenient ones. The technical aspects of the insurance business had been subordinated to marketing considerations between the 1850s and the 1890s. But as public criticism of insurer practices mounted, first in the 1870s and then, more seriously, at the turn of the century, the entrepreneurial ideology espoused by the companies began to give way to a more politically palatable managerial ideology rooted in the idea of technical expertise. The scandals uncovered by the Armstrong Commission in 1905 rocked the life insurance industry and forced many top executives to leave the country.[10] In the aftermath of the scandals and the personnel changes that resulted, the entrepreneurial ideology was publicly abandoned. A new generation of top managers favored a more politically sophisticated ideology based on four main tenets:

1. Insurance companies are members of an established industry, one whose existence is secured by the commercial need for security from risk on one hand and the crucial role of insurers as public trustees and financial intermediaries on the other. Thus there need be no public doubt about the viability of the industry or the prominence of its position in American society.

2. Insurance companies possess a wealth of technical and managerial expertise which enables them to continuously and effectively perform the social task of providing security while not endangering the funds of those who have invested in the enterprise (by investment or policy purchase). The keys to successful social performance are adherence to sound underwriting standards and pursuit of sound investments.

3. There is an intimate association between insurance and the public interest, and regulation by insurance commissions is both inevitable and legitimate. As the commissions develop the technical expertise necessary for effective regulation, they will join the insurers in a "partnership" to safeguard the public interest.

4. Insurers are directed by professional managers who are technically skilled in underwriting, actuarial, and investment matters and who are especially cognizant of their public responsibility in all facets of the business.

The Postindustrial Period

The insurer ideology that emerged in the early 1900s has prevailed to the 1970s with relatively minor refinements. Societal ideology, however, has changed dramatically during the twentieth century. The development of major social insurance programs during the 1930s, exemplified by the Social Security legislation of 1935, signaled a new period in the debate over the appropriate ends and means of insurance. The period introduced by that legislation is now commonly referred to as *postindustrial* in nature.

According to Daniel Bell, postindustrial society is characterized by a shift from goods production to a service economy, a preeminence of professional and technical occupations, an emergence of theoretical knowledge as the basis for innovation and policy-making for the society, an orientation toward controlling technology and assessing its impact, and the creation of an "intellectual technology" for decision-making.[11] For the insurance industry, the opening round of postindustrial developments occurred with the formation of public insurance programs predicated on principles of social interdependence, not individual risk or loss. Policy-making based on such considerations reflects a transition from an "economizing mode" of thinking to a "sociologizing mode" in which social criteria replace narrow efficiency criteria. This transition is characteristic of a society's passage to a postindustrial stage of development and emphasizes a crucial social change–the importance of the political system and public policy. Bell has argued that as a postindustrial society emerges, it becomes clear that the autonomy of the economic order (and the people who run it) passes in favor of new, varied, and different control systems. The control of society becomes primarily political, not economic.[12]

In the post-World War II period, the status of the insurance industry as a provider of new coverages deemed important by the public has been a central policy topic. Frequently, this question has appeared as an ideological struggle between an emerging societal ideology of the "sociologizing mode" and a prevailing industry ideology of the "economizing mode." During the late 1950s and 1960s, for example, as the automobile became firmly established as the principle means of transportation, public demands for guaranteed access to auto insurance were met with industry opposition. To insure all drivers, it was argued, was only possible with an unbounded rate structure. The only way to maintain a system of auto insurance at "reasonable rates," insurers contended, was to insure only the "best" risks–that is, those with the lowest probability of becoming involved in accidents. The companies remained bound to the principle of each risk bearing a proportionate cost of insurance, not an equal share.

The provision of fire insurance coverage to inner city and ghetto properties was another underwriting case in point. The demands of inner city property owners for such coverage did not, according to insurers, warrant the issuance of coverage because of the disproportionately high risks involved. That the inability of such owners to secure insurance further contributed to the decay of inner cities and the impoverishment of families whose property was destroyed did not sway the "economizing" mind of the insurers.

A third, and most current, example of the pattern involves health insurance. The industry's long-time opposition to both the Medicaid program for the aged and Medicare program for the elderly is well documented,[13] as is its long-standing opposition to a program of national health insurance. In each case, the industry arguments have involved elements of efficiency, underwriting standards, and cost. The arguments have been of an "economizing mode," and they have, at times, failed to carry the legislative day.

Through the 1960s, insurers continued to adhere to and refine the managerial ideology that took original form in the early 1900s. It emphasized the primacy of the private insurer, the technical nature of insurance calculation, the professionalization of management, and the unification of insurer interest and the public interest. That this ideology wore thin as postindustrial society emerged seems to have gone unnoticed by insurance executives through much of the 1960s.[14] As will be seen, the growing gap between societal and industry ideology since the late 1960s has once again proved to be the stimulus for the engagement of public policy. Table 2-1 summarizes the material presented in this chapter.

Notes

1. On the theory of risk see Greene [61], Denenberg [41], and Crowe and Horn [35]. A classic work is Knight [86].

2. Stalson [151] p. 6.

3. In general see Houston [73]. Regarding fire insurance risk see Swadener [154], Kenney [83]; regarding life insurance risk see Belth [9].

4. The Equitable is a classic case in this regard. See Buley [22].

5. On the importance of ideology to social change see the discussion in Lauer [90].

6. Bendix [10] p. 2.

7. See Cochran [30, 31].

8. See James [78], Williamson and Smalley [166], Kimball [84], and Stalson [151].

9. Douglass [43].

10. See New York State [114]. The investigations are discussed at greater length in Chapters 5 and 6.

Table 2-1
The Ideologies of Insurance

Preindustrial Period

Societal Ideology:
Risk is a community problem and must be shared by all members of the community.

Insurer Ideology:
Social institutions and organizations are created to facilitate the sharing of risk among a "community" (e.g., tribes, guilds, merchant groups).

Industrial Period

Societal Ideology:
Risk is a private, not community, concern. It is the responsibility of the individual to protect himself and his property against risk by whatever means will enable him to preserve his interests and safeguard his independence. This individual responsibility extends to providing for one's own family and kin.

Insurer Ideology:
a. Insurance provides a means whereby the individual can preserve his independence, yet protect himself, his property, and his family from risk.

b. Insurance is an industry that meets vital public needs for protection, and, through such service also provides credit for investment. The industry's expertise in underwriting and investment and the public's interest in their performance makes insurance an appropriate matter for regulatory review. These public and private concerns are melded and joined in the professional managers of insurance companies who are cognizant of their responsibility to the public.

Postindustrial Period

Societal Ideology:
Society can, and should, assume many risks that impact unevenly on individuals (socialization of risk). Public insurance programs may be the necessary means for accomplishing this end.

Insurer Ideology:
The private-carrier insurance industry should be the primary provider of insurance protection. When it cannot provide protection, or can only do so under uneconomic conditions, cooperation with public programs may be necessary. In this regard, the private sector and the public sector are in "partnership" for meeting the needs of society.

11. Bell [8].

12. Bell [8].

13. The industry press is the clearest indicator. An examination of the *National Underwriter* and *Best's Review* (Life Edition) discloses the factual and editorial opposition involved.

14. Some exceptions exist, primarily in the life insurance industry where a number of "statesmen" emerged during the 1960s. See Oates [115].

3 Evolution of the American Insurance Industry

Antecedents of the American Insurance Industry

According to a number of historical accounts, the practice of insuring property and lives was common as long ago as the ascendancy of the Babylonian, Phoenician, Indian, Greek, and Roman civilizations.[1] The property involved in such early transactions typically included cargo being shipped, as well as the vessels that carried it. Insuring the lives of slaves was also common, slaves being considered "property" having an insurable value.

Relatively little is known about the organizations providing such insurance. However, it is generally agreed that among the early antecedents of the modern insurer were the Greek and Roman burial societies and guilds that provided religious burial services for members. In time, the religious element passed in favor of a straight-forward cash payment to the deceased member's heirs. Trennery indicates that these societies were numerous during the second, third, and fourth centuries in Rome and that an individual's membership in several societies was a sign of an intention to provide an estate for heirs.[2]

Financial goals were not the dominant purpose of insurance until many centuries later however. Through the middle ages, when guild societies dominated town life, mutual aid was the dominant purpose of such organizations. It was not until the 1600s and 1700s that commercial purposes began to significantly shape insurance practice.

Marine insurance was one of the first areas in which an insurance market developed. Private underwriters undertook to insure cargos against destruction on sea voyages and also issued policies on the lives of the ship captains for the purpose of indemnifying the shipowner or sponsoring merchant.[3] Brokers also became important parties in insurance transactions by the latter part of the sixteenth century, operating to place insurance with willing underwriters.

Private underwriters continued to write virtually all casualty and property insurance in England until well into the eighteenth century. In 1698, however, the first life insurance company without any other financial or business activities was created. The Society of Assurance for Widows and Orphans was limited to 2000 members, attempted to base its rates on basic mortality information, gave a written policy to subscribers, and was selective in accepting risks.[4] It was, in short, one of the first associations to resemble modern insurance organizations. More important to the evolution of insurance enterprise was the Society's appointment of a manager who had a financial interest in increasing the membership. His compensation depended upon quarterly payments from members and a commissionlike fee for each new member. Even with such inducements, however, the 2000 member limit was never reached.

Stalson viewed the Society's appointment of a manager to secure members as the first identifiable attempt to market life insurance. In a broader sense, however, the differentiation of tasks within the organization suggests that more specific functions were evolving within insurers. The emphasis on enlisting members that accompanied a flurry of newly organized insurers between 1700 and 1720 in England, and which has been fundamental to the life insurance business since then, denotes an important step in the organizational evolution of insurers.

Various technical variations of the pooling principle characterized insurance practice in England throughout the early 1700s. In general, however, the organizational characteristics of these insurers were alike. Typically, they involved a technical component–a person or department–devoted to underwriting and rate-setting activities. This was the core of the insurance enterprise and was highly dependent upon the existence and collection of statistical information.[5] Although such information was poor by modern standards, insurers of the time did estimate risks along a variety of mathematical lines, relying on such devices as Pascal's probability theory and the mortality records of towns, villages, and churches. In marine insurance, correlates of risk included the seaworthiness of the vessel, the length of the voyage, and planned ports of call.

A second important organizational contribution of the English companies was the creation of the *agency system.* The Westminster Society, organized in 1792, established a selling organization that would come to dominate insurance practice into the twentieth century. The company did not hire salesmen and pay them a salary; rather, it granted commission contracts to bankers and lawyers that allowed them to keep 5 percent of the premiums collected in the first and all succeeding years of a policy's life.[6] The Westminster agency system broadened the geographic scope of insurance sales operations. But since it was no longer possible for the insurer's directors to strictly review each application, insurability had to be determined by geographically distant agents. The company had to, *seriatim*, delegate the underwriting function, establish general underwriting standards, and place faith in their agents. This problem of harmonizing technical underwriting requirements with the desire for increased sales would continue to plague insurers into the twentieth century.

The development of a technical basis for the selective underwriting of marine, fire, and life insurance on one hand and the formation of an elementary sales system on the other were outcomes of a largely primitive insurance organization that was highly susceptible to external stimuli. Public opinion was an especially powerful factor, and, indeed, one of the underlying reasons for the Westminster agency system was to take advantage of "country buyers" who were less aware of the hazards of insurance schemes than their city counterparts. Thus such insurers were amoebic, in the sense that economic, social, and political influences all affected their existence.[7] Those that survived appear to have done so less on the strength of their original conception and organization than on their ability to adapt to new circumstances.

Emergence of the American Insurance Industry

The core of technical knowledge necessary to the development of an insurance industry was not transferred to the American colonies prior to the Revolutionary War. Rather, British underwriters–especially marine underwriters–continued to operate solely from London and other British ports. But the growth of trade originating in the colonies and the transportation and communication difficulties involved in dealing with British companies soon led colonial merchants to develop alternative insurance sources.

Sea trade was a vital commercial link for the American colonies, and marine insurance was a crucial aspect of sea trade. The impracticality of relying on distant English underwriters stimulated the development of a complex system of self-insurance. Merchants who were about to embark on a voyage typically approached a broker or agent who issued a "policy"; a premium was paid by the merchant for the coverage. The broker, in turn, sold shares of the policy coverage to other merchants. In this way, the merchants shared the risk of sea voyages among themselves.

By the mid-1700s, groups of these merchant underwriters formed formal underwriting associations. In 1757, for example, Thomas Willing of Philadelphia, an innovator in the colonial insurance industry, organized the first marine underwriting firm, Thomas Willing & Company. Willing's firm, like others that would develop, combined two of the requisite insurance functions: they served as both the brokers and the actual writers, the role previously filled by other merchants. In so doing, the new underwriting firms secured both the broker's commission and the underwriting profits resulting from the excess of premium receipts over insured losses.

Relatively little is known about rate-making during the colonial period. Apparently, rates reflected some collective judgment of the mercantile community about the risks to be encountered. The length of a voyage, the condition of the ship, ports to be visited, and current or rumored wars all influenced specific rates.[8] Since relationships between underwriters, brokers, and merchants continued to be relatively informal through the early 1800s, nothing approaching uniform rates or standardized underwriting developed.

A major transition in the marine business began during the last decade of the 1700s when the Insurance Company of North America was established (1792). Marine underwriting had been a generally profitable venture until this time, and the practice of sharing the risk of a single voyage among a number of underwriters was still common. The Insurance Company of North America, however, was promoted as a corporation of large capitalization with widely held shares of stock. The company offered 60,000 shares at $10 per share, thus it had a stated capitalization of $600,000. Eleven days after the stock had been placed on the market for sale, over 5000 individuals subscribed for 40,000 shares.[9] The widely spread ownership minimized the risk to individuals while it allowed for a concentration of capital large enough to underwrite larger and potentially more profitable voyages.

The Company was incorporated in Pennsylvania by special charter and was empowered to sell fire, life, and marine insurance. In the early years, the company concentrated largely on marine coverage and proved so profitable that it paid dividends of 28.75 percent in 1796 and a first half dividend of 20 percent in 1797.[10]

The inherent risk in marine insurance was as much political as atmospheric and climatological. The Naval War with France, commencing in 1798, cut seriously into the profitability of marine insurance, and the Insurance Company of North America suffered large losses. Although a large award was eventually paid to the company by the joint committee on claims established by the Jay Treaty, the company began a process of prudently shifting some of its capital out of marine insurance and into fire insurance. Although marine insurance would remain an important line of business for some years, the company's adverse experiences began to dictate tighter underwriting standards as well as some diversification.

The importance of underwriting as a scientific basis for insuring property and lives was bolstered by the existence of the larger companies. As the Insurance Company of North America continued its operations, it began to accumulate underwriting data that became a technical substitute for the merchant consensus that characterized the informal underwriting associations.[a] The company's business practices began to reflect this scientific approach.

The company's secretary examined applications within hours of their submission, evaluating all the particulars associated with a specific voyage. The company retained a retired sea captain to inspect vessels for seaworthiness; following inspection, the secretary passed on a recommendation to the board of directors. The board rarely deviated from the recommendation of the secretary.[11] Rates continued to reflect prevailing money market conditions and information about political affairs. Thus premiums varied widely, ranging from about 2.25 percent of stated cargo value to over 30 percent for a voyage to the French West Indies.[12] Despite rate flexibility, however, rapidly changing conditions (such as those in 1798) did produce large losses.

[a]One of the company's founders was Samuel Blodgett, Jr., who had previously engaged in various tontine associations (a combination life insurance and gambling device) and was a statistician who developed early estimates of national wealth.

The manner in which money was apportioned is also instructive about the technical aspects of insurance practice. The Insurance Company of North America apportioned its funds into three separate accounts: capital, surplus, and reserve. The capital account was maintained at $600,000 and invested. The surplus account reflected net earnings. The reserve account held premiums paid on policies still in effect. When a claim was filed, it was paid out of the reserve. If the reserve proved insufficient, funds were taken from surplus. If both were insufficient, resort was made to the capital account. Standard commercial practice of the time dictated that reserves not be permanently maintained on a continuing basis, but that separate reserves be set for each policy. Also, earnings in the surplus accounts were normally distributed in full, with no funds being channeled into the capital account. Hence there was no growth in capital.[13]

The investment of capital funds constitutes the second important technical aspect of insurance activities. By the early 1800s, insurance companies had become important financial intermediaries in the nation's commercial growth. Although records are limited, there is evidence that insurance companies were important suppliers of capital and purchasers of government bonds and bank stocks.[14] The Insurance Company of North America's investment practices are illustrative.

In 1794 the company had its $600,000 capital invested in bottomry loans (loans secured by ships and cargo), the Lancaster Turnpike, and the stock of the Bank of Pennsylvania. In 1807 half of its $750,000 of assets were invested in government notes, about $300,000 in cash and other notes, and the remainder in such social capital projects as highways, toll roads, canals, as well as other insurance companies and banks.

The dual technical nature of insurance—underwriting and investment—made it both financially complicated and potentially lucrative. The ability to use other people's money to invest in other people's ventures, yet keep whatever profits resulted proved a powerful attraction for entrepreneurs. By 1800 there were over 30 nonlife insurance companies in the United States; in 1824 the estimate is that New York alone had 34 companies, Boston, 20, Philadelphia, 11, Baltimore, 9, and their combined capital exceeded $25 million.[15] Growing out of the social need for trade and commerce and the derived economic need for marine insurance, the insurance industry had become, by 1825, an important financial intermediary as well as an important supplier of insurance services. And within specific companies, this dual set of activities would continuously vie for power and influence.

Diversification and Risk

The marine insurance business was the industry's foundation and provided a basis for the development of actuarial and underwriting skills. But concentration of assets in a single risk area was nearly as fraught with danger as using all assets to insure a single ship. For companies such as the Insurance Company of North America, diversification was the basic response to the risk of being in the insurance business itself. For many companies, this risk-avoidance strategy led to the shifting of capital into fire insurance.[b]

Fire insurance, while not as old as marine insurance, had a considerable history of its own. Kimball notes that the demand for organized fire insurance originated in the ashes of the great London fire of 1666.[16] But, as with marine insurance, actuarial experience was limited and companies frequently failed as a result of great fires, thereby further limiting their ability to gather long-term data. Indeed, to be able to survive the losses of a great fire became, in time, an indication of the quality and soundness of an insurance company's management.

The development of fire insurance was stimulated by a set of factors quite different from those that spurred the growth of marine insurance. Whereas marine coverage grew out of an inherent commercial need, fire insurance–especially in the United States–was more of a social phenomenon. In Philadelphia, for example, the first American fire company–the Union Fire Company (1735)–was organized as a result of a newspaper campaign begun by Benjamin Franklin, advocating fire protection for the city.[17] Indeed, the Company was as much a social club as a fire-fighting group. The thirty or so members were provided with the fire-fighting equipment of the day (leather buckets, fire hooks, and so on) and were pledged to fight fires anywhere in Philadelphia. To maintain the fraternal fervor of the group, and to emphasize the organization's good works, solidarity dinners were held monthly. In time it would be imitated by other groups using names such as "Fellowship" and "Heart-in-Hand."[18]

The insurance aspects of these ventures began about 1750 when the members of the Union formed a mutual fund with which they insured their own houses. Two years later the group was reorganized and expanded to become the Philadelphia Contributorship for Insurance of Houses from Loss by Fire. The Contributorship marked the beginning of the American fire insurance industry.

The special nature of fire insurance is reflected in the fact that from the outset fire prevention was as much a purpose of these organizations as the provision of insurance. Since premiums immediately reflected losses, the mutual fire companies undertook to encourage members to reduce losses by minimizing hazards. The Philadelphia Contributorship, for example, established such practices as inspecting the houses of applicants, ordering the removal of fire hazards before granting approval of applications, and periodically reinspecting insured properties to reevaluate risks.[19] Such preventive measures were reinforced by a rate schedule that was flexible in nature, rates being set in proportion to risk. As Douglass relates, the Contributorship assessed members an initial fee ranging

[b]Interestingly, diversification out of the insurance business itself became a basic strategy of insurers in the 1960s and 1970s, when specific lines of insurance have proven too risky or unprofitable.

from $17.50 to $25.00 per thousand dollars of valuation for a seven-year premium.[20]

Since the organization was a mutual, the premium constituted both a payment for the cost of insurance and an investment in the company's reserves. The manner in which those reserves were themselves invested, in turn, affected the overall rate structure for the members of the mutual.[c] Thus fire insurance operations began to develop, as did marine insurance, a technical core consisting of the underwriting of risk and the investment of capital funds.

As the fire insurance market evolved, it became attractive for more marine insurers, such as the Insurance Company of North America, to enter the market. Diversification became a useful way of spreading a company's total underwriting risk and an important means of increasing total investment funds. For the insurer, expansion into the fire insurance business was a managerial response taken to facilitate better acquisition of resources and to stabilize conditions for performance of the technical function.

As might be expected, the initial problems in the fire insurance business were technical in nature. Yet, flexible rates and selective underwriting generally enabled the companies to return a profit in the absence of a major catastrophe. When catastrophes did occur, however, the companies responded by further restricting their underwriting standards. The Philadelphia Contributorship, for example, had $2 million of insurance in force by 1781, the year in which it refused to insure houses surrounded by trees because of a conviction that such structures were likely to be struck by lightning. That restriction served to stimulate the formation of the Mutual Assurance Company, a company organized for householders who wished shade and insurance at the same time.[21] The merit of the restriction remains a point of historical debate, however, since both the Contributorship and the Mutual Assurance Company have survived into the 1970s. Other underwriting restrictions and practices did matter, however, and the mortality of fire insurance companies before the 1800s remained high.

Fire insurance increased in economic importance as the nineteenth century began. Competition for acceptable risks was vigorous in the larger cities, a situation that sometimes prompted rate cutting and relaxation of underwriting standards. These practices added to the conditions that precipitated insurer insolvency.

A second and ultimately more important by-product of such competition was the transition made by some firms from purely local to regional and even national insurers. The Insurance Company of North America was chartered from its beginnings to write fire insurance coverage. It remained local for a brief period of time, but the growing number of competitors in Philadelphia soon led

[c]The difference between mutual and stock companies has been persistent in the American insurance industry. In the *stock company*, underwriting and investment surpluses (profits) are distributed to shareholders as dividends. In the *mutual company*, underwriting and investment surpluses are distributed to the owners—the mutual's policyholders—as either dividends or in the form of reduced rates.

the company to offer to write fire insurance anywhere in the United States. In 1796 over $10,000 in annual premiums was being received.[22] And in 1797 the company appointed an agent, its first, in Baltimore. Although such early agents were restricted to soliciting potential policyholders for the company, they were eventually allowed to actually issue policies on the behalf of the company. The fees for such policy writing were small, thereby forcing most agents to operate on a part-time basis. Yet, by the early 1800s the basic agency system had been introduced to the United States.

On the investment side, the capital assets of the fire and general insurance companies rose quickly. According to Kroos and Blyn, in 1830 there were 8 marine insurers in New York City with $3 million in capital; 20 fire insurance companies in the same city (including 16 formed after 1815), capitalized at $7.5 million; and in Massachusetts 48 companies, capitalized at $9.4 million.[23] These firms were becoming increasingly important sources of capital funds for commercial growth.

The process of becoming major suppliers of capital was interrupted by catastrophe, however. In 1835 a severe fire swept the city of New York and forced most of the city's insurers into bankruptcy. The ability to survive such losses became a mark of managerial acuity and financial soundness, qualities that were emphasized in the marketing of the surviving companies, many of which were located in Hartford, Connecticut.

The investment policies of companies that survived underwriting catastrophes were apparently quite conservative in nature. The Philadelphia Contributorship invested nearly all of its assets in real estate and mortgages. In 1846, for example, it owned 481 shares in four companies, $460,000 in real estate and mortgages, and $30,000 in other assets.[24] And although some companies did invest in somewhat more speculative ventures, this generally did not occur until the mid-1800s.[25] Thus through the early decades of the nineteenth century insurance investment seems to have been largely confined to real property and social capital projects, such as toll roads, canals, and highways. Nevertheless the slow shift in investment thinking did point to a broadening of considerations by investment managers and a relaxation of the view that "insurance is insurance, pure and simple."

New lines of insurance also began to develop during the first half of the 1800s, including, in particular, inland transportation coverage. These new insurance products signified, as did the agency system and new investment forms, an expanding notion of the purpose of the insurance enterprise and the nature of its technical function.

Risk and Organizational Form

The American insurance industry has been characterized by organizational and conceptual diversity since its earliest days. Indeed, new organizations have been a standard social response to the absence of other risk-avoidance mechanisms. When existing insurers refused, or were unable, to assume new classes or types of risk, new kinds of insurers were formed. So prevalent was this pattern that even the operations of the technical core of the enterprise (underwriting and investment) were often determined by the founding organizational scheme—e.g., tontine, mutual benefit society, or fraternal association.

Kimball's study of the legal and public policy aspects of insurance in the state of Wisconsin suggests the great variety of organizational forms taken by insurers during the nineteenth and twentieth centuries.[26] Included were private underwriters, unincorporated associations, stock corporations, mutual corporations, town mutual, city and village mutuals, the reciprocal or interinsurance exchange life insurance companies, mutual benefit societies, fraternal societies, and commercial assessment companies. All were essentially private in nature (as opposed to government sponsored), though their organizational purposes varied considerably, some seeking profits, others only protection for members. Not surprisingly, most developed during the nineteenth century when commercial needs were diversifying.

By the mid-1800s, the private underwriter of the colonial period had largely disappeared or had, in any event, become a relatively unimportant provider of insurance. Even syndicates of underwriters, organized along the lines of Lloyd's of London, were infrequently used as a major provider of insurance coverage by the latter part of the nineteenth century.

The development of the corporate form was especially important to insurance companies that, unlike businesses that depended on the device in order to raise capital, especially needed the corporation's perpetual existence. As Kimball has noted, the long duration of an insurance contract makes it more desirable that the legal existence of the insurer be continuous. For life insurance, perpetual existence is a virtual necessity.[27] The corporate form was an understandably popular one, therefore, although there was some tendency among state legislatures in the early 1800s to limit the life of insurance companies for fear of monopoly and perpetual power.[28]

The early nineteenth century insurance corporation was usually formed by special charter of the state legislature. Terms and powers varied from grant to grant but frequently included monopolistic privileges in a geographic area and the power to require assessments of additional capital from shareholders. Fire insurance companies constituted the first major line of business to be incorporated, though most others followed rather quickly.

Stock companies were organized for profit, and their growing numbers reflect the readiness of investors to form insurance companies whenever a new product or geographic demand seemed to exist. The formation of such companies reflected more than the enthusiasm of growing commercialization. It indicated an increasing appreciation of the independent markets that were developing for insurance products of all types. In the early 1800s it was still common to organize a single company to perform banking and insurance functions; a number of special charters that included powers to write marine and inland insurance were similarly granted to transportation companies.[29] As the nineteenth century progressed, such mixed enterprises became specialized in their actual operations, in their organization, and, perhaps most importantly, in the public mind.

Stock companies distribute their unretained profits as dividends to stockholders. But, unlike other industries where initial capital investment needs are large, start-up capital is generally small for insurance companies. Apart from basic office facilities, only legally required reserve amounts are usually necessary. If no reserves are required to begin operations—a situation that was common until the late 1800s—there is virtually no impediment to starting an insurance enterprise. Moreover, the rationale for having stockholders is undermined. It was precisely this type of situation that led to the formation of many mutual insurance companies during the 1800s.

Beginning as a reaction to unacceptably high fire insurance rates and the restrictive underwriting of established companies, or as a response to a shortage of funds, mutual assistance organizations (in the tradition of the Union Fire Company) were formed in many newly developing communities. These companies were nonprofit in nature, and returns on the investment of reserves were either returned to members or applied against future premiums. In time, specific trades and industries, as well as local communities, formed mutual organizations to meet insurance needs. One of the first successful trade mutuals was the Brewer's Mutual (1868) of Wisconsin. The principle of mutual insurance took root especially in the Midwestern states, and mutual companies soon entered into lines of coverage other than fire insurance. Many of these original mutual ventures have survived and become prominent twentieth-century insurance carriers.

As the mutuals became more concerned with the technical aspects of the business, including underwriting standards, the need for protection continued in capital-scarce communities. For the same reasons that the early mutuals were created, town mutuals developed in many Midwestern communities. The reluctance of more prosperous local inhabitants to join these risky ventures in favor of established commercial companies was often short-lived, given the failure of commercial companies due to catastrophic city fires (e.g., the Chicago fire of 1871) and the attempts of survivor companies to tighten underwriting and loss settlement practices. Stories of insurer refusal to pay claims spread quickly, and local citizens were reduced to placing their faith and dollars with the local mutual insurer. Kimball notes that the rise of the Grange proved a major boom to the development of the town mutual and that in some states cooperative arrangements arose under the aegis of the Grange itself.[30] A number of these companies have also survived into the twentieth century.

Less successful than the town mutuals were city and village mutual companies. Organized in the same manner as the mutuals, they suffered the fatal defect of population density. A single fire often involved many insured losses in a city or village. Given the frequency of city fires before twentieth-century fireproofing, it is not surprising that many of these ventures failed as a result of fires that destroyed whole sections of cities and villages.

Attorneys were among the principal developers of new organizing schemes, and hence it is not surprising that one alternative to the corporate form involved a very basic legal device: the power of attorney. The *reciprocal* or *interinsurance exchange* was simply a multilateral contract in which participants paid premiums, in advance or by assessment, to the attorney who received a commission. These funds formed the reserve used to pay claims of participating members. Although not as widely used as the stock corporation or mutual company, the reciprocal did prove a useful means of dealing with a single line of insurance and for insuring large risks.[31]

The business of life insurance spawned its own set of organizational forms, including some that resembled modern versions of the ancient Greek burial societies. Some of these mutual benefit societies aided widows and orphans in addition to paying burial expenses. A number also provided assistance during illness or injury. These societies were often associated with churches, guilds, or labor unions and were usually local in character.

Somewhat analogous to the town mutuals that provided fire insurance were various types of fraternal life associations. Usually more complex in their operations than the simple mutual benefit society, they often included such arrangements as assessments of members for deficits and the maintenance of reserve funds. Grange-sponsored associations were popular during the late 1800s in some areas and grew, as did The Patron's Benevolent Aid Society of Wisconsin, by building their membership and inveighing against exorbitant premiums, intricate and complicated policy conditions, excessive and unreasonable management salaries, and the aggressiveness of general and district agents and subagents who were said to resemble locusts upon the land.[32]

The companies to which the fraternals were reacting were known as *legal reserve companies*, a term that embraced both stock and mutual companies selling life insurance and operating with an eye toward profit or surplus. By the terms of their charters, they normally were required to maintain legal reserves against claims. Whether stock or mutual, the original founders of these companies or their appointees usually retained operating control of the company, frequently voting themselves the high salaries and trappings of affluence against which the Grange and others inveighed.[d] This form of management domination was not confined to insurance organizations, of course, but in the latter decades of the nineteenth century the insurance companies became the focus of considerable public and regulatory interest. The specific subjects of this interest were the life insurance companies that had grown so quickly and to such gargantuan proportions in the second half of the 1800s.

[d]In a mutual company policyholders theoretically have voting control; in a stock company such control is vested in the shareholders.

Growth of Life Insurance

The life insurance industry has been an important supplier of capital funds to the economy since the late 1800s, and the detailed story of its phenomenal growth has been recorded in a number of histories.[33] Especially important in the context of the present work is the manner in which the industry passed through a number of distinct stages of development.

The American life insurance industry was primitive in development until about 1845. Although a number of life insurers had written policies as early as 1759 when the Presbyterian Minister's Fund was formed to insure the lives of members of the ministry, early developments were of limited significance. Pelican of London did establish an agency in Philadelphia in 1807, marking the first U.S. encounter with life insurance agents; the Pennsylvania Company, a level-premium life company,[e] sold its first policy in 1813; the well-known Massachusetts Hospital Life Insurance Company was founded in 1823 to do a life insurance and trust business but came to ignore insurance in favor of a lucrative trust business; and the idea of mutual companies spread to life insurance by 1840 and stimulated the formation of a number of new life companies. With the exception of the formation of mutual companies, however, these developments had little permanent influence on the shape of the industry.

Unlike marine and fire insurance, which became commercial necessities by the mid-1800s, life insurance did not become an important item of purchase until major marketing efforts began in the mid-1800s. Whereas marine and fire insurers underwent a relatively long period of technical development (i.e., erratic underwriting experience), the technical aspects of life insurance were considerably simplified by the mid-1800s through the existence of mortality and actuarial data. Thus, while a fairly large body of technical knowledge could be drawn upon for purposes of setting rates and selecting insurable risks, the major problem for life insurers was to interest the public in the life insurance product.

Securing necessary resources for the organization, including policyholder premiums in this case, is a managerial subsystem function. By the mid-1800s life insurers had recognized the necessity of aggressively approaching the public. In the 1840s the agency system was employed by mutual companies to increase the number of salesmen. Advertising campaigns were developed and run in local newspapers, and the "hard-sell" techniques of insurance sales began to evolve. By the decade's end the mutuals were issuing large dividends, thereby encouraging more new companies to enter the field. Life insurance in force rose from

[e]*Level premium* refers to a premium that is constant over the life of a policy. In the early years of a policy, the individual pays a much larger premium than is actuarially necessary. Part of the excess is attributable to *loading*, an assessment of administrative costs and company profit, the remainder being used to establish a reserve that is invested by the company for the policyholder and allowed to accumulate at compound interest. As the policyholder grows older, the surplus is used to offset the rising natural cost of the insurance while the premium remains level.

$4.65 million in 1840 to $14 million in 1845 and to $96 million in 1850. Such figures barely indicated the scope of growth yet to occur, however; by 1870 life insurance in force would approach $2 billion.[34]

The influx of new companies encouraged a number of bad practices, including the payment of high dividends in excess of earned surplus. Such dividends were payable only in company scrip, however, a device designed to encourage additional purchases of life insurance by policyholders. Thus sales increased without creating an immediate drain on assets. But future liabilities increased precipitously, ultimately driving a number of smaller companies into insolvency and others to the brink. The survivors did so only by increasing new premium income and investment profits faster than inflated claims were being filed.

Another dubious sales technique involved allowing policyholders to pay part of their premiums with *premium notes*, which were later redeemed from policyholder dividends. This allowed a person to purchase more life insurance than he could presently afford and had the effect of undermining the financial soundness of company capital structures.

By far the most important sales technique to emerge out of the 1840s, however, was the aggressive "hard sell." In the 1850s newly-formed insurers joined existing companies in advertising insurance products and employing armies of agents, raising commissions from 5 and 10 percent to 15 and 30 percent on initial premiums and 5 percent on renewals, and raiding each other's sales forces continually. The pressure on salesmen to sign up new policyholders and get the first year's premium contributed to the industry's aggressive image. A rhyme of the period characterized the prevailing situation: "No one has as much endurance as the man who sells insurance!"

A second phase in the development of the managerial subsystem in life insurers involved internal administration. As sales volume grew, the companies were forced to both expand in administrative size and specialize in administrative detail. The transition from primitive organizations to hierarchical structures was well underway by the 1850s.

By 1860 the simple storefronts and few clerks had given way to large buildings and immense staffs. The specialization of the two-sided technical function gave rise to a number of departments, including underwriting, actuarial planning, accounting and statistics, and investments; the managerial subsystem's activities stimulated the growth of sales, claims, agency, and finance departments. Overseeing this range of activities and receiving the legion of reports that filtered through the pyramidlike structure were the company's chief officers—president and secretary—and, ultimately, the board of trustees or directors. The boards of life companies were usually composed of leading businessmen and citizens (usually including at least one minister), whose presence was intended to contribute to the image of success, financial strength, and moral rectitude believed necessary for the retention of public confidence. Such boards suggest that the importance of an institutional subsystem responsible for legitimizing the company's existence in the eyes of the public was well recognized by insurers of the late nineteenth century.

The marketing experience and organizational development that had occurred before the Civil War prepared many life insurers for the wealth of opportunities that would develop as the decade progressed. Yet their success before 1860 only hinted at the potential that lay ahead.[f] During the last three decades of the 1800s life insurers would multiply their assets 32 times, from $24 million in 1860 to $771 million in 1890, and reach a point where, in a *single* year, one company alone (Equitable) would be writing more than $300 million of new insurance, an amount nearly one third greater than the total of all life insurance in force in 1860.

A number of factors apart from the Civil War contributed to the industry's growth. Much is accounted for by the recognition that selling, not underwriting or investment, was the dominant aspect of the life insurance business and that sales efforts reached full bloom during this period. Great emphasis was placed on the creation of both new insurance products and new selling methods.

By consensus, the high priest of life insurance salesmanship during the latter half of the 1800s was Henry Baldwin Hyde, legendary salesman, agency organizer, and founder of the Equitable Life Assurance Society of the United States.[35] The influence of Hyde's innovations transcended the Equitable and affected the entire life insurance industry. Hyde's innovations resulted, in part, from his questioning of the traditional role of insurers as providers of basic family protection.

Traditionally, the premiums paid by a policyholder had been used to establish a reserve against the policy that the policyholder could claim in cash or use to purchase paid-up life insurance or limited-term insurance equal to the face value of the policy. Under such a system, the investable funds available to the company were limited to the reserves plus the annual loading charge.

Hyde's entrepreneurial talents and his desire to spur capital growth led to the introduction of an updated version of the old tontine principle. Under the Equitable's tontine plan, the beneficiaries of policyholders who died received the face value of the policy. If a policy had lapsed, however, the beneficiary received nothing. Those policyholders who kept their policies in force for a stipulated period of 10, 15, or 20 years were paid the face value of the policy, plus their own accumulated dividends, plus a share of the dividends of those who died, plus a share of the accumulated gains of those who let their policies lapse. The tontine policy was, therefore, more than simple family protection; it was a speculative venture in which the policyholder bet, in effect, that he would outlive the majority of the participants thereby gaining a speculative return.

---

[f]The most successful companies of the 1850s were the mutuals. Of the $205 million of life insurance in force in 1860, $125 million had been written by five mutual companies: Mutual of New York ($40 million), Connecticut Mutual ($26 million), Mutual Benefit ($25 million), New York Life Insurance Company ($16 million), and New England Mutual ($16 million).

The tontine proved immensely popular and, when coupled with aggressive salesmanship, became the product with which the Equitable catapulted itself into industry sales leadership. The tontine enabled insurers who sold them to accumulate large reserves for investment. Life insurance assets between 1860 and 1890 increased from $24 million to $771 million, an average annual increase of nearly 25 percent.

The second product innovation accounting for the growth of life insurance was the introduction of industrial life insurance. Whereas regular life insurance was sold predominantly to the middle and upper classes, who possessed discretionary income, industrial life insurance was an attempt to get at the petty savings of the millions of lower-class and lower-middle-class population segments. Industrial life insurance had originated in England in the mid-1850s and made its first major appearance in the American market in 1877 when it was offered for sale by the Prudential Insurance Company.[36]

Industrial life insurance had unique marketing characteristics. The policies had a small face value—$25 in some cases—as opposed to the $500 minimum face value on regular policies; it was sold door-to-door and premiums were collected weekly (also on a door-to-door basis) by company salesmen. And, industrial life insurance was at least as profitable as other life policies because its total price per dollar of coverage was much higher than regular policies. Most importantly, to a segment of the population excluded from other forms of risk avoidance, industrial insurance offered an affordable means of meeting that need.

The principal sellers of industrial life insurance—Prudential, Metropolitan Life, and John Hancock—quickly became important actors in the industry, expanding from relatively small sales volumes to positions of industry leadership in just a few years.[g]

As industry assets grew in size, company pressure for greater investment latitude and discretion was applied to state legislatures that had previously tended to restrict insurance investments to government securities, real estate and mortgages, and high quality bonds.[37] By the 1890s the companies' investment powers were broadened considerably by state legislatures and insurance commissions. The types of investments that could be made were expanded in terms of scope and permissible risk and, most importantly, geographic restrictions, which prevented funds from being taken from one state and invested in another, were removed. A national capital market was being formed, and the life insurance companies were becoming major holders of capital assets.[38]

As described previously, the rise of the life insurance enterprise in the latter half of the 1800s is an example of how managerial subsystems, concerned with securing resources (policy premiums), create the conditions that enable the technical subsystem (underwriting and investment) to function. Moreover, the

[g]Metropolitan was eighteenth in size in 1875 ($25 million in force) and rose to first by 1910 ($2 billion in force). The Prudential had $250,000 in force in 1876; it rose to $139 million by 1890.

managerial subsystem dominated the character of the enterprise. The quest for expanding sales preoccupied life insurers of the day, and underwriting standards were generally not allowed to present a technical barrier. In a sense, the entrepreneurial philosophy of the late 1800s seems to have been rooted not in the precision of acturial estimates but in the law of large numbers. As long as sales continued to grow at a constant or increasing rate, the capital base became ever larger, thereby generating a flow of funds sufficient to meet current claims.

Inevitably, perhaps, a version of the law of large numbers also began to affect the organizational structures of the life insurers. With success came large bureaucracies, monumental headquarters buildings, internecine relationships with other financial institutions, and the elaborate trappings of a profitable industry based on "other people's money."

The size of the home office bureaucracies was an obvious indicator of a company's overall prosperity and growth. In 1883 the Prudential had a home office staff of 89; in 1890 it numbered 250.[39] Metropolitan Life had a home office staff of 1081 by 1897, and the home office boasted that it had more typewriters than any other office building in the world.[40]

Headquarters building also approached monumental proportions. Boorstin has noted that the history of the American skyscraper is illustrated by monuments to the growing insurance industry. It became fashionable–and virtuous if one is to believe the corporate rhetoric–to construct structures as impressive and lasting as the companies themselves. The Prudential building, which opened in 1892, was intended to exemplify moral qualities of fairness and love for fellowmen.[41] With prose approaching the skyscraping proportions of the structure, the New York Life building was referred to as a modern temple of humanity.[42]

Of greater long-term significance was the growing interlock between the large life insurance companies and other financial intermediaries. Common directorships among such life insurers as the Equitable, Mutual of New York, and New York Life and a number of leading banks, investment brokerages, and trust companies intensified to such an extent that they came to constitute a powerful "money trust." Later, this would provide fuel for the scandals that would engulf the industry.[h]

The growth of capital assets and interlocking relationships with other financial institutions made the life insurance industry a primary participant in the so-called Age of High Finance between 1890 and 1920. Investment became the predominant technical and managerial preoccupation during this period, underwriting and claims administration being relegated to a clearly subordinate position. Holdings of industrial stocks, including especially heavy holdings in the

[h]Krooss and Blyn [89] p. 113 point out that such decay in the business structure, coupled with excessive salaries and assorted forms of mismanagement contributed to a continually declining net rate of return. In 1871 the net rate of return was 6.90 percent; the rate dropped to 5.10 in 1890.

railroads, attested to the liberalized regulation of investments. But, most importantly, the life insurance companies became deeply involved with the banks and investment companies that were the core of financial power. The complexity of the resulting financial alliances has long been a topic of interest to government commissions and students alike.[43]

During the early 1900s mandated reforms included a tightening of investment rules and marketing practices; ultimately these served to prevent the industry from suffering as greatly as other financial intermediaries during the Depression of the 1930s.[i] Life insurance in force did fall–from $107 billion in 1931 to $96 billion in 1933–but it had recovered by 1937, reaching a new high of $107.8 billion in that year. Asset growth continued despite declining interest rates, rising from $17.5 billion in 1929 to $21.8 billion by the end of the decade.

Following the reform period of the early 1900s, land and mortgages reassumed an important position in the industry's investment portfolio. Viewed as consistent with prudent and conservative investment management, the concentration of insurance funds in real estate and mortgages would ultimately prove to be a source of losses during the Depression as forfeitures increased. So numerous did delinquencies and foreclosures become that the companies actually developed field staffs to manage the properties. More importantly, the companies proved reluctant to invest further in real estate and shifted to government bonds and public utility bonds as primary components of investment portfolios. In this way, insurers acquired considerable influence in the government bond markets.

The Depression stimulated a number of other trends that adversely affected the industry. Policy loans had increased during the late 1920s to facilitate stock purchases. By 1929 they accounted for nearly 14 percent of life company assets. But by 1932, with high unemployment, policy loans approached 18 percent of total assets (about $3.8 billion).[44] Cancellations also ran high during the 1930s, $6.7 billion of life insurance being cancelled in 1932 as compared to $2.7 billion in 1929. Given these drains on insurer assets, the ability to maintain liquidity became a major problem for investment departments.

Lapse rates also increased during this period, especially on individual insurance. As the difficulty of paying the weekly premiums increased for lower income families who were its primary purchasers, industrial life insurance suffered lapse rate increases from an already high 42 percent in 1929 to 54 percent in 1933.[45] Once recovery began and discretionary incomes accelerated, as they did throughout the 1940s and 1950s, the future of industrial life insurance faded in favor of ordinary and group life coverages.

Group life insurance was one of the few lines of business to experience

[i]So successful were some of these reforms that, according to Krooss and Blyn [89] p. 203, Metropolitan had only one percent of all its assets in stocks at the time of the 1929 stock market crash.

significant expansion during the 1930s, having increased from $9 billion in 1929 to over $15 billion in 1940. Its share of total life insurance in force also rose, from 8.8 percent to 13 percent over the same period. Thus, by the inception of the post-World War II period, the life insurance industry had acquired new contours. While group insurance expanded, industrial life insurance showed little growth. It amounted to $33.4 billion in 1950 and only $38.8 billion in 1968. All ordinary insurance increased from $149 billion to $650 billion over the same period; group insurance increased from $48 billion to $438 billion; and credit life insurance from $2.5 billion to $75 billion.[j]

This shift in the product mix of life insurers had a major effect on their role as savings institutions and, consequently, as a supplier of funds to capital markets. Between 1950 and 1965 life insurance assets as a percentage of total capital declined from 15 percent to 11 percent. Significant changes in the disbursement of these funds also occurred. Life insurers became major suppliers of funds for mortgages and industrial bonds, a shift that would ultimately generate important issues for managements during the 1960s.

The failure of life insurers to grow during the post-World War II period stimulated a trend toward the formation of holding companies and diversification into new fields. Such changes enabled insurers to participate in the growth of inflation-resistant products, such as mutual funds and variable annuitites. By the 1960s this market became a fast-developing portion of the insurer's business.

The movement in favor of diversification by life insurers signaled a development that had begun a decade earlier for the nonlife insurance companies. Ultimately there was a convergence of interest among life and nonlife companies, and by the 1960s growing numbers of holding companies and multiple-line insurers were being formed. These consolidations served to bring within a single management structure life insurance and nonlife lines of business. Against a background of major social and political (as well as economic) change the newly formed insurance holding companies would have to face a wide range of market and nonmarket issues. The number and importance of the issues are perhaps the clearest indicator of the evolving interpenetration of the industry and society. These issues are further discussed in Chapter 7.

Nonlife Insurance between 1890 and 1960

The spectacular growth of life insurance overshadowed the steady, albeit less spectacular, growth of the nonlife insurance business. The assets of nonlife insurance companies nearly tripled between 1860 and 1890, and total insurance in force in both stock and mutual companies grew from approximately $1.6 billion to $19.6 billion. Premiums increased from $30.8 million in 1860 to

[j]Credit life insurance is issued to a lender to cover the payment of a loan, installment purchase, or other obligation in case of the debtor's death.

$156.8 million in 1890, and surplus rose from $8.8 million to $31.5 million over the same period.[46]

The pattern of growth that began after the Civil War continued into the twentieth century. Although not characterized by the product or managerial innovations of the life insurance business, nonlife insurance adapted to social change with sufficient speed to remain profitable. For the industry as a whole, the crucial market change was the relative lack of growth in fire and marine sales and the growing importance of casualty and liability insurance. As an increasing amount of adverse claim experience occurred in the marine and fire business (the San Francisco earthquake of 1906, for example, bankrupted many fire companies), the need for diversification became increasingly obvious. The actual movement toward diversification became prominent in the post-World War I years.

Casualty and inland marine insurance were two fast-developing lines of business. Although the railroad had undermined inland water travel, the inland marine insurance business came to include coverage on all forms of cargo being transported, whatever the mode of carriage. Moreover, the development of the automobile in the early 1900s made casualty insurance a promising, if not immediately successful, line of business. Since casualty insurance was a line that most fire and marine companies were not chartered to write, however, action had to be taken to amend charters or to establish affiliates in anticipation of growing casualty markets. This limited form of diversification, resulting from growing commercial needs, and the steady growth in the total amount of nonlife insurance in force characterized the general insurance business through the 1920s.

The scandals that had rocked the life insurance business in the early decades of the 1900s did not generally extend to nonlife insurers. That freedom from scandal and the growing importance of general insurance as a commercial necessity preserved the business and generated the assets that were largely invested in common stock portfolios. When the stock market crash occurred, however, the face value of the insurers' stock portfolios declined precipitously and threatened the solvency of many companies. To avoid nationwide insurer collapse, the National Convention of Insurance Commissioners authorized insurers to value securities above market prices according to what became known as *convention values.* The Reconstruction Finance Company also extended loans to a number of companies, thereby helping to preserve their solvency.

General operating revenues also declined during the 1930s, largely because of the decline in commercial activity. Data from the Insurance Company of North America illustrate the situation. In 1929 marine revenues were $9.2 million; in 1932 they were $4.6 million. Marine losses fell proportionately less, from $4.2 million in 1929 to $2.5 million in 1932. Operating expenses were relatively insensitive to falling sales revenues, however, declining from $4.1 million to only $2.8 million between 1929 and 1932. The result was that the company's net marine insurance profits of $956,000 in 1929 were turned into a $529,000 loss in 1932. The fire insurance branch had a similar experience, profits falling from $2.1 million in 1929 to a $1.4 million loss in 1932.[47]

As commercial activity increased in the late 1930s, nonlife insurers began to recover. Momentum built, and in the post-World War II period this growth accelerated so that assets increased by more than 8 percent annually. Unlike the past when all insurance innovation seemed to involve life insurers, nonlife companies began a major process of innovation during the 1950s.

The central development during this period was the creation of the *multiple-line insurance company*. A structural device used to unify a number of lines of insurance under a single management, the multiple-line concept had been prohibited for many years by state regulations.[k] Those regulations had generally been enacted by compliant legislatures at the turn of the twentieth century when home-grown mutuals sought to protect their geographic markets. The history of small-insurer responses to the competitive threats of large Eastern insurers is closely linked to the use of state legislative power and will be discussed further in Chapters 5 and 6. The ultimate competitive effect was to prevent the union of marine, fire, casualty, liability, and life insurance lines of business for nearly a century. That barrier gave way in the 1930s when a trend toward "fleets" of affiliated companies began; it accelerated in the late 1940s and evolved to the multiple-line company movement during the 1950s.[48]

Formation of multiple-line insurers had a number of managerially related effects. First, it improved the ability of insurers to "market the whole consumer"—that is, to fill the full range of a single client's needs to manage risk.[49] The multiple-line companies prospered as the convenience and loss settlement advantages of a unified marketing approach became more obvious to both insurer and insured.

A second advantage of multiple-line organizations involved administrative economies of scale. As the Depression experience had demonstrated, operating costs did not directly vary with current sales volume. Many administrative costs were relatively fixed. The merger of several single-line insurers into a multiple-line company allowed for organizational consolidation and cost savings. Coupled with the marketing advantages mentioned above, these cost-saving and operating efficiencies stimulated a wave of nonlife insurance mergers in the 1950s. In New York, for example, the number of companies with multiple-line powers expanded from 48 in 1949 to 360 in 1957. The significance of monoline companies has continued to wane ever since.

The formation of multiple-line companies was one major nonlife trend in

---

[k]New York's Appleton Rule was the primary cause. Dating from the early 1900s, the rule prohibited companies doing business in the state from engaging in any line of business in *any* state that was not allowed to companies chartered in the State of New York. Since the New York market was a major one, which national companies could not afford to ignore, the net effect was to give the New York rule extraterritorial effect throughout the United States. See Michelbacher and Roos (106).

the post-World War II period. A second was the emergence of the so-called specialty groups or specialty companies. A *specialty company* is one that develops a single line of business and, by using nontraditional methods, such as continuous policies, direct billing, and payment in advance, creates maximum cost efficiencies. The most important source of cost reduction is the development of direct-marketing techniques and the abandonment of the general agency system. Nonlife stock company insurers had long depended upon the independent insurance agent or broker to serve as the salesman for the companies' coverages. These agents placed a customer's insurance requirements with an underwriter of the agent's choosing. Hence the insurers' true customers were the independent agents. The specialty companies used salaried or exclusive agents instead of independent agents and brokers. By having standard policies, uniform underwriting through a central office, salaried claims representatives, and so forth, the specialty companies (mostly mutuals) were able to effect significant cost reductions, estimated at up to 20 percent. Being mutuals, these savings were passed on to policyholders through reduced costs or dividend payments. The growth of such specialty companies as State Farm, Allstate, and Nationwide far exceeded the industry average. Between 1949 and 1959 net premiums for these companies increased by 463 percent, as opposed to an average increase of 175 percent for the largest stock agency groups.[50]

The success of specialty companies in a single line of business (e.g., automobile insurance) carried over as the companies began to write fire insurance, casualty and liability coverage, and even life insurance by the early 1960s. As these firms expanded, and as the use of the multiple-line organizational form increased, competition increased, especially on a marketing level. These developments also made clear by the early 1960s the increasingly perilous position of the independent agency system as the primary sales device in the nonlife business.

Summary

Insurance is an industrial society's response to the existence of risk and the desire for security. Insurance companies have been a primary instrument in the provision of means to the accomplishment of that end for several hundred years. During those centuries, an evolution of organizations has occurred in both the life and nonlife branches of the industry.

In their early primitive forms insurers had simple organizational structures and were generally affected by social, economic, and political forms of environmental change. As industrialization commenced, general insurance coverages–especially marine and fire insurance–became commercial necessities, and insurance premiums, a standard cost of doing business. Thus the status of the nonlife insurance business became securely embedded in the nation's social and economic way of life. Life insurers had no comparable flow of events to establish their existence as a necessary part of American life. Hence the development of the life insurance industry was retarded until such time as the per capita national income included a significant amount of discretionary income and the public became convinced of the desirability of the life insurance purchase.

Marketing, not underwriting, was the key to the growth of life insurance. Unlike marine and fire insurance, where the technical core of the business developed as the industry itself grew in size, the underwriting and actuarial side of life insurance was well developed before its major growth occurred. This comparative experience was reflected in the technical versus managerial orientations of the two industry segments for most of their history.

The dependency of the life insurers on public confidence led to the early emergence of an institutional subsystem, including boards of directors composed of prominent community figures. The nonlife companies were somewhat slower in this regard, but they too developed an organizational subsystem that performed these legitimizing activities.

The second technical side of both the life and nonlife branches of the business involved the investment of capital funds, including legal reserves. The great volume of funds held by insurers–especially life companies in the late 1800s–involved them in many of the high finance machinations of the 1890-1920 era. Once disclosed, the rationale for public regulation needed little further embellishment.

In the twentieth century both nonlife and life insurance have grown, though at a slower rate than in their halcyon years. The maturity and importance of the private-carrier industry was well-established by the 1950s, despite the establishment of a number of public insurance programs. As the 1960s began, it appeared that the industry's greatest challenges were competitive in nature, involving multiple-line companies and the rapidly growing specialty groups.

Notes

1. Stalson [151] and citations to Trennery [159] therein; also Kimball [84].

2. See Trennery [159] and Stalson [151].

3. Stalson [151], Douglass [43].

4. Stalson [151] p. 38.

5. See Stalson [151] pp. 35-37 regarding some early English statistical developments in the area of life insurance. Regarding American developments see Vinoskis [162] and American Conservation Co. [2].

6. Stalson [151] p. 41.

7. The distinction between amoebic and hierarchical organizations is discussed in Preston and Post [135].

8. Douglass [43] p. 56.

9. Douglass [43] p. 56, James [78].

10. Douglass [43] p. 56, James [78].

11. Douglass [43] p. 57.

12. See Krooss and Blyn [89] p. 37, and Douglass [43] p. 57.

13. Douglass [43] p. 57.

14. Krooss and Blyn [89] p. 37.

15. Krooss and Blyn [89] p. 36.

16. Kimball [84] p. 10.

17. Douglass [43] p. 58.

18. Douglass [43] p. 58.

19. Douglass [43] p. 59.

20. Douglass [43] p. 59.

21. Douglass [43] p. 59.

22. Douglass [43] p. 60.

23. Krooss and Blyn [89] p. 63.

24. Krooss and Blyn [89] p. 84.

25. For example, the Union Fire Insurance Company in 1860 had $400,000 in assets, including $270,000 in stocks and bonds. Krooss and Blyn [89] p. 84.

26. Kimball [84] also contains a full discussion of these mechanisms.

27. Kimball [84] p. 39.

28. Livermore [95] pp. 259-260; also cited in Kimball [84] p. 39.

29. Kimball [84] p. 41.

30. Kimball [84] p. 45.

31. See Hensley [71].

32. See Kimball [84] p. 50.

33. See Stalson [151], Keller [82], Kimball [84], Buley [21, 22], and various company histories [29, 78, 79, 102, 137, 153] in this regard.

34. Douglass [43] p. 157.

35. Hyde's story is a colorful one. See Stalson [151], Buley [22], and Equitable [48].

36. May and Ousler [102].

37. The market for securities of all types was well-developed by the Civil War, the New York Stock Exchange having been in operation since 1817. See Sobel [149].

38. For details of how specific companies invested their assets see Buley [22] and James [78].

39. May and Ousler [102];

40. James [79].

41. Boorstin [16] pp. 173-174.

42. Boorstin [16] p. 174.

43. See Keller [82].

44. Krooss and Blyn [89] p. 205.

45. Krooss and Blyn [89] p. 207.

46. See Krooss and Blyn [89] p. 113.

47. See James [78].

48. See Bickelhaupt [15] regarding this transition.

49. Williams and Heins [165], especially chapter 1, "The Risk Management Concept."

50. Krooss and Blyn [89] p. 241.

4 Critical Interpretations

Insurer Behavior and Social Change

Have insurers generally reacted to a changing environment or has the industry engaged in a concerted effort to shape the environment for its own purposes? Previous analyses of the history of the relationship between the industry and society have argued on behalf of one or another of these interpretations. One reason for analyzing the industry and society as social systems is to bring a new perspective to this question. In this chapter we initially discuss the principal interpretations of insurer behavior, pointing out that conventional interpretations of organizational behavior always imply an assumption about the status or underlying relationship between the industry and society.

As discussed in Chapter 1, there are two principal models of organizational behavior in the literature, one emphasizing reaction to environmental change, the other stressing action to promote environmental change. These modes of behavior describe general patterns of response to an environment of changing social expectations. Yet, as one favorite historian often noted in his course on historical methodology, history is full of revisionists. The point, of course, is that what appears adaptive to one historian will appear manipulative to another, especially if he proceeds from a different perspective or reviews the same facts at a different point in time. The lesson is useful in the study of insurer behavior. Based on the same basic facts described in Chapter 3, interpreters of insurance history have variously concluded that the industry was a shrewd interpreter of public needs and wants or a corrupted manipulator of public fear, emotion, and concern. These interpretations, and the assumptions underlying them, are examined in this chapter, with special attention being given to the theoretical bases for such interpretations. The critique of these approaches, and a note about the alternative that systems analysis provides, will help prepare the reader for our own revisionist analysis that continues in Part II.

The Insurance Industry as a Study of Adaptation

Adaptation as a Mode of Corporate Behavior

An important, yet implicit, question in the analysis of organizational response to social change is "Why do organizations act?" The question is a deceptively simple one. It may be argued that organizations act because their management causes them to act. But that answer assumes that organizations are the tools of their founders and/or managers, and it raises a great many questions about what forces or stimuli prompt managers to make the organization act in a particular way.

Questions similar to these have long been asked about individual behavior, and, by analogy, some hypotheses about organizational action may be raised. One is that any organization is subject to social control through the means of values, norms, and sanctions. Smelser has noted that *values* refer to beliefs legitimizing the existence and importance of specific social structures and kinds of behavior occurring in social structure; *norms* refer to standards of conduct regulating the interaction among individuals in social structures; and *sanctions* include both rewards and deprivations and refer to the use of various social resources to control the behavior of personnel in social structures.[1] In the context of the organization, we can argue that the value of "free enterprise," for example, legitimizes the pursuit of profit by business firms; contract and property law establish norms by which such pursuit may be conducted in specific situations; and sanctions, in the form of ridicule, appeal to duty, while coercion serves to establish roles in particular business firms, induce individuals to perform those roles, and control deviations from expected performance.[2]

By considering norms, sanctions, and values as the basic means through which social control is exercised in a society, we can begin to understand the range of stimuli accounting for organizational behavior. At one level, the shared values of the organization's members (board of directors, management, employees) form a stimulus that is the product of collective initiative.[3] These values may be dominated by one or another of the organization's memberships (e.g., management) and then reinforced throughout the organization by a variety of incentives and social sanctions designed to unify other memberships and enhance their commitment to the goals of the firm. The manner in which employee profit-sharing plans reinforce management values of growth and profit are an example of such a relationship.

Norms, especially explicit legal norms, form a second set of stimuli, inducing behavior that is largely involuntary in nature. Because norms are also reinforced by explicit social sanctions,[4] conflicts can arise between the values of the organization's members and the social norms specified in law (through legislation or judicial decisions). These create for management the dilemma of either complying with the legal norm or with the social values prevailing within the organization.[5]

Between the voluntary situation where organizational initiatives (values) prevail and the involuntary where legal norms compel action lies an intermediate situation in which various forms of public pressure are directed against the organization by relevant publics in an attempt to influence and affect the organization's action. Here management faces another dilemma, for it can neither claim that it must comply with the law nor can it always perceive a consensus among its members as to the appropriateness of a given response. Management is forced, in effect, to seek a coalition among its various internal (e.g., employees, shareholders) and external relevant publics that will support a chosen course of action with regard to the social claim.[6]

In this context, organizational *adaptation* is essentially a reactive response to the changing legal norms and public pressures confronting the organization. With respect to legal norms, it ranges from minimum compliance at one extreme to compliance with the spirit as well as the letter of the law; with respect to public pressure it involves those concessions necessary to stabilize the environment and permit the organization to continue its operations. In both situations changing performance requirements (demands and expectations of relevant publics) stimulate changes in organizational behavior. Thus *reaction* to changing performance requirements is the essence of adaptation.

Ackerman's study of organization responses to changing social demands illustrates both the uses and the limitations of the adaptation concept in describing and analyzing responses to changing social demands.[7] His study concentrated on the responses of two large, decentralized corporations in the areas of environmental protection and minority rights. The result of this observation was the identification of a three-step process, involving a recognition phase wherein the company, through its chief executive officer, becomes aware of the social issue and responds in an ad hoc fashion; a specialist phase where the organization gathers technical expertise about the issue and its implications for the firm; and a policy implementation phase where the systematic implementation of policy is undertaken by integrating the policy into the resource allocation and management evaluation process of the firm. When the process has been completed and the policy institutionalized,[8] the result is a regularized and effective response by the organization to the social demand. This is viewed as an optimal result for the organization. Stability has been achieved in the environment through organizational adaptation, and "rationality" has been extended to an area of previous uncertainty.[9]

The cogency of the Ackerman model masks the narrowness of its scope. First, the time period under consideration is ill-defined, ranged from initial social concern to the development of full social consensus.[10] Of major importance, though unanswered, is the question of the nature of the forces prodding the organization to action. The environmental texture received only cursory mention in Ackerman's discussion and is portrayed in the broadest terms.[11] The problem is that the objective environment is less important than the perceived environment in shaping the organization's responses; management perceptions, in turn, are likely to vary with the amount and types of pressure being applied by relevant publics. Thus, with regard to both time and pressure, Ackerman's model is unduly general.

A second shortcoming involves the restricted definition of social demands.

Ackerman describes responses to particular social issues, not to trends or to relevant publics. In so doing, the discussion is focused on the tactics of response, not strategies of response. To discuss the latter, it is necessary to understand management's total perception of the environment, not merely perceptions relating to a single issue. By concentrating on a single issue, the model is confined to the narrowest manifestation of social change. A broader focus, incorporating social trends and evolving coalitions of relevant publics is required for a more thorough analysis of responses to social change.

Thirdly, Ackerman characterizes the end result as an adaptive response. The response he describes is essentially reactive, calculated to comply with prevailing legal norms and to avoid overt social sanctions. This conception assumes that the stimulus for organizational action must lie outside the firm, that is, the organization cannot initiate action with regard to either the issue or the relevant public(s) involved. But it is precisely because we know that organizations can and do initiate action with respect to issues and relevant publics that we look beyond the adaptive organization. What kinds of initiatory action actually occur depends greatly on the values of management and their perceptions of the issue and/or relevant publics involved.

Philip Selznick is among the more prominent theorists who have considered organizations and values. He has argued that there is an important distinction to be drawn between organizations that are simply rational instruments for accomplishing the definite goals of their founders and command no personal investment or commitment and organizations that have taken on a distinctive character, become prized in and of themselves, and command the loyalties and personal commitments of people.[12] The latter are *institutions*, and they become institutions through a process of organic development whereby the organization responds to the strivings of internal groups and the values of the external society.[13]

Charles Perrow has questioned the usefulness–but not the validity–of the distinction between organizations and institutions, arguing that the more basic and essential difference is between the inflexible and unswerving organization, deriving its goals from its participants, on the one hand, and the flexible, outward-looking organization that responds to the values of the community, on the other.[14] Selznick himself has noted that any organization that survives for some time will be affected by the process of value infusion, and, as if to reinforce Perrow's point, Selznick stresses that the degree of institutionalization varies with the freedom for personal and group interaction. Hence the more precise the goals and the more technical and specialized the operations, the less opportunity there will be for social forces to affect the organization's development.[15] Thus adaptiveness to social change and community values varies with organizational characteristics.

The use of the term *institutionalization* to describe this evolutionary and maturing process is somewhat confusing. Since all organizations that continue for even a brief period of time are in the process of becoming institutions, the term connotes a general pattern. But since, as Perrow shows, institutions can be inflexible as well as responsive, it forces us to conceive of institutionalization as a process whereby flexible organizations can also become inflexible institutions. The point is that institutionalization refers to a microlevel process of change; but institution is also a macrolevel characterization of a *class* of organizations, not the universe. This dual usage gives institutionalization a confused and imprecise meaning; the term is therefore specifically rejected as a description of the process by which organizations are shaped by the values, norms, and standards of their environment.

A number of empirical studies in the tradition of Selznick's *T.V.A. and the Grass Roots*[16] have described processes by which organizations have found their purposes eroded away by time and events,[17] have acquired purposes other than those with which they originally began,[18] or have established a client relationship with a new public.[19] All identify, in part, a broad process of interaction between the organization and those aspects of society that constitute its environment, and all refer in part to changes in the values of the organization and its members. Such studies are, however, restricted to a single case, and empirical attempts to describe a general process of organization-environment interaction have largely been confined to analyses of only a few environmental variables, such as technology or labor market changes.[20]

Adaptation and Insurance

The insurance industry has not been explicitly studied as a case of organization or industry adaptation to change. However, a number of studies have developed themes that imply that the pattern of industry or firm development has been primarily adaptive in nature.

One of the premier studies of the insurance industry is Stalson's analysis of the marketing of life insurance.[21] The study is considerably more than a history of marketing, for it brings together the threads of organizational growth, entrepreneurial innovation, and changing market demands for life insurance. Originally published in 1942, Stalson's analysis stops near the end of the 1930s Depression period and does not, therefore, deal with any post-World War II developments. But the history does establish a clear model of life insurer behavior. In Stalson's view, marketing is the quintessential adaptive response of insurers to changing internal (organizational) factors, such as actuarial knowledge, and to changing external social and political conditions. The history of the industry is the story of continuous adaptation by the industry to social stimuli, all in the basic framework of the marketplace. Thus Stalson's work is an adaptive action model in association with a market status model.

One of the leading analyses of the legal history of insurance is Spencer

Kimball's study of insurance and public policy based on the Wisconsin state records.[22] This history is a landmark in attempting to weave into a single cloth the economic and social purposes giving rise to pertinent insurance legislation, court rulings, and administrative decisions over the course of one hundred twenty-five years of development in Wisconsin. Kimball's thesis is that the law is a means for accomplishing social and economic purposes and that the analysis of legal records discloses much about the implementation and true purposes of public policy. The status model that Kimball employs is obviously a legal one, wherein the suprasystem develops the rules of the game to which the organization responds. In Kimball's study, therefore, two lines of analysis are continuously developed. The first describes the events, interests, and debates occurring in society (e.g., the failure of Eastern life insurers to finance development in Wisconsin) and the public policy responses that evolved; the second describes how the microorganizations (e.g., the Eastern insurers) responded to those policies. Generally, the response is portrayed as adaptive in nature, the insurers reacting to legal change. At times, however, Kimball does describe insurer actions that are more manipulative in character and, of course, not theoretically consistent with the legal status model. In this sense, such activity is treated as a deviant form of action but not one that undermines the basic legal model.

Although not plentiful in number, there are a few insurance studies that treat insurer actions as adaptive to the environment, but only in the sense that they constitute a continuing search for new areas of exploitation. Several of these studies have focused on pricing patterns and policy differentiation as areas in which life insurers have continuously sought to exploit a confused and unsophisticated buying public.[23]

The technostructure model of industry-society relations has been implicit in the various writings of Herbert Denenberg and explicit in his actions as a Commissioner of Insurance in the Commonwealth of Pennsylvania.[24] Denenberg has treated insurer relations with society as involving a situation in which the technocrats (insurance company managers and insurance commission staffs) have developed an identity of interests that dominates the public's expectations with respect to both the industry and its regulators. The adaptive action model is most dramatically portrayed in Denenberg's own attempts to create a state of countervailing power in Pennsylvania by adopting a "maverick" posture as insurance commissioner and demanding that the insurers respond.[25] To the extent they did react the insurers were responding to a situation where technocratic identification existed between the commission staff and the industry experts, but not between the commissioner and the industry. The situation is appropriately characterized in terms of adaptive insurer behavior viewed from the perspective of a technostructure status model.

Overall, therefore, most studies of the insurance industry tend to assume the adaptive action model. Company histories frequently describe the perceptions of founders and managers in responding to changing public needs, goals, and aspirations.[26] Even studies of such specialized aspects of the industry's history as the development of multiple-line insurers tend to treat insurer action as an adaptive response to social change,[27] not an attempt to manipulate the environment for organizational purposes.

The Insurance Industry as a Study of Manipulation

Manipulation as a Mode of Corporate Behavior

Scholarly analysis of the manipulative type of organizational action is not nearly as well-developed as that of the adaptive type. There is an apparent preference for treating manipulative acts as the deviant case of organizational action. However, the number of reported instances of manipulation or attempted manipulation are numerous and some theorizing is possible.[a]

A starting point for theorizing about the manipulative mode of organization behavior involves organization goals. But the study of goals is, itself, an area of some complexity. Organizations are created to pursue specific goals and their raison d'etre is the service of those goals. Once formed, however, organizations acquire their own needs, and these needs may vary greatly from the original goals.[28] Thus goals are dynamic not static, and they reflect the influences of numerous—and changing—internal and external factors and pressures.

In terms of a model of organizational action, an organizational goal is a state of affairs that the organization is attempting to realize; it is the state of affairs that the organization, as a whole, is trying to bring about.[29] In terms we have used before, the goal is a preferred state, and the organization's activity is directed toward achieving that state. But, as Etzioni also points out, the organization is not always (or ever) able to bring about this desired image of the future. And, even if it is achieved, it then ceases to be a goal but becomes a reality; a new goal then emerges as the next preferred state to which the organization aspires.

By definition, goals are the creations of individuals, either individually or collectively. A goal does not remain constant; it really is an abstraction distilled from the interests of members, pressures of the environment, and desires of the organization's internal subsystems. Indeed, as one looks at the history of the insurance industry there is clear evidence that the balance of influence between the technical, managerial, and institutional subsystems of the firms shifted and influenced the goals that were pursued for periods of time. One task of a firm's top management may actually be to keep organizational goals in a form sufficiently abstract as to permit adjustment to changing circumstances while

[a]The many cases of illegal political and business payments that have been reported in the recent past reinforce the conclusion that what has heretofore been viewed as isolated acts of deviance is a more widespread pattern of "normal" organizational behavior.

still providing useful reference points for all members of the organization. Such a purpose, however, raises a necessary and important distinction between official and operative organizational goals.

Perrow distinguishes between the general purposes of the organization as stated in the charter, annual reports, and public statements of top executives—the *official goals*—and the *operative goals*, which designate the ends sought through the actual operations of the organization; they tell us what the organization is really trying to do, regardless of what official proclamations identify as the goals.[30] It is this emphasis on what the organization actually is trying to do that identifies the critical distinction between adaptive action and manipulative action. If management has perceived a state of affairs preferable to that which prevails, and if it attempts to move the organization toward that preferred state by changing the environment rather than positioning the organization, the action is manipulative in character.

The difference between adaptive and manipulative action is most clearly drawn when one examines why organizational goals change. Hall describes three basic reasons for goal change in organizations: first, direct pressures from external forces that lead to a deflection from the official goals; second, pressures from internal sources that may lead the organization to emphasize activities quite different from those originally intended; and third, altered environmental and technological demands that force a redefinition of goals.[31] Organizational behavior, then, is either a response to these factors or an attempt to modify them and thereby preserve the goals.

One consequence of direct external pressure can be the deflection away from the original goals. As long as the pressure continues, the original goals cannot be achieved. If those goals are still the preferred state, however, action will be taken to eliminate the external pressure—that is, to change the environment. Bargaining, competition, cooptation, and coalition formation have all been described as means of changing an environment to make possible the attainment of the preferred state.[32] Each involves action taken toward a relevant public or publics: bargaining is an attempt to gain *x* by giving *y*; competition is an attempt to gain support through exchange; cooptation involves bringing new elements (or relevant publics) into the decision-making process; coalitions involve the seeking of common goals. Each can be intended, and actually serve to operate, as a means of shaping the environment, not simply responding to it.[b]

Goal displacement reflects changes in goals attributable to internal sources. Michel's analysis of socialist parties and labor unions in Europe during the early 1900s is a classic study in this regard and the source of the "iron law of oligarchy" thesis. In that case, the need for the organization (Party) to

[b]Many authors treat this as a case of interorganizational action; that is, the environment is composed of other organizations. Such treatment ignores, for the most part, the unorganized character of some relevant publics with which every organization must interact.

accomplish revolutionary purposes led to the establishment of leaders within the organization. The leaders, in turn, sought to preserve their positions rather than further revolutionary goals. Hence the revolutionary goals of the Socialist Party were displaced to serve the interests of the new leadership.[33] Examples of the same pattern which are closer to the American scene in the twentieth century can be found in the life cycle analyses of the independent regulatory agencies, first proclaimed by Bernstein in the 1950s and subsequently refined by Lowi, Kohlmeier, and Chatov.[34]

Changing environmental, cultural, and technological conditions that impact on an organization more indirectly than the direct efforts of a relevant public form a third force effecting goal change. The indirect impact of these factors makes it difficult for management to initiate action that will change the environment; the environment is too unstructured to normally permit direct dealings with relevant publics. There are some exceptions, however, as for example, where an organization attempts to shape the technological environment in its industry by developing a dominant arrangement of patents. IBM, Polaroid, and Kodak all represent variants of an organizational strategy directed toward the preempting of technological competition, not toward responding to it.[c]

Manipulation and Insurance

Although not as numerous as those that have treated insurer activity as adaptive in nature, a number of studies have treated insurer behavior as manipulative in character. As with the adaptation studies cited above, these studies also explicitly or implicitly assume a status relationship between insurers and society.

The capture and use of regulatory agencies for insurer purposes is perhaps the clearest case of manipulation that has been reported. Kimball, for example, describes a number of occasions when insurers chartered in the state of Wisconsin prevailed upon the insurance department to issue rulings that created a special burden for out-of-state firms seeking to do business in the state.[35] Although Kimball quite clearly prefers to see such behavior as deviant examples of insurer action not inherently consistent with the legal status model, his description portrays organizations with goals that are being deflected because of the external pressure of competition. When a firm cannot, or does not choose to, compete by improving product quality or lowering prices, one alternative is to convince the regulatory agency that oversees the industry to impose more stringent regulation on major competitors. In Wisconsin this led to the imposition of special taxes on out-of-state insurers.

[c]The technological environment in such cases is, of course, somewhat structured by the patent system. Where patents fail to afford real protection, the technological environment becomes unstructured and therefore difficult to manipulate.

The operative goal of a protected competitive environment that one can impute to the insurers in the Wisconsin case has been extended to a more general statement of the industry's desire for a secure and protected existence. Keller, for example, describes the manner in which the life insurance magnates of the late 1800s proclaimed the social importance of their enterprise and sought federal regulation of life insurance because it seemed to provide an opportunity for the great companies to prevent the emergence of a fragmented state regulatory system such as that which afflicted the fire insurance business. This would, in turn, provide an opportunity for the large companies to continue their great growth and market dominance.[36] In this context, manipulation of the Congress and the political environment was not a deviant form of insurer action; it was the necessary result of the intimate relationship between politics and life insurance. It was a business that was involved in, and had demands to make upon, an extensive state regulatory system, and it stood to gain by influencing the shape of that system.[37] As to the regulatory system, Keller assumes an exploitation relationship between insurers and society; as to the public that purchased life insurance, Keller seems to perceive a market relationship, but one that evolved into an exploitive one as the life insurers assumed gargantuan size in the last decades of the nineteenth century. The point of Keller's study of life insurance enterprise between 1885 and 1910 is that manipulation was a mode of insurer action that proved immensely successful throughout much of the period. Eventually, legislative, regulatory, and social pressures would curb the overt manipulative activities of insurers but not until the industry had acquired a protected, quasi-public-utility character quite unlike the robber baron image it garnered in the 1870s and 1880s. This protected state was achieved, not by responding to the environment, but by manipulating the environment so as to make a protected state of affairs possible.

The most recent study of the insurance industry to treat insurer action as manipulative in nature is Orren's analysis of the credit and mortgage lending practices of life insurers.[38] This study presumably deals with the life insurance industry's Urban Investment Program, announced in September 1967, and which originally committed the industry members to extend a special one billion dollars of mortgage credit for inner-city properties. This action, often described as a socially responsible commitment to urban improvement, is analyzed in terms of its impact on housing tracts in the Chicago area. The result is a condemnation of the scheme as a hoax and an attempt to manipulate public opinion away from any serious consideration of mandatory investment legislation that would require insurers to invest their funds in specific socially desirable projects.

Orren's larger thesis is that the goal of all insurer activity is to free resources in the form of investment funds so that management may invest them as it chooses. The investment pattern that results will inevitably lead to an exploitation of citizens who purchase life insurance but reside in areas that are "redlined" as unsuitable investment areas by insurance companies, thereby receiving no mortgage or improvement capital. What permits this state of affairs to continue is a sophisticated and intensely political environment in which the insurers have captured and dominated regulatory and legislative bodies. One result of this manipulative activity is the regular defeat of mandatory investment legislation whenever it is proposed, and a general thwarting of the public purpose.

Orren's use of status models runs the gamut, and she assumes, in rapid-fire succession, that the legal model yields a look at cooptation of the legislature and the regulatory agencies, that the market model fails to describe everything except the way in which insurers actually choose to avoid investment in the inner city, that exploitation of both insurance policyholders and the inner city is the result and purpose of these legal and market considerations, and that insurers have succeeded in creating an identity of values between themselves and regulatory officials and legislators (at least in Illinois where between 25 percent and 58 percent of the members of the legislature's two insurance committees between 1961 and 1968 were engaged in the insurance industry).[39] In each respect it is the intensive activity of insurers to shape their environment that has permitted profits to be made and abuses to continue uncorrected.

In conclusion, then, manipulation has been treated as a basic mode of insurer action in situations where external pressures have directly threatened reform (e.g., mandatory investment laws), where uncontrollable change has indirectly portended departures from the normal way of doing business (e.g., the urban investment program as a response to riots), or where new internal needs (goals) have recommended a new preferred state (e.g., federal regulation). In each case, the response of the insurers has been interpreted as being less a reaction to environmental change than an overt (or covert) attempt to shape the future contours of the business environment. But these theories of insurer behavior, like the adaptive theories discussed earlier, cannot account for all specific actions. Keller noted, in his study of life insurance enterprises at the turn of the century, that the managers demonstrated unparalleled purpose and skill in attempting to control their business environment. Yet their efforts eventually came into conflict with limiting factors that imposed significant checks on their power and altered the life insurance enterprise.[40] It is this apparent truth—that manipulation can prevail but not forever dominate a relationship—that is the Achilles' heel of the manipulation theories. Just as the effort of organizations to manipulate an environment undermines the pure adaptation theses of insurer conduct, the necessity of adapting *at times* to external demands undermines a pure manipulative theory of insurer behavior. Within the parameters described by these weaknesses is the need for further research into the modes of organization action.

Interpenetrating Systems and Corporate Behavior

The singular shortcoming of both the adaptive and manipulative theories of corporate behavior is that they cannot independently explain key developments in the industry's evolution without characterizing some significant part of that evolution as the result of essentially deviant behavior (i.e., theoretically inconsistent with the market, legal, exploitation, or technocratic status models). The difficulty with such a result is that such deviant behavior is often quite permissible within the framework of the American political economy. Hence, deviant is not synonymous with illegal, despite its otherwise pejorative connotations.

The interpenetrating systems model of the management-society relationship resolves this problem by focusing on the actual process of interaction between an industry (or firm) and society rather than attempting to theorize about causality. While lacking the theoretical elegance of the classicial economic (market, exploitation, technocratic) or political (legal) models, the treatment of the firm and society as social systems that interact and directly and/or indirectly influence one another permits an inductive analysis of the actual manner in which these systems behave. In practice we expect that both adaptive and manipulative behavior patterns will be identified. However, it is possible that other patterns of behavior may exist, and it is certain that neither adaptive nor manipulative behavior will be considered deviant unless it is clearly outside the scope of legally permissible social, political, or economic activity.

The social processes through which an industry (or firm) interacts with society include the market process and the public policy process. In Chapter 3 we discussed the history of insurer-society relations in terms of market developments. But as it was repeatedly emphasized, the market system in the insurance business has long been recognized as being affected with the public interest. Hence the workings of the insurance market are entirely dependent upon the public policy setting. If, as has happened on a number of occasions, the public collectively determines that changes must be made in the working of the market or even that the market be abandoned as a means of providing insurance, the public policy process is the setting within which those decisions are made.

The history of the changing public policy environment for insurance is an extensive one and deserves consideration distinct from that given to market matters. Hence, in Part II our consideration of the evolution of the industry-society relationship focuses on those broad areas of changing public policy involving regulation of the insurance enterprise and the regulation of insurer behavior.

Notes

1. Smelser [148] p. 27.
2. Smelser [148] p. 28 employs the term *institutionalization* to describe

the harmonious integration of these elements of social interaction and social control. In his terms, institutionalization refers to the distinctive and enduring expectations created by integrating values, norms, and sanctions.

3. Such initiative may be the product of consciously or unconsciously shared values. See Chatov [26].

4. For an example, see Muir [110].

5. The difficulties in implementing affirmative action programs to eliminate racial and sex discrimination form the outstanding recent example in this regard. See Collins and Ganotis [33]. For an example dealing with the implementation of the U.S. Supreme Court school prayer rulings, see Muir [110]. Stanley Milgram's psychological studies in the area of behavioral obedience offer provocative suggestions regarding the need for authoritative reinforcement of behavioral norms not naturally reinforced by the values of involved individuals. See Milgram [108].

6. This is an essentially political act and points to the political character of modern business. See Chamberlain [24] and Schlusberg [142]. The participation that is attendant to this phenomenon is discussed in Preston and Post [135].

7. Ackerman [1].

8. This usage of the term suggests that institutionalization is synonymous with adaptation. If this usage is accepted, however, it portrays the organization as being most effective when it engages in a processs of reaction, rather than initiative-taking.

9. This formulation is suggested by Thompson [156].

10. Ackerman [1] estimates a cycle of six to eight years in length. That estimate seems limited to the specific issues studied, discrimination, and pollution. Indeed, with regard to discrimination, a strong argument can be made that the cycle most recently began with the U.S. Supreme Court's *Brown v. School Board* decision in 1954.

11. See Emery and Trist [45] and Terreberry [155].

12. See Selznick [146] pp. 5-21.

13. Perrow [126] p. 190.

14. Perrow [126] p. 191.

15. Selznick [146] p. 16.

16. Selznick [146].

17. See Gusfield [65] regarding the Women's Christian Temperance Union.

18. See Selznick's discussion of the TVA [145] and Scott's [144] study of sheltered workshops for the blind.

19. Selznick's study of the TVA [145] and Sill's analysis of the National Foundation for Infantile Paralysis (March of Dimes) [147] are two classics.

20. See Lawrence and Lorsch [91] and Woodward [167].

21. Stalson [151]. Buley's studies of the industry [21, 22] are comparable.

22. See Kimball [84].

23. In the muckraker tradition see Dacey [37]; a more factual and scholarly treatment is found in Belth [9].

24. Regarding his writings, see Denenberg [40, 41]; regarding his tenure as Insurance Commissioner, see Grotta [64].

25. An example is Denenberg's treatment of Pennsylvania Blue Cross and Blue Shield. See Grotta [64].

26. Among the more notable company histories in this regard are James [78, 79], May and Ousler [102], and Williamson and Smalley [166].

27. See Bickelhaupt [15] for example.

28. Etzioni [49] p. 5.

29. Etzioni [49] p. 6.

30. Perrow [125] p. 855.

31. Hall [66] pp. 87-88.

32. Selznick's study of the Tennessee Valley Authority [145] is the classic reference. Also, see Thompson and McEwen [157] for a typology of possible actions.

33. Michels [107].

34. See Bernstein [13], Lowi [99], Kohlmeier [87], and Chatov [27].

35. See Kimball [84].

36. Keller [82] p. 32.

37. Keller [82] p. 31.

38. Orren [120].

39. Orren [120] p. 51.

40. Keller [82] p. 33.

Part II
Public Policy and Public Interests

5 Regulation of the Insurance Enterprise

Insurance and Public Policy

In the sense that public policy refers to generally accepted social principles, the sale of insurance products has long been recognized as a matter involving the public interest, and hence, public policy. Whether manifested as direct, ad hoc interventions by the executive or legislature or as continuing regulation by commission, government has acted to both promote and control insurance activities for several hundred years in the United States. The history of this governmental concern with insurance suggests the changing focus of public policy. At one time the primary concern of the state was the existence of insurance as a legitimate commercial activity; over time that focus has changed and the role of the industry and the actions of companies engaged in selling insurance have become matters of primary importance.

Current public policy principles regarding insurance had their genesis in the late nineteenth century when two sets of developments coalesced and prompted a major public debate on the status and activities of American insurers. The first, and perhaps more important, set of developments involved the evolution of the industry from an essentially technical character to one that was, in Parsons' terms, in the process of becoming more managerial and institutional in nature. This line of development transformed insurance companies from primitive entrepreneurial enterprises into huge and complex hierarchical structures, seemingly impervious to the demands of the public.

A second line of development that shaped public policy involved the growing number of legal interactions between the public and insurers. Insurance policies are contracts that, over several centuries of Anglo-American judicial interpretation, have acquired a unique legal character. The frequency of law suits against insurers, the appearance of one-sidedness in insurance policies, and the mind-boggling increase in insurer assets and power kept the insurance companies in the public eye, often in an unfavorable light. It was a situation not unlike that of the railroads during the late nineteenth century. Insurers gave the appearance of growing in size and power at the expense of the innocent public that increasingly had to sue insurers to preserve its rights. Such an impression was a sure invitation to public scrutiny and pressure for the formulation of regulatory standards.

Public policy refers to those widely shared and generally acknowledged principles directing or controlling actions that have broad implications for society.[a] There are structural, substantive, and procedural aspects to public policy. In one sense, public policy is the result of the interaction of various individuals, groups, and organizations whose existence and relationship to one another is a continuing and dynamic one; it is also the body of principles upon which societal consensus exists; and it is a process by which society modifies, replaces, or reaffirms those principles that it values.

In a substantive sense, public policy is formed when the inputs of public opinion, expert knowledge, and the views of interest groups (all reflecting current social forces) are channeled into a series of objectives. The determination of which objectives are to be pursued at a given time, and in what order, is a policy matter of the first importance.

The formation of public policy objectives and the setting of priorities is one aspect of the public policy process. A second aspect involves the manner in which policy objectives are pursued through the use of various instruments. The instruments of policy implementation typically include executive branch activities, legislation, the application of administrative rulings, and, in some instances, the decisions of courts.

Since many public policy objectives exist at any time and the capacity to implement is limited, it is also necessary to establish priorities for policy implementation. The setting of implementation priorities is also influenced by systemic pressures from the environment, thereby forcing a continuing public reappraisal of both policy objectives and their priority. In addition, public policy implementation is influenced by the success or failure of previously selected implementation devices. Thus policy objectives are both formulated and implemented in a manner that reflects current social demands and past experiences. This simple model is illustrated in Figure 5-1.

Policy Objectives

Spencer Kimball, whose study of insurance and public policy was based on an intensive study of the Wisconsin insurance records, has concluded that there have been five major public policy objectives with regard to insurance.[1] These are: (1) to set limits on those types of insurance activities that might be permissably conducted as legitimate commercial activities; (2) to create an insurance fund from which incurred losses can be paid; (3) to maintain and protect the integrity of the insurance fund against dissipation by those entrusted with managing it; (4) to determine those persons who were legitimately entitled to share in the insurance fund; and (5) to enhance the social usefulness of insurance while mitigating the adverse social impact of large insurance organizations. The relative priority of these objectives has fluctuated considerably over the course of the 200-year history of the American insurance industry.

[a]This definition implies that public policy is more firmly rooted in social consensus than in the specific actions of government.

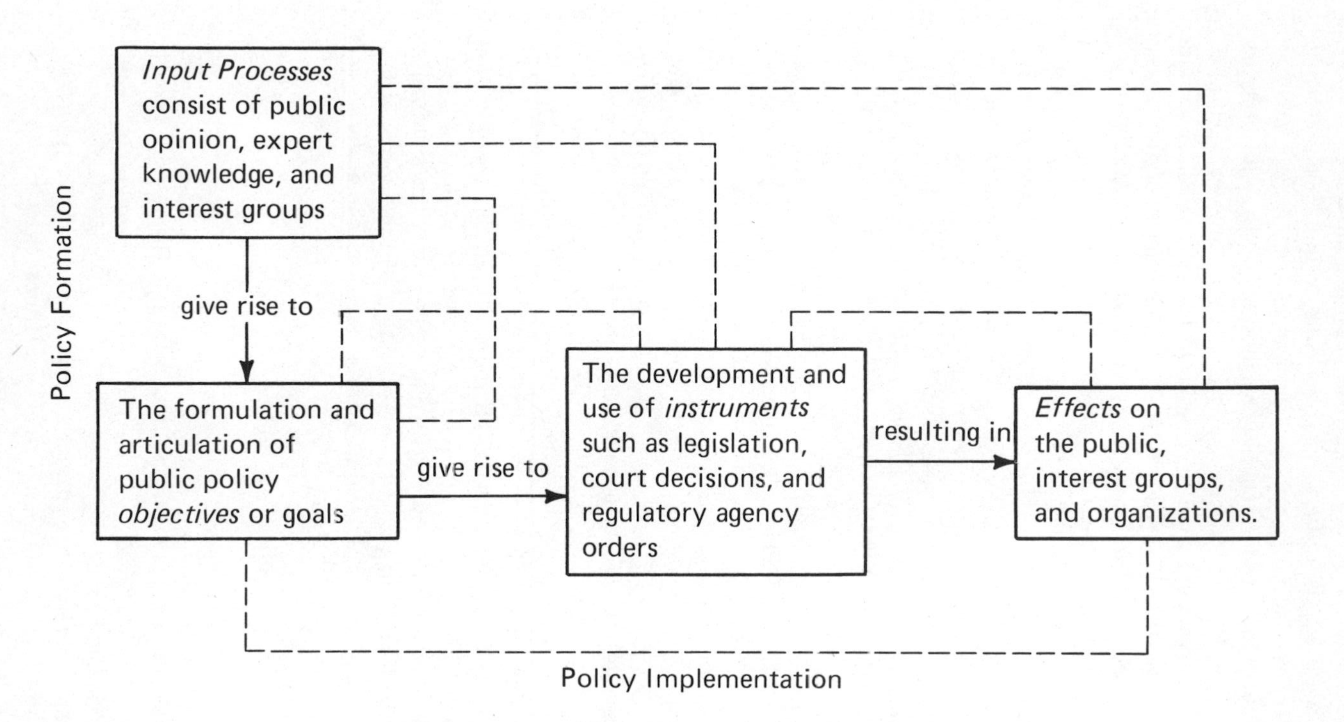

Note: Dotted line represents information feedback.

Figure 5-1. The Public Policy Process.

In general the public policy objectives regarding insurance during the preindustrial period related to the permissable kinds of insurance that might be sold and to the creation of an adequate insurance fund. As industrialization progressed, however, and as insurers became more numerous and the types of coverage they provided more extensive, the issue of who was entitled to payment from the insurance fund became an important one. In the twentieth century, various questions relating to the social usefulness of the insurance principle as a device for social protection and the private carrier industry as a means for providing this protection have become paramount.

The evolution of issues and public policy objectives has followed the industry's evolution from a technical to a managerial and, eventually, an institutional character. To generalize, it is possible to say that the cutting edge of public policy development during the preindustrial period was technical in nature, involving the provision of insurance; during the industrial period it was related to the managerial matters of sales methods and the distribution of funds; and in the postindustrial period it has involved issues relating to the social performance and social role of the industry. These matters have overlapped one another, of course, generating contradictory pressures in some instances, cumulative pressures in others. Friedman's conclusion that public policy regarding insurance has long suffered from the absence of a coherent and systematic economic theory of regulation has substantial justification.[2] Public policy at various times and in various states has been both contradictory in purpose and inconsistent in application. Consequently, the effects of public policy, reflecting these forces, have sometimes been contradictory as well.

To discuss this wealth of history, a distinction must be drawn between public policy directed toward the existence or status of insurance as a legitimate activity and important industry on the one hand, and policy that is directed toward the control of insurer behavior on the other. In this chapter we shall discuss the manner in which public policy has approved insurance as a legitimate area of commerce and encouraged development of a private insurance industry. In Chapter 6 the focus will turn to a consideration of the control of insurer behavior. This distinction will also prove useful in preparing the reader for public policy developments of the 1960s and 1970s.

Policy Instruments

The early policy instruments regarding insurance were direct orders from the state, usually in the form of specific legislation designed to limit or eliminate an entrepreneurial practice. This was particularly true with regard to schemes, in both England and America, that crossed the line between genuine insurance and lotteries.[3] In the early 1800s the state legislatures extended this line of governmental activity by granting to companies special charters that specifically enumerated and limited the powers of firms to engage in insurance enterprise.

The importance of legislative action changed in the mid-1800s when general incorporation statutes replaced the special charter. Many of the powers previously granted on a limited basis to individual insurance companies were thereby made available to any newly incorporated insurer. Modification of general incorporation statutes has occurred from time to time, but in general the influence of direct legislative action as an instrument of public policy has diminished in the twentieth century. Although legislative inquiries and investigations have been potent instruments of public policy at times (as evidenced by the Armstrong Investigation in 1905-1906, they are of primarily historical interest. A number of legislative investigations by the federal Congress in the late 1960s and early 1970s, however, have demonstrated the importance of legislative hearings as a forum for inputs into the formation of policy goals and objectives.

The primary instruments of public policy in the twentieth century have been the insurance commissions established by the states. New Hampshire established the first insurance commission in 1851 and Massachusetts did so in 1855. By 1873 twelve states had some form of institutionalized regulation, a number that grew to 17 by 1890 and 22 by 1905.[4] Today the National Association of Insurance Commissioners (N.A.I.C.) constitutes an important fact-finding and policy-coordinating coalition of state commissioners.[5] Although regulatory supervision of the industry has grown in a fragmented and incremental way, reflecting shifting public pressures and concerns, regulation today is generally comprehensive, extending to most aspects of the business. In many states all changes in rates, policy forms, and underwriting standards must receive prior approval from the commissions. In other areas, such as advertising, the commissions generally intervene after the fact to restrain questionable practices. Overall, the insurance commissions are unquestionably the principle instrument of policy implementation.

The courts have played a crucial, but limited, role as articulators of public policy regarding insurance. In terms of the public policy model described above, the courts serve primarily as a feedback device, communicating to the public, the companies, and the regulatory agencies various shifts in prevailing social consensus or breakdowns in the implementation of public policy objectives. In a few instances, however, they have also been the focal instrument for articulating new public policy or modifying existing policy.

In both England and America the courts ruled that one might not enter into a contract of insurance with regard to property or the life of another person unless the purchaser had an insurable interest. This doctrine, intended to restrain the proclivities of those who would prefer the payoff of the insurance contract to the continued existence of the insured property or person, was an important step in the validation of insurance as a legitimate commercial activity.

The courts—and especially the United States Supreme Court—also contributed to the development of public policy by articulating the legal basis for regulation of insurance. Although the state courts have heard most insurance-related cases, two decisions of the U.S. Supreme Court have provided the legal foundation upon which the present system of insurance regulation rests. In 1869 the Court held in *Paul v. Virginia* [8 Wall. 168] that insurance was not commerce and that under the U.S. Constitution, therefore, the states, not the federal government, were free to tax and regulate insurance. This decision, coupled with a line of cases holding that the insurance business was clothed with a public interest and thus subject to the police power of the states, formed the legal basis for insurance regulation through the early 1940s.[b]

The second crucial Supreme Court decision had the effect of providing the federal government a legitimate legal basis from which it too could regulate the insurance business. In November 1942 the U.S. Department of Justice secured an indictment against the Southeastern Underwriters Association and 198 member fire insurers on the grounds that their rate-making activities violated Sections 1 and 2 of the Sherman Antitrust Act.[6] Specifically, they constituted a conspiracy to fix prices and an attempt to monopolize trade and commerce in the fire insurance business across state lines. The Supreme Court was obliged to decide whether insurance across state lines constituted interstate commerce because, if so, federal statutes regulating such commerce–including the Sherman Act–would apply. The Court reached an affirmative conclusion on that issue by a 4-to-3 majority on June 5, 1944 when it announced its decision in *United States v. Southeastern Underwriters Association* [322 U.S. 533]. The decision established the underlying power of the federal government to regulate insurance as interstate commerce. Although the McCarran Act[7] was quickly passed by Congress to allow the states to continue to function as the primary regulators of the insurance business, it was clear that the absence of federal regulation was a permissive, not mandatory, feature of the legal environment. By the 1960s a number of inroads on the McCarran legislation had occurred and the federal power to regulate insurance was beginning to be exercised.

Policy Effects: Status and Behavior

The effects of public policy are usually matters of considerable debate. Every public policy action tends to generate both intended and unintended effects. Proponents tend to emphasize the positive intended effects; critics are prone to highlight the unintended and negative effects. It is probably impossible to examine all the intended and unintended effects of public policy as it applies to insurance, and it is certainly impossible to do so in one chapter. Hence our discussion of policy effects will be divided, those dealing with the existence of the insurance enterprise being considered in the remainder of this chapter, while the effects of behavioral regulation will be discussed in the following chapter.

---

[b]The principle case in this regard was *German Alliance Insurance Company v. Lewis* [233 U.S. 389], a case the U.S. Supreme Court decided in 1913 upholding the validity of a state rate regulation law. For a discussion see Michelbacher and Roos [106].

Any consideration of the impact of public policy on the status of the insurance enterprise must begin with the recognition that the manner in which economic activities are to be carried on is a fundamental policy question in every society. There are three broad alternatives: the activity may be left to the development of market forces, the state itself may perform the activity as a public enterprise, or the state may regulate—to some greater or lesser extent—the development of market forces. Along with the activity's legitimacy, the question of economic organization is a matter of status. Public policy with regard to insurance has evolved in the American experience first from a market orientation to an increasingly regulated framework; in the twentieth century, a further evolution toward the development of public enterprise ventures has occurred. These two transitions will be discussed in turn.

The Road to Regulation

The existence of insurance as a legitimate social activity was tempered in colonial America by a distrust of the gambling and wagering schemes that infested English insurance practice during the late 1600s and early 1700s.[8] And although there was considerable public support for most entrepreneurial ventures, insurance enterprises were not intuitively attractive. Part of the problem stemmed from English legislation of 1719 and 1741 which prohibited the formation of stock company insurers as competitors to two crown insurers; even mutual companies were rare before the Revolutionary War.[9] The position of private insurance companies improved only slightly after the War as the states, perhaps recalling the experience of the English monopolies, proved reluctant to grant special charters to would-be insurers.

Eventually, of course, the market for insurance coverage began to expand and, especially for companies writing marine coverage, the grants of power in special charters became broader, allowing more flexibility to company managers. Nevertheless, the legislatures tended to adhere to the concept of the monoline insurer—that is, one whose power is limited to the writing of a single line of coverage. In Kimball's terms, this was an attempt to both validate the enterprise on the basis of technical expertise and to safeguard the insurance fund from the uncertainties of risk in nonallied insurance lines. Thus specialization among insurers was encouraged for both technical and political reasons.

Arguments favoring private enterprise and unlimited rights to incorporation eventually led to general incorporation statutes as a replacement for special legislative charters. Legislative standards for incorporation made it possible for all who could meet the standards—primarily related to capitalization—to form insurance enterprises. Thus by the mid-1800s the right to form insurance companies had become a general one, and state legislatures had largely abandoned direct intervention in the insurance business.

Coupled with such fundamental legal doctrines as insurable interest, the general incorporation laws allowed the insurer of the mid-1800s to operate in an environment that generally favored entrepreneurial initiative and the expansion of product and geographic markets. It was a period of maximum reliance on the market as a device for normalizing social conduct and on competitive pressures as the means of satisfying the public's demand for insurance.

The primacy of the market as an organizing principle for the insurance business was never absolute. The early legislative reluctance to grant unlimited powers to insurers was regularly reaffirmed by the developing Midwestern and Western states. Kimball's analysis of Wisconsin legislative developments during the middle and late 1800s suggests that the great variety of state restrictions on out-of-state insurers arose from fears of concentrated power; it is also reflected in the encouragement given the formation of local, mostly mutual, fire insurance companies.[10]

An early precursor of regulation was state reliance on tax revenues from insurers. Insurance companies, with their large cash flows and financial reserves, were long identified as potential sources of tax revenues for needy state legislatures. A tax could be levied on the stock of insurers organized under the state laws or upon the premium income collected in the state. Foreign insurers (those formed in other states) could avoid the stock tax but their local agents could be reached. In order to effectively tax insurers, however, it was necessary to devise a system of registration, data compilation, annual reports, and penalities for nonpayment of taxes. The states' need for tax revenues served to both stimulate a rudimentary regulatory system that would require extensive reporting by insurers and to solidify the status of private insurers as a basic means of organizing the insurance business.

A second precursor of regulation was the attempt of some states to require annual operating reports of insurers. Massachusetts, for example, required all domestic insurers to report on their affairs to the legislature as early as 1807; in 1818 the issuance of an annual report to the public was made a standing provision of the law.[11] Eventually similar provisions were extended to out-of-state insurers as well. Regulation by publicity would prove to be a short-lived phase, to be sure, but it did indicate an early legislative reluctance to rely solely on market forces for the disclosure of information necessary to the public's protection.

The transition from a predominantly market framework to one of regulatory administration was a slow one. The actual transition apparently occurred in three steps. The first step involved the continuing attempts of state legislatures to directly control the business. Given a tendency to keep enforcement machinery to a minimum, early enforcement was primarily a system of *adversary regulation*—that is, the bringing of law suits against violators of legislative provisions or the institution of legal action to rescind a company's charter on the basis of a violation of charter terms. Annual reports and various filings of information were also made directly to the legislatures. Eventually, however, the whole process became overloaded to the extent that the handling of such reports was delegated to nonlegislative officials who were required to report their summarized findings to the legislature.

The second stage in the transition toward regulation involved the delegation of supervisory power to existing state officials, such as the state treasurer, auditor, or controller, who administered the revenue aspects of the early laws. Even as nonrevenue legislation was passed, the tendency existed to add new administrative responsibilities to these officials. In New York the first supervisory official was the controller. In other states regulatory power was passed to the secretary of state who also granted charters.

The multiple responsibilities of early supervisory agencies limited the effectiveness of regulation. By the mid-1800s the inadequacy of this system led to the creation of special insurance commissions in a number of states. The special commission phase of the transition to regulation began in the 1850s when New Hampshire, to be followed by Massachusetts and other states, created several-member commissions to undertake the annual examination of insurers.

The most famous of the early insurance commissions was that of Massachusetts, which was changed from a three-member board to a two-member board in 1855. One of the members was Elizur Wright, frequently referred to as the "father of insurance regulation."[12] By the 1860s and 1870s even the two-member commissions had been replaced by a single commissioner, normally an appointed official, who continued to report to the legislature. With the development of the office of insurance commissioner supervision of the industry was placed a framework of *administrative regulation.*[c]

Prior to the development of insurance commissions, the status of insurance as a legitimate commercial activity had been solidified by a combination of factors involving the growing need for protection, the existence of the courts as a device for implementing the rules of the game according to which insurers sold insurance and paid claims, and the general incorporation statutes that had democratized the formation of insurance companies. The development of the insurance commissions, however, operated to solidify the existence of the private-carrier insurance industry as the primary means of supplying insurance protection to the public.

The very basis of an insurance company's existence was the insurance fund.

[c]The rise of administrative regulation, especially in the late 1800s, is in part the result of the perceived failure of adversary regulation. Lawrence Friedman [54] notes that insurance claims were the friction point where aggregated capital met the common people on a plane of inequality (p. 387). Insurance litigation was frequent by the late 1800s. Keller [82] indicates that there were as few as 100 reported cases on life insurance to 1870. Fire and marine cases were more frequent but still not numerous among all appellate court decisions. By the 1890s appellate decisions on insurance law had mushroomed in number. As Friedman points out in the West Company's *Century Digest*, which briefs all reported cases down to 1896, the heading "Insurance" covers 2,808 pages. This volume suggests an absolute increase in lawsuits on all levels (pp. 476-477). Insurance law had exploded as a major area of litigation, and the insurance commissions would prove to be, in order, first a result, then a cause, and eventually an impediment to these legal challenges to insurers.

The creation and management of that fund constituted the technical core of the business. As long as the company's managers were relatively free to invest that capital fund in land and mortgages, the stocks of banks, railroads, or other insurers, and government securities of their choice, their own existence as a viable entity could be fairly well assured. Thus it is not inappropriate to argue, as some have done,[13] that insurers have continuously sought freedom from investment restrictions. Unwittingly the insurance commissions assisted in this purpose.

Safeguarding the insurance fund by inspecting the financial solvency of companies was a long-standing regulatory practice. And since the determination of reserve levels, evaluation of the quality of investments, and the setting of taxation levels were relatively technical matters about which the public was generally uneducated, it became possible for regulators and insurers to arrive at harmonious understanding about these problems. Agreement as to the manner in which the technical core of the business should be conducted thereby served to further ensure the survival of insurance enterprises by imposing a regulatory imprimatur on company practices.

Insurance regulation was also the outcome of the fear and public mistrust of the financial power of the large companies and an impression that the insurers were cheating the public. Such fears were not easily translated into legislation however. The demand for specific regulatory programs was diffuse, generally resulting in programs that were weak. The general demand for regulation resulted in an immense amount of legislation that may have symbolically satisfied the public but that did little to substantively affect the status of insurers.[14] The Massachusetts law to amend and codify the statutes relating to insurance, which was passed in 1887, for example, contained 112 sections of tightly written text.[15] Rather than serving as an expression of public priorities about policy objectives, such legislative outpourings were strictly expressions of public wishes. The establishment of policy priorities was left to the primary instruments of policy implementation, the regulatory commissions themselves.

The insurance commissions, however, became instruments of insurer competition as well as public policy. The interests of insurers were readily communicated to regulators, and corruption was common in the late decades of the 1800s; in New York the state legislature conducted investigations of insurance regulation in 1870, 1872, 1877, 1882, and 1885.[16] When not corrupt, the commissions were often half-hearted in their regulatory efforts.

The unification of insurer and commission interests proceeded in a predictable fashion.[17] The early commissions concentrated on developing an expertise in the financial and underwriting areas that constituted the technical core of the business. Indeed much of Elizur Wright's notoriety as insurance commissioner in Massachusetts derived from his prior experience as a developer of actuarial tables. The harmony of interest that developed between insurers and commission staffs on such matters as actuarial standards, insurer solvency, taxation, dividend policies, and reserve requirements all served to protect the industry from public criticism through the appearance—and incoherence—of technical regulation. The complexity of these technical matters made public understanding difficult and public action unlikely. On matters such as policy terms, however, where the public had both a concern and understanding of their effects, legislation was passed to mitigate those rules and clauses that made a policy void if an applicant made false or misleading statements.

Policy forms and marketing practices were managerial matters, tied to the selling of insurance and the administration of claims; they were not at the technical core of the business. The distinction is important because the industry's existence was safeguarded by regulatory acceptance of the technical aspects of the business. Individual companies might fight for their own survival in terms of sales schemes and claims practices and thus prompt regulations on insurer actions, but the industry's viability and status were secure. Even at the height of the public criticism directed at insurers during the early 1900s, the thrust of criticism was directed toward the behavior of individual companies, not at the legitimacy of the entire industry.[d]

Toward Public Enterprise

The shift from reliance on the market as a regulator to reliance on the state as regulator—first as an adversary, later as an administrator—constituted one major transition in the public policy evolution of the insurance industry. The second major transition occurred when new concepts about the socialization of risk began to garner public support in the twentieth century.

Socialization of risk refers to public recognition of the social interdependence of people, irrespective of wealth and private circumstances, and the inherent propriety of spreading risk over a population composed of dissimilar individual risks. The idea challenged the contemporary insurance practice of the early twentieth century, for it undermined the actuarial principle of selective underwriting and the creation of risk classes. The workmen's compensation laws, originally written in the first decades of the 1900s, provide an interesting example of the challenge to normal insurer practice that was posed by socialization of risk concepts.

As industrialization progressed, occupational injury and death rates rose precipitously. In the period 1907-1908, for example, 4534 workers were killed in railroading and 2534 were killed in bituminous mining; total deaths in 1908 from industrial accidents were estimated at between 30,000 and 35,000.[18] The number of occupational injuries caused an immense increase in the cost of disability insurance.

The courts were the articulators of early public policy toward occupational

[d]The effect of this criticism on behavioral regulation is discussed in Chapter 6.

disability, deriving a body of rules regarding employer liability from the common law. Three especially important legal rules resolved most cases in the employer's favor. First, under the common law, servants (employees) were denied recovery for injuries arising from a fellow servant's negligence. Hence, if one employee's negligence was the cause of another's injury, no action would hold against the employer. The second rule was the assumption of risk principle, which made the hazards of an occupation noncompensable. An employee could not collect from an employer for injuries suffered from a risk inherent in the job because, it was felt, wage rates of an occupation reflected its hazards. Thus in accepting a job at a given wage, an employee assumed the risks inherent therein. A third rule, that of contributory negligence, further sealed the injured employee's fate. At common law an employee injured in an accident in the course of his work could only collect through a personal injury suit against the employer. To succeed, the employee had to show that the job-connected injury arose from the employer's negligence. Although a master owed his servants due care, the servant had to be entirely without negligence on his own part in order to recover. Contributory negligence on the employee's part, even in the slightest amount, would defeat his cause of action against the employer.[19]

The volume of injuries and the paucity of adequate damage awards culminated in many legislative attempts to articulate new public policy in the late nineteenth century. Many states enacted employer liability legislation between 1885 and 1910 that attacked the fellow servant, assumption of risk, and contributory negligence doctrines. Progress was slow, however, and public sentiment continued to build in support of a system of comprehensive workmen's compensation to replace the employer's liability legislation. Favorable experience with such a system in Germany, England, and a number of other European nations was documented in numerous investigative reports. New York finally passed a workmen's compensation statute in 1910; but it was declared unconstitutional in 1911.[e] A Wisconsin statute in 1911 was successful. Other states quickly followed; by 1948 the last of the holdouts, Mississippi, had also passed a workmen's compensation statute.

The principle upon which workmen's compensation laws is based is that of liability without fault. In abandoning fault as a basis for liability, the employer's risk of liability was changed from a probability into an automatic judgment. The risk of disability to employees was thereby socialized and spread over an entire population. The risk of employer liability is simultaneously elminated in favor of an automatic process of injury reimbursement. Hence the workmen's compensa-

[e]In *Ives v. South Buffalo Railway Co.* [201 NY 271, 94 N.E. 431 (1911)], the court wrote: ". . . . This is a liability unknown to the common law and we think it plainly constitutes a deprivation of liberty and property under the Federal and State Constitutions. . . . (If) the legislature can say to an employer, 'You must compensate your employee for an injury not caused by you or by your fault,' why can it not go further and say to the man of wealth, 'You have more property than you need and your neighbor is so poor that he can barely subsist; in the interest of natural justice you must divide with your neighbor so that he and his dependents shall not become a charge upon the State'?"

tion laws are an expression of broad public policy that took cognizance of the fact that employment of labor posed a risk of disability and that such risk was not to be borne by the injured or disabled employees alone.

The workmen's compensation legislation raised an important policy question regarding the status of insurers. The agreed-upon plans had many insurance features. Employers were to be required to contribute to a fund that would then be used to pay disabled employees. There was initial company and insurance commission opposition to the state compensation plans; once it became obvious that legislation would pass, however, the commissions and the companies collaborated to guarantee private carriers a share of the new market. Thus most states provided that employers be allowed to secure their workmen's compensation coverage through private insurance carriers as well as state insurance funds.[20] Through a unified insurer-commission coalition a new market was opened to private carriers, although the underlying principle—nonselective underwriting—was not a technically acceptable one in the industry. The promise of state action in the area, however, stimulated the companies and the commissions to stake out a place in the newly socialized area of risk.[21]

The workmen's compensation laws were the first in a long line of social legislative actions in the twentieth century extending the concept of socialization of risk. The Social Security Act of 1935, its subsequent amendments, unemployment insurance, new forms of occupational disability insurance, and Medicaid and Medicare were all extensions of public policy that favored socializing the risk of injury, illness, old age, or other social infirmity. Throughout this evolution the private insurance industry, including life and nonlife carriers alike, frequently objected to such proposals, eventually agreed in principle, and ultimately took steps to secure a share of the newly created insurance markets. What has been accepted as a matter of public policy itself, is the status of the private insurance mechanism as a fundamental means of insurance delivery. Even in the face of a new societal ideology that emphasized societal goals (a sociologizing mode of thought, in Daniel Bell's terms), the status of the industry—that is, its place in the scheme of things—has been preserved.

Notes

1. Kimball [84], pp. 6-7.

2. Friedman [54] p. 388. Also, see Kimball and Denenberg [85] regarding alternative rationales for regulation.

3. See Ezeel [50].

4. Keller [82] p. 19.

5. See annual reports, National Association Insurance Commissioners [112].

6. 26 Stat. 209, 15 U.S.C.A., secs. 1-7.

7. Public Law 15, 79th Cong., approved March 9, 1945, 15 U.S.C.A. secs. 1011-1015.

8. See Stalson [151].

9. Michelbacher and Roos [106], Douglass [43].

10. Kimball [84].

11. Michelbacher and Roos [106].

12. O'Donnell [118].

13. See Orren [120]; also Keller [82].

14. See Edelman [44].

15. Friedman [54] p. 388.

16. See Stalson [151], Buley [21], and Keller [82].

17. The pattern is described by Bernstein [13] as a life cycle through which regulatory agencies tend to pass.

18. Data are drawn from Turnbull et. al. [160], p. 309.

19. Turnbull et. al. [160], pp. 308-319.

20. Three options generally exist for employers. They may utilize a private carrier, contribute to a state insurance fund, or prepare an acceptable self-insurance plan. The private carrier provision is allowed in 44 of 50 states. Turnbull, et. al. [160], pp. 318-319.

21. According to Buley [21] the state insurance plans often involved state-created mutual companies. Private companies could then write workmen's compensation policies at a rate no higher than that of the state company (pp. 410-411).

6 Regulating Insurer Behavior

Policy Effects: Insurer Behavior

While the regulation of status has generally reflected the successful efforts of the industry to secure for itself a permanent position in American society, the regulation of action or behavior has reflected public efforts to specify norms and standards or acceptable insurer conduct. In fact, public policy has formalized those norms and standards with respect to many of the technical and managerial aspects of the business.

The analysis of how this comprehensive regulation developed involves several themes. First, the regulation of insurer activities followed, not preceded, the regulation of matters of status, such as the legality of the insurance product and the insurance enterprise. Most regulation of behavior developed at the turn of the twentieth century, and unlike regulation of insurer status, passed almost directly from an unregulated to an administratively regulated stage, bypassing the adversary regulation that was so prominent in regulating the insurance enterprise.

Second, the regulation of insurer action initially focused on such technical aspects of the business as financial solvency and actuarial standards; this was followed by a concentration on such managerial facets of the business as marketing and sales practices; then by the early 1900s the focus shifted toward institutional practices, such as management control, political corruption, and interlocking directorates.

Lastly, the courts were a more prominent instrument for public policy implementation in the area of insurer action than they were in dealing with status. Although the legislatures also were concerned with insurer action, the creation of the insurance commissions was their principal contribution to the exercise of social control. Indeed it has been the commissions that, in the twentieth century, have been the primary means of regulating insurer behavior. But during the late nineteenth and early twentieth centuries it was the courts that worked out concepts of acceptable and unacceptable action by insurers.

Specific attention is given in the following sections to three main areas of insurer action: the regulation of insurance products, public policy regarding insurance pricing, and public policy actions taken to regulate a number of other historically important insurer practices. Together they constitute a framework for understanding the continuing regulation of insurer behavior.

Product Regulation

Because the insurance product is really a promise by the insurer to pay under specified conditions in the future, an early area of state regulation involved insurer solvency—that is, the ability of insurers to ultimately deliver the product. The insurance law of each state normally stipulates the minimum capital and surplus a domestic insurer must possess in order to transact business and the manner in which funds may be invested. Similar provisions are also applied to foreign (out-of-state) insurers.

The states have also limited those types of coverage that a single company can write. Through the late 1940s many states specified and restricted the kinds of insurance that might be written by insurers operating within the state. Life insurance and annuities were reserved for life insurers, title insurance for the special title insurance companies. Other companies could choose from among a set of approved lines that were classified into *casualty and surety* insurance (including accident and health, water damage, burglary and theft, glass, boiler and machinery, elevator, animal, collision, personal injury liability, property damage liability, workmen's compensation and employer's liability, fidelity and surety, and credit insurance) and *fire and marine* insurance (including fire, miscellaneous property, water damage, collision, motor vehicle, aircraft, marine, and indemnity insurance).[a] Although some exceptions existed, the general purpose of such product classifications was to restrict the underwriting powers of companies to related sets of products.[1] These classifications provided the basis for the monoline character of life, fire and marine, and casualty and surety companies.

Regulation of the financial structure of the firm and restrictions on the types of insurance it could write went to the heart of the enterprise. As discussed in Chapter 1, investment constitutes one aspect of the technical core of the insurance business. The policy objectives with regard to financial regulation are fairly simple and straightforward. They involve protection of the existence and integrity of the insurance fund through the stipulation of legal reserve levels, limitations on the nature and types of investments that may be made with premium funds, capital, and surplus, and through the filing of regular and standardized financial statements and reports.[2]

Policy objectives other than the preservation of solvency have led to regulation of the manner in which insurers normally invest their funds. During the late 1800s, especially, regulatory interest and legislative action focused on the manner in which insurers moved large amounts of capital across state lines. This movement had a great impact on local communities and prompted a rash of legislation by the states designed to control the effects of capital relocation. These laws especially affected the life insurance companies that possessed large

[a]These classifications are drawn from appropriate New York statutes. Similar classifications are used in other states.

reserves and surpluses.[3] The most objectionable of all the laws of the period was the Robertson Act of 1907 in which the state of Texas required that life insurers invest 75 percent of their Texas policy reserves in the state's public or corporate securities. Twenty-nine companies withdrew from the state rather than adhere to the compulsory investment provisions.[4] Although the Robertson Act was rescinded in 1967, state interest in this aspect of the insurance business persisted through the 1960s, when the question of the contribution of insurers to urban decay and retarded urban redevelopment heightened legislative interest in the larger question of insurer flow of funds.[5]

Public policy concerned with underwriting underwent a similar evolution. Historically, underwriting practice was focused on estimating the risk associable with physical hazards affecting the risk of loss or premature death. Whether it involves the brick building versus the wooden building or the lawyer versus the man who handles explosives, both situations involve relative degrees of risk. As insurers grew and the construction of insurance policies became more sophisticated, clauses began to appear that excluded certain types of property from coverage (e.g., lumber stored in the brick building) or conditioned coverage on the continuance of important risk considerations (e.g., as long as the lawyer didn't go near the plant of the explosives manufacturer he represented). These terms served underwriting standards but also angered a public that was frequently barred from collecting on their insurance because of such restrictive terms. By the late 1880s public policy began to reflect a concern with not only the sale of insurance but with the ability of the insured to collect insurance proceeds.

The underwriting issues of standards, terms, and conditions received a new focus in the twentieth century as insurance increasingly became a commercial, if not personal, necessity. Public opinion began to build in favor of compelling insurers to insure all risks. The financial responsibility laws regarding automobile usage that ultimately required that insurance be provided to all drivers introduced a new type of underwriting problem, the legal hazard.[6] *Legal hazards* refer to risks that insurers must assume and, also, to a variety of absolute liability doctrines established by the courts (e.g., product liability) that serve to broaden the scope of liability beyond that which was originally underwritten.

Another changing aspect of underwriting has involved challenges to the moral hazard component, which underwriters have seen as inherent in all risks. *Moral hazard* refers to deviations or departures from standards of conduct prevailing in a society and that, therefore, are assumed to increase the risk of loss. In practice the moral hazard issue has been used to justify insurer inquiry about an applicant's personal habits, life style, claims consciousness, racial background, police record, employment experience, and other social habits. Whatever the merit of such considerations (a matter about which there is disagreement), it was clear that by the 1960s such conceptions were undergoing change. When coupled with trends toward mandatory insurance programs, these changes indicated that underwriting was no longer the stable activity of an earlier time.

Price Regulation

Public policy regarding the pricing of insurance evolved in a manner similar to that regarding the insurance product. Regulatory concerns were initially technical in nature, relating to the creation of an insurance fund that would prove adequate over time to meet the commitment undertaken in issued policies. By the late 1800s these issues were replaced by public concern with the excessiveness of rates and the unfair and discriminatory manner in which they are applied. In the twentieth century increasing concern has been paid to the underlying principle of price discrimination among classes of risks. As risk has become increasingly socialized, fundamental questions have been raised about the legitimacy of discriminatory rate-making.

Product pricing, or rate-making as it is known in the industry, has been a subject of public policy in both the life and nonlife segments of the business for over 100 years. In both areas pricing was originally a matter to be determined by the market. Over time there was a marked shift in favor of some regulatory scrutiny of the rate-making activity.

Insurance pricing differs in important respects in the life and nonlife businesses, a condition that has given rise to differing regulatory histories. Pricing of such insurance as fire or marine coverage was usually based on judgment. The materials of which a building was constructed or the destination of the vessel were the risk factors upon which an underwriter made a judgment. While marine underwriters continued to rely on judgment rating for many years, nineteenth century fire insurers moved in another direction.

Local boards of insurance men were formed as early as 1819 with the purpose of establishing uniform premium rates to which board members agreed to adhere. The success of such boards was uneven at best. Losses seemed to occur in cycles. When loss ratios were low, profits would appear high and thereby attract new competitors. Without required reserves for losses, an illusion of profitability could be created as long as sales expanded faster than claims were paid. In the quest for sales, premiums were often cut. Then, when large losses did occur, claims could not be paid and the companies were driven out of existence.[7]

In 1866 the National Board of Fire Underwriters was founded for the purpose of systematizing rate-making on a national level. The Board's domination by large insurers, however, led the smaller companies to break away from the arrangement, and they continued to cut fire premium rates. The Board received a new life during the 1870s, however, amid the ashes of the great Chicago and Boston fires in 1871 and 1872. Regional fire-rating associations were formed and state and local boards were revitalized. The effect was to organize the fire insurance business very rapidly. As rate-making power shifted from the national to the local boards, a drama of localized price fixing was played out in the American insurance industry. Kimball has noted that the legal validity of price fixing in insurance as compared to the railroads may have occurred because it was not industry-wide, nationally oriented trusts but local bodies that were fixing the prices.[8]

The ease with which insurers could be formed, however, provided a continuing stream of new competitors who were not bound by the local boards' fixed rates. Rate wars were frequent occurrences, and stronger means of local control were necessary to prevent fire insurer failures. In some areas local boards were replaced with a *compact system*, which emphasized the locality as the scene for agreements wherein local agents would abide by the rates established by compact managers. This system, with its special local flavor, was particularly prevalent in Missouri and parts of the Northwest during the 1880s.[9]

The development of the compact system occurred, however, at a time when the antitrust movement was gaining popular support in the United States. Thus between 1885 and 1907 the anticompetitive features of the system stimulated the legislatures of some 20 states to enact anticompact legislation. While the statutes do not appear to have been effective in stemming rate-setting in concert, they do reflect a public awareness of the dangers of such practices. Nevertheless, the legislation seems to have been primarily symbolic in nature.[10]

By the late 1800s proposals for rate regulation had been made in a number of states. In New York a joint legislative committee was appointed to investigate the nonlife insurance field. The Merritt Committee's report (1911) found that unrestricted competition had been generated by the anticompact laws, thus inviting rate wars and leading to a deterioration in the quality of available insurance protection. The Committee concluded that anticompact legislation had failed and that collaborative rate-making was desirable. Legislation was passed in 1911 that permitted such rate-making in concert by rating associations or bureaus, provided a filing of rates was made with the purpose of ensuring that they were not unfairly discriminatory. The New York law became a model for other states seeking to replace anticompact statutes with supervised rate-setting.[b]

Commission regulation of rates continued until the U.S. Supreme Court's decision in the *United States v. Southeastern Underwriters Association* case (1944) wherein it held that insurance was "commerce" and was, therefore, subject to federal law. Specifically, the case involved the Justice Department's

[b]A Kansas statute of 1909 charged the Kansas Insurance Commissioner with requiring adequate, but not excessive, fire insurance premiums. The law was challenged by the German Alliance Insurance Company on grounds of unconstitutionality. The case eventually reached the U.S. Supreme Court where, in the 1913 decision, it was announced that regulation of fire insurance is permissible because the industry is "affected with the public interest." *German Alliance Insurance Co. v. Lewis* [233 U.S. 389 (1913)].

challenge to the underlying price-fixing features of fire rating boards as a violation of the Sherman Act's antimonopoly provisions. Insurers predicted chaos following the decision, and Congress hastened, under appropriate insurer prodding, to pass the McCarran-Ferguson Act. The Act declared that regulation of insurance by the states was in the public interest and that the federal antitrust laws were to be applied only to the extent that the insurance business was not regulated by the states.

The National Association of Insurance Commissioners, in cooperation with the industry, drafted two model bills that were framed in a manner that would preserve the status quo and demonstrate that rate-making—especially bureau rate-making—would be explicitly regulated by the states. The NAIC-All Industry bills, eventually enacted by over 40 states, served to establish a new system of prior approval laws under which the state insurance commissioner's approval is required before new rates may be applied.[c]

The policy objectives of such nonlife rate regulation were twofold: to preserve the integrity of the insurance fund and thus preserve the insurer's existence and to protect the public against excessive rates. The first objective—the *adequacy* objective—has been assessed as actually inhibiting competition and thereby adversely affecting the consumer's interest in the property and liability industry.[11] The second, or *fairness* objective, refers to unwarranted discrimination among policyholders in the setting of rates. Under the bureau rating system, classes of risks are established and rates determined for each class. The question of unwarranted discrimination really refers to the propriety of assigning a particular risk to a specific risk class. Under newly developing concepts of socialized risk, an even more fundamental question about the propriety of any form of risk discrimination has been raised on a serious and continuing basis.

In the life insurance business where the practice of rebating through agents' commissions was prevalent in the late 1800s, the problem of discriminatory pricing has been a more serious problem. The tontine policies that Henry Hyde's Equitable Life Assurance Company popularized in the late 1800s generated a huge surplus of funds that managers were free to manipulate. In the 1870s this led to increasing agency commissions as the giant life insurers battled for market supremacy. The higher commissions gave the agents the funds with which they might spur sales through rebates. Because the rebates were not uniform to all policyholders, they operated in a discriminatory fashion. A number of states moved to regulate rebate practices on this basis as early as the 1880s.[12] In general, however, rebating was only a symptom of the larger problems being caused by excessive cash flows. The full scope of the problems would not be appreciated until the Armstrong Investigation disclosures in 1905.

---

[c]In general, under a prior approval rating system, the insurer determines rates according to formulas established by the rating bureau and accepted by the commission. A company not wishing to use bureau rates normally has the option of filing deviated rates for one or more classes of risks or submitting an independent filing. Both options demand commission approval before they may be implemented by the insurer.

The pricing problems in the life insurance business tended to be sales related and involved the efforts of companies to intensively market life insurance products.[d] The life insurance premium is composed of three parts: an actuarially estimated cost of coverage, a calculated return on investment of previously paid-in premium funds, and an administrative expense component. The exact relationship between these components varies with the type of policy, thus accounting for major variations in life insurance prices. In addition, there are many variables in each of the three components (e.g., mortality estimates vary with age, occupation, sex, and so forth), further adding to the range of possible price variations.

The estimated cost of coverage and the calculated return on investment are both technical matters about which insurers and insurance commissions have worked out technical compromises. The administrative expense component (or loading charge) that is attached to each policy, however, has been subjected to a reasonableness standard by regulatory agencies. The emergence of a reasonableness standard occurred during the late nineteenth century when the life insurers' quests for growth and the symbols of wealth caused administrative expenses to mushroom. The administrative cost per dollar of insurance in force rose rapidly during that period, steadily eating away at the accumulated surpluses created by high premiums. The unreasonableness of these expenses was highlighted by testimony received at the Armstrong hearings and resulted in legislation to control the legal expense associated with the administration of insurance policies. Today administrative costs are reported upon annually by life insurers.[e]

Regulation of Other Practices

Apart from the regulation of insurance products and the manner in which those products are priced, public policy has also evolved with regard to many other types of insurer activities. In this regard, the category is something of a catchall, composed of practices variously relating to the technical core of the business, its managerial (especially marketing) aspects, and the institutional relationship

[d]There were relatively fewer problems of adequacy in the life insurance business after the mid-1800s. Technical information based on mortality tables and actuarial prediction had improved greatly by the mid-1800s, and companies were relying on a variety of mortality tables for rate-making. Only a few states, especially Wisconsin, made any attempt to establish maximum rates for life insurance. Kimball [84] pp. 110-111. Competition tended to keep rates below maximum levels. Adequacy problems only became acute during business cycle depressions when insurer investments tended to deflate rapidly. For this reason legislation and insurance commission rulings required the establishment of legal reserves as a means of preserving the solvency of the life insurers.

[e]Disclosure of the excessive loading charges of the large life insurers reinforced the case being made by Louis Brandeis in Massachusetts for legislative approval of savings bank life insurance. Such insurance, it was promised, would prove a cheaper alternative to the expensive life insurance company policies. See Keller [82]. The original argument can be found in Brandeis [17].

between the business and society. It is the great scope of such behavioral regulation, rather than its categorical consistency, that makes it noteworthy.

The scope of insurance practices affecting public interests and the extent to which insurers had deviated from publicly acceptable standards of conduct became apparent during the Armstrong investigation. The Armstrong Committee was created by the New York State legislature in 1905 to investigate questions relating to the public struggle over the control of the Equitable Life Assurance Society. Its founder, Henry Hyde, had died in 1899 and control was intended to pass to his son, James Hazen Hyde, in several phases through the use of a trust arrangement. The younger Hyde's exploits in high living, including a much publicized predilection for French actresses, aroused the concern and objection of other Equitable stockholders and employees. The squabble soon became a public one and much doubt was cast on whether the integrity of the Equitable could be preserved under such circumstances. The Armstrong Committee was appointed to investigate the matter and Charles Evans Hughes, later to become the Governor of New York, a U.S. Supreme Court justice, and presidential candidate, was named the Committee's chief counsel.

In a social environment that included such disparate elements as a healthy number of robber baron personalities and attitudes, a budding philosophy of "trustbusting," and a growing number of journalistic muckrakers, the Armstrong investigation began to systematically disclose the methods and practices that enabled the life insurers–especially the Big Three (Equitable, New York Life, and Mutual of New York)–to achieve and maintain their size, power, and influence. Corruption, political influence, discriminatory and unfair practices, unbridled competition, and public swindle all came to the foreground during the proceedings. As a result of the report issued in 1906, extensive remedial legislation was passed in New York. Similar investigations were initiated in other states, and public confidence in the insurance industry seemed badly shaken.[f] In New York, alone, legislation was passed that established new election machinery for mutual companies, prohibited rebates, barred political contributions, attacked false advertising and false bookkeeping, required lobbyists to register, put an end to tontine dividends, established nonforfeiture provisions on policies, prohibited discrimination among policyholders, limited the amount of new business companies could add each year to a percentage of previous insurance in force, provided for four standard policy forms and gave the commissioner power to approve others, and mandated that boards of directors approve the salaries of company officers.[13] The volume and variety of regulatory provisions passed in the wake of the Armstrong legislative inquiry publicly identified insurance as a corrupted and socially irresponsible industry. Whatever the ideology of responsi-

[f]Discussions of the Armstrong investigation generally focus on the life insurance business. Yet the Committee's report also affected insurance commission practices in the nonlife industry. At the least, the commissions were stimulated to look longer and harder at the competitive and political practices of the nonlife insurers.

bility preached by its leaders, the facts pointed to the need for major reform and social control.

Beyond all else the Armstrong investigation established a rationale for a scheme of comprehensive administrative regulation of the industry. Within a few years the especially onerous aspects of the legislation would be muted or removed, but the principle of full regulatory supervision would remain. The Armstrong investigation highlighted the extent of the industry's interpenetration with American society; the legislation that followed and the regulatory principle that survived directly manifested the public's interest in the industry. Today there is no aspect of the life or nonlife insurance business that is not subject to public policy. The Armstrong investigation highlighted a fundamental relationship between the industry and society: in its existence and in its behavior, the insurance industry is a creature of public policy.

The regulation of insurer practices was more systematic than either product or price regulation, the problems having emerged at a single time, thereby facilitating a systematic attack on insurer abuses rather than resorting to a series of incremental regulatory adjustments. Among the technical practices that were included were declarations of dividends. Early state legislation had tended to establish maximum dividend levels for insurers so as to protect the insurance fund against dissipation. Mutualization was a means of avoiding these restrictions and was managerially desirable, provided that the risk of policyholder voting control could be eliminated. Toward this end a number of companies had successfully connived to achieve state legislation that eliminated policyholder voting in mutual companies.[14] Such laws were either voided or revised in the wake of the Armstrong disclosures, and mutualization was actually encouraged by legislatures as a means of safeguarding policyholders against corporate mismanagement.

The managerial facets of the insurance business were a primary target of post-Armstrong legislation. The Committee had found that the very size and power of the Big Three was a serious policy matter and recommended legislation that would prevent similar abuses of insurer growth. Rebating was one particularly invidious practice attacked during the hearings and the legislative debates that followed. Moreover, it was also shown that rebating was actually part of a much larger problem involving the entire general agency system of marketing.[15]

Large sales forces were the means by which the insurance industry underwent its great expansion during the late 1800s, and the general agency system was the dominant selling organization. General agents were regional representatives for insurers, appointing local agents, collecting premiums and forwarding them to home offices, and paying all local operating expenses. General agents were normally paid on a commission basis, a device that served to stimulate sales growth. The insurers competed vigorously for the loyalty of general agents, raising commissions, offering bonuses, and attempting to steal away the best agents of competitors.

The growth and success of the general agency system, both in sales volume and in profitability, ultimately led to problems of coordination and control, however. The insurers were prompted to attempt the consolidation and systematization of operations in an effort to lower administrative costs and improve profitability. The large life companies began to appoint special agents who were free to go anywhere in pursuit of large sales accounts. General agent hostility was a natural response. Moreover, the life companies began to create branch offices under the supervision of salaried superintendents who replaced the general agents who had been paid on a commission basis. The branch offices reflected the trend toward the centralization and rationalization of company operations. More importantly, the trend toward centralization reflected a desire for consolidated power, responsible to a single source. The vision of such an organization inspired many of the autocratic presidents of the late nineteenth century life companies.

The pressure on agents for sales and the incentives for rebate twisting[g] and rate discrimination afforded by the dual agency and commission systems led to major regulatory changes in the post-Armstrong period. Such practices were specifically outlawed, and agents were made subject to licensing, certification, and residency requirements. Steps were also taken to prohibit misleading and unfair advertising and unscrupulous public relations practices.

The importance of the courts as an instrument of public policy was most obvious in an area of insurer practice that the Armstrong investigation avoided—the interpretation of warranties. By the 1890s the large insurers had begun to retain lawyers on a full-time basis and proved more willing to contest lawsuits by claimants and policyholders alike. Much of this litigation involved the policy contract that had become increasingly legalistic in its terms and aleatory in its nature. Chronologically, the first part of the insurance contract was the application. It was with regard to representations made in the application that the rules of warranty were applied.

The essence of the *rule of warranty* in insurance cases was that any false statement by an applicant permitted the insurer to avoid contractual responsibility. The reasoning was that if the insurer had known of the falsity, it would not have entered into the contract. In legal practice no distinction was drawn between misrepresentations that were large and significant and those that were trivial and insignificant. In sales practice the situation differed considerably, agents always pressing for greater sales volumes and commissions. The underwriting staffs at insurer's home offices understood the tendency of agents to shade information or even encourage misrepresentation by the applicant in order to get the sale. But within the home offices the underwriters carried less

[g]*Twisting* refers to the practice of encouraging a policyholder of one company to forfeit his policy and purchase a policy from another company. This practice was inherently injurious to the policyholder because the highest cost and least dividends occurred at the beginning of a policy's life. Allowing the policy to lapse resulted in a forfeiture of all accrued dividends.

influence than the agents and their managers, and the companies were pressed continuously to expand sales volume and cash flow to cover past commitments. To be sure, a company's integrity could be endangered if it knowingly paid claims on policies that were issued on the basis of false information. But to fully investigate all applicants at the time of application would have been outrageously expensive and unnecessary. Since only a limited number would eventually file claims, expenses could be minimized by waiting until the claim was filed. Then, if any misrepresentation was disclosed, the claim could be avoided and the integrity of the insurance fund preserved. Meanwhile the company would have had the benefit of the applicant's premium payments as investable funds during the years between the application and the filing of a claim.

Through the 1890s insurers insisted on strict interpretation of the warranty rule, and such dreadful misrepresentations as the color of one's eyes, hair color, place of birth, year of citizenship or marriage, or the failure to note such injuries as lacerations requiring three stitches, or neglecting to include a mole on one's left shoulder as an ailment were likely to be used as a basis for an insurer's charge of breach of warranty. The exaggeration of warranties by insurance lawyers was so extreme as to be a case of overservice by the profession.

By the early 1900s the warranty doctrine was under severe attack, and the courts were articulating the public dissatisfaction with the insurance lawyers' overservice. A number of ameliorative court doctrines developed: statements on applications were to be treated as representations, not warranties; evidence was allowed that either the companies or their agents had waived application requirements; and the admission of evidence was permitted to show that oral (or parol) waivers by agents had modified the written contract.

The courts also expressed public policy when they disallowed policy cancellations because of late premium payments on the basis of waivers by the company or its agents, the minor nature of the delayed payment, or other exceptional circumstances. Similar expressions of judicial imagination characterized the interpretation of other policy clauses and conditions. All in all, the courts began to move in the direction of construing contractual terms against the companies whenever possible as a matter of public policy, because of the one-sided nature of the arrangements. The protection of the policyholder became a policy goal expressed and implemented through the courts.[h]

The objectionable practices of the insurance companies went beyond the technical and managerial aspects of the business and reached the highest levels of organizational behavior. As with many of the technical and managerial issues, the Armstrong investigation was the principal instrument for disclosing the

[h]Philosophically, the early 1900s were a period of the ascendancy of the so-called sociological school of jurisprudence in American law, which was characterized by the view that the interest of the parties before the court ought to be balanced in arriving at a decision. As between the insurance company and the policyholder then, the courts were finding that the specific interests of an individual policyholder tended to outweigh the more general interests of the insurers. See Berman and Greiner [11] chapter 1.

objectionable institutional practices and abuses. In large measure the institutional abuses related to the acquisition and maintenance of managerial power and control. The fight over control of the Equitable exposed not only that company's internal politics but served as a springboard from which Charles Evans Hughes was able to inquire into the internal practices of Mutual of New York, New York Life, and others. The disclosures were a muckraker's dream: systematic attempts to secure insider control by eliminating or negating the voting power of unsympathetic shareholders or policyholders; payment of excessive salaries and bonuses to executives, managers, and political allies; nepotism and the treatment of companies as personal fiefdoms; interlocking directorates; and a system of lobbying and political alliances that was oiled by millions of dollars of company funds that were used to purchase legislation and regulatory officials.[16] So widespread was this pattern of insider control and sanctioned corruption that the top managements of virtually all the largest life insurers were ousted in the wake of the Armstrong disclosures. Relatively few criminal indictments were returned, but many insurance executives were forced to repay funds to companies, seek new avenues of entrepreneurial adventure, or prudently set off on extended foreign vacations.[i] That the smaller companies escaped the spotlight of such disclosure seems attributable to their lesser prominence rather than to their innocence. But the legislation that was directed at the behavior of the largest companies applied to the smaller ones as well.

A new ethos began to emerge after the Armstrong investigations. Responsibility to the public was preached widely, and the innovative, entrepreneurial, and autocratic spirit of the pre-1905 period was replaced by protective bureaucratization. The regulatory agencies and state legislatures continued to refine their control of insurer action. Of course, the generally understaffed condition of the commissions made enforcement in all but the largest states erratic, if well-intentioned. And in the largest states, such as New York, Illinois, and California, insurers continued their attempts to influence the passage of legislation and the enforcement of regulations. But even the sweeping investigations of the Temporary National Economic Committee (T.N.E.C.) during the 1930s generally failed to disclose new forms of reprehensible insurer action. Ironically, one of the T.N.E.C.'s criticisms of the industry was that it was bound to the safest sort of investments and had not been a source of venture capital. The irony, of course, was that this was the very antithesis of the Armstrong Committee's alarm. The new spirit of the insurance industry after the Armstrong disclosures was the cultivation of public trust and confidence. Charles Peabody, the new president of Mutual of New York, spoke of making it the "soundest company" rather than the largest. And Paul Morton, former Secretary of the

[i]One of the conditions imposed by Hughes before taking charge of the Armstrong investigation was that no criminal indictments would be brought as a result. Much to Hughes' chagrin apparently, a politically motivated New York District Attorney ignored the agreement thereby prompting a number of the more odiously portrayed company officials to depart for Europe.

Navy and newly named Equitable president, proclaimed a desire to see it known as the strongest company, morally as well as financially.[17]

The acquiescence of the insurers in the spirit of the reforms as well as the structure of the new regulatory regime manifested the deep wounds left by the Armstrong investigation. The life insurance industry, in particular, had portrayed itself as the protector of widows and orphans. To be publicly displayed as the persecutor of stockholders and employees and the corruptors of politicians and regulators caused more than a little ideological schizophrenia. Conservative behavior became a shibboleth in the twentieth century. As if by unwritten agreement, insurance companies were committed to a policy of not exposing themselves again to the pointed attacks of an incensed public.

Conservatism proved a prudent and successful strategy, and insurers stayed with it long after the end of the Depression. Both sectors of the industry prospered and firms adjusted to the protection as well as the scrutiny of an administrative regulatory system. It would take another period of public dissatisfaction, quite distinct from that which preceded the Armstrong inquiry, to shake the industry as a whole and stimulate some firms to act in a distinctively innovative manner. The insurance industry was not moribund during the twentieth century—but there was a strong industry identification, an ideology that favored conservatism as a management style, and a recognition that a stable and profitable industry, protected by regulatory standards, was better than an energetic industry that was exposed to public criticism.

Notes

1. Michelbacher and Roos [106].

2. Patterson [124]. The standardization of reports has been advocated and furthered by the work of the N.A.I.C. See annual reports, N.A.I.C. [112].

3. See Keller [82], Orren [120], and Kimball [84].

4. Orren [120] p. 36 and Kimball [84].

5. Orren [120]. Through the early 1960s over 250 proposed mandatory investment laws had been introduced in various state legislatures. See Wright [169].

6. See McGill [105] for a discussion of the concept.

7. See Kimball [84], and Keller [82].

8. Kimball [84].

9. Kimball [84].

10. See Edelman [44].

11. See Joskow [80] for a critique of this system from a consumer and social welfare perspective.

12. Kimball [84] p. 10.

13. Stalson [151] pp. 551-552 also contains a useful discussion of the Armstrong Committee's impact.

14. New York State [114].

15. Regarding the evolution of the general agency system see Stalson [151].

16. See New York State [114].

17. Keller [82] p. 268.

Part III
Private Insurers and Social Change

7 The Changing Agenda

New Dimensions of Interpenetration

From the perspective of the mid-1970s the past decade appears to have been the most significant period of social change for the industry since that of 1900-1910. A number of important trends, some underway before 1960, others originating during the decade, impacted on the industry. Beyond these continuing trends, new matters, such as equal employment, urban decay, crime, the impact of the automobile, changing life styles, and new concern for the environment, emerged as issues of public concern and influenced insurance as well as other industries. In general, they were matters about which little public concern had been previously manifested. That condition would change dramatically before 1970, and the scope of such change, as well as the intensity of the public feeling involved, has posed a continuing set of problems for the industry.

As we have discussed throughout, the interpenetration between the insurance industry and American society has been shaped through two distinct social processes—the market and public policy. These processes do not exhaust the full range of industry-society relations however, and during the 1960s other types of social interaction occurred between insurers and their relevant publics. Many of these contacts were grounded in conflict and involved groups or relevant publics that were not related to the industry through the market and who were unable, or believed themselves unable, to successfully use the public policy process. The most notable example involved the urban poor, whose desire for change and whose inability to effectively use either the market or public policy was manifested in the riots of the middle and late 1960s.

Overall, therefore, the interpenetration between the insurance industry and American society took on a new dimension in the 1960s. In a sense, the management-society relationship had evolved to a new threshold, whereby action by a relevant public was directly used to elicit insurer response. Given the continued evolution of market interpenetration and the trends associated with it, as well as those associated with expanding public policy, this social conflict constituted a new and significantly different element in the relationship between the industry and its relevant publics. Moreover, the process of direct contact between relevant publics and insurers interacted with the market and public policy processes. By the 1970s the most challenging problem for management was to divine the manner in which social conflict, public policy, and the market were operating *in concert* to affect the industry.

Organizational Trends

During the 1950s the most significant organizational developments in the industry involved the popularity of the multiple-line structure and the success of the specialty companies. During the 1960s the most important development involved the usage of the holding-company structure. It has been pointed out that the insurance holding company has had three stages in its development.[1] At first it was an easy way to conduct an active insurance business, the holding company serving to coordinate the top management activities of a number of subsidiaries established to conduct individual lines of business or to operate in particular states.

By the mid-1960s the purpose of the holding-company form became flexibility. Life insurers, for example, used affiliates to market a variety of variable, inflation-resistant investment products. Property and casualty companies began to diversify into new product and investment fields and contributed to speculation that insurers were intent on diversifying away from the conventional insurance business. Among other effects, this served to generate concern among regulators still concerned with insurer solvency and policyholder protection.

A third phase in the use of the holding-company form emerged by the late 1960s, when conglomerates began the external takeover of insurance companies.[a] The thought of major insurance companies being under the control of managers without insurance backgrounds caused considerable concern among regulators and insurance managers alike. Some pressure arose to ban the holding-company device entirely, but in general the insurance commissions seemed more intent on identifying significant points of contact between insurers and their noninsurance affiliates where conflicts of interest could arise and taking steps to subject these to familiar regulatory techniques.[2]

The holding-company device and the tendency toward multiple-line underwriting discussed in Chapter 3 have had the combined effect of changing basic aspects of the industry's structure. Stock companies, in particular, unified their subsidiary companies under strong central managements. Decentralization continued to characterize most operating divisions, but policy and planning were clearly a function of the holding company's top management.

Market Trends and Issues

By the 1960s the interpenetration between the industry and public policy was so substantial that no major market issue or trend existed entirely outside of the regulatory framework. Predictably, perhaps, regulation proved an asset to insurers in some instances, a detriment, in others. In any event, as a former

[a]The most notable example was I.T.T.'s takeover of the Hartford Fire Insurance Company.

general counsel to one large insurer pointed out, life in the regulatory fishbowl has been a way of life for several generations of insurance managers and most could not imagine insurance as an unregulated business.

Market regulation in the insurance industry has steadily come to focus on three related areas: the price of insurance products, the quality of insurance products, and the availability of insurance products to the public.[3] While the relative importance of each area has varied over time, the 1960s proved unique because major industry issues developed in each area, while at the same time, still other issues involved all three areas in such a broad way as to defy narrow regulatory resolution. No-fault automobile insurance was the outstanding example of the phenomenon in the property and casualty business; national health insurance had a similar effect for life and health insurers.

Problems of Availability

As we have discussed, the decision of an insurer to offer a particular type of coverage deeply involves the organization's technical subsystem. Actuaries estimate probable losses, establish underwriting standards, conditions, and requirements, and frame the context within which the company will commit itself to covering the risk. This reliance on the technical subsystem for a determination of the conditions under which risk will be insured by the company accounts for some of the major availability problems that developed during the 1960s.

The first type of availability problem involves new kinds of risk. If a person or organization wishes to procure insurance against a particular risk, they may approach an insurer and solicit coverage. The tradition of American insurers is to view new risks with suspicion, pending the gathering and analysis of pertinent loss data. Hence coverage is usually slow in forthcoming, if it is offered at all. The second type of availability problem is closely allied to the first and involves situations where a currently insured peril becomes both unpredictable in character and catastrophic in its consequences. In this instance, insurers are prone to not only withhold further coverage but actually withdraw existing coverage. Should no alternative sources of coverage exist, a major availability problem may develop.

A third instance in which availability becomes an issue is when an insurer perceives a particular group of insureds as consistently costing more in claims and expenses than they contribute in premiums. In such cases, the insurer may choose to either limit or restrict the type of insurance coverage or the amount of coverage available to such an insured.

During the 1960s availability issues of all three types emerged in both the property-casualty and the life-health businesses. The health insurance market, in particular, was an instance in which the inability or unwillingness of insurers to provide significant health insurance coverage to the elderly and the poor at affordable prices became a critical issue. The emergence of the availability of health coverage for the elderly as a major issue can be quickly grasped by referring to the chronology of events described in Table 7-1. The chronology suggest the slow pace of private insurer innovation in providing medical insurance coverage to the public.

Among the segments of the public most in need of medical insurance coverage and least able to secure it under existing plans were the elderly. The long public debate and numerous opportunities for private insurer initiatives simply failed to stimulate the development of a workable means of providing such coverage that was acceptable to the elderly, the insurers, and other relevant publics. Medicare was not the inevitable entry of the federal government into the

Table 7-1
Private Sector Health Insurance Innovations, 1950-1966[a]

1950	The National Association of Insurance Commissioners promulgates the Uniform Individual Accident and Sickness Policy Provisions Law.
1951	First small group hospital and surgical insurance policy introduced to cover groups of five or more employees.
1952	First noncancelable and guaranteed renewable hospital-surgical-medical policy issued providing protection for the lifetime of the policy.
1952	First guaranteed renewable hospital and surgical policy offered on an individual basis.
1954	First comprehensive major medical group insurance offered as it is known today.
1955	First guaranteed renewable hospital-surgical policy issued becoming fully paid-up at age 65.
1955	First guaranteed renewable lifetime hospital-surgical policy designed for older age people.
1957	First mass enrollment plan offering hospital-surgical insurance regardless of medical history to persons 65 and over.
1957	First senior citizen hospital-surgical policy issued using a group insurance principle.
1958	First comprehensive major medical individual insurance plan issued.
1959	First comprehensive group dental insurance plan written by an insurance company.
1961	First state enrollment plan made available to persons 65 and over on a state basis and under special enabling legislation allowing the pooling of risks by a group of insurance companies.
1962	First lifetime and noncancelable and guaranteed renewable hospital-surgical policy offered.
1963	First fully paid-up guaranteed renewable lifetime major medical insurance introduced by an insurance company.
1966	Program of governmental health insurance, Medicare, for people age 65 and over became effective July 1. Federal entry into health insurance.

[a]Adapted from Health Insurance Institute, *1970 Source Book of Health Insurance Data* (New York: Health Insurance Institute, 1970).

health insurance business; it was the result of an inability to otherwise make available the quantity and types of coverage that the public sought.[4]

The second type of availability issue involved situations where coverage was withheld or withdrawn because risks significantly changed in their character (predictability) or consequences. The urban riots of the late 1960s served to virtually dry up the available sources of fire insurance for inner city buildings. The seeming unpredictability of such losses and the extensiveness and "total loss" nature of the losses transformed the coverage of such properties from a calculated assumption of risk to a gamble without actuarial basis. A related availability problem involved crime insurance, which also disappeared from the inner city insurance market in the wake of rising crime rates and civil disorders. Yet in both cases the need for insurance was so manifest and critical to the continued survival of the inner city[b] that great public pressure supported the development of some scheme to provide coverage.[5]

The third type of availability problem—limited coverage because claims and costs exceed premiums—became critical in the automobile insurance business during the 1960s. As loss ratios became increasingly unsatisfactory, and as regulatory agencies limited the companies' ability to pass along rate increases, auto insurers turned toward writing as little bad risk or high risk business as possible. This was a traditional industry response and usually served to restore a favorable margin between claims and costs and premium revenues. A variety of special automobile rating plans had been developed during the 1950s to deal with the problem, but these plans had the side effect of antagonizing those segments of the driving public who were refused coverage or who could only procure such coverage at greatly inflated premium levels. This pattern was repeated throughout the 1960s.

The traditional underwriting (or technical) response proved increasingly unsatisfactory in a society where the automobile, more than any other single development, had reshaped the way of life in the twentieth century. The post-World War II love affair with the automobile, and the resulting restructuring of American population and housing patterns, made the auto an indispensable item. The natural increase in losses that followed from many additional drivers and automobiles served to further reinforce the need for insurance protection. Without such protection, drivers were forced to use an essential good devoid of any means of protecting those who might be injured as a result. Unable to secure insurance, the driver placed himself and all of his assets in peril whenever he drove. Automobile insurance had become as much of a social and economic necessity as the automobile itself.

Legislative and regulatory steps were taken to ensure the public of the coverage it needed. Financial responsibility laws were passed in some states,

[b]Without proper fire insurance coverage, mortgage funds were virtually unavailable from market sources. Without crime insurance, businessmen were virtually unable to secure commercial loans using inventory as collateral.

requiring that automobile owners give proof of liability insurance coverage or minimum financial ability to compensate wrongfully injured parties; compulsory automobile insurance laws were passed in other states. An initial regulatory step was to impose restrictions on the freedom of insurers to cancel automobile insurance policies or to refuse to renew existing policies upon their expiration. But the remedies produced additional problems. Distortions became apparent as the demand for automobile insurance increased while the willingness of insurers to make coverage available was tempered by underwriting considerations. Eventually many states were forced into developing plans whereby the least desirable purchasers of insurance on an underwriting basis would be assigned on a pro rata basis to insurers doing business in the state. In this way the social burden of the worst risks was borne by the companies writing the preferred risks. But, as with the other availability problems, the market and regulatory systems were so entwined, one with the other, that incremental measures seemed only to exacerbate and worsen the overall situation.

Problems of Quality

The quality issues are, at first glance, more nebulous than those involving the availability of insurance; yet in fact, most of the quality issues proved more susceptible to regulatory action than the availability issues described above. Policyholder expectations about the types of coverage are probably more unclear than a policyholder's knowledge of whether or not he has been denied insurance coverage. Nevertheless, public expectations about insurer performance are crucial to any assessment of actual insurer performance, and therefore, they constitute an important area of regulatory interest.

Although most quality issues had less widespread popular support in the 1960s than the availability issues, a number of them did emerge as significant matters by the decade's end. More importantly, a number of issues lent support to the general criticism of business that would be called the *consumerism movement* by the early 1970s.

There are several vital qualitative aspects to the insurance product. Certainly the solvency of the insurer and its ability to satisfy in the future the obligations being undertaken in the present is a matter relating to the quality of the insurance product. Indeed, as discussed in Chapter 5, an early and continuing rationale for state regulation of insurers was the protection of the public against insurer insolvency.

Beyond insurer solvency, issues relating to policy terms and claims practices surfaced as important qualitative matters. The one-sidedness of the insurance transaction creates a *caveat emptor* situation in which the insurer can impose conditions, limitations, and other restrictive terms designed to narrow the scope of circumstances under which indemnification must be made. In theory this power is somewhat mitigated by regulatory approval of policy forms and changes therein.[6] Yet, as consumers increasingly came to understand during the 1960s, state regulation can serve to deflect rather than focus criticism and to deter rather than generate change. Reliance on professional groups within the industry have produced similarly frustrating consumer results.[c]

Another set of qualitative issues involved product innovation.[7] Life insurers, for example, had long been subject to criticism for portraying life insurance as a sound consumer investment. The manner in which the industry had vigorously promoted life insurance as an investment during the 1950s and 1960s was criticized because of the fixed nature of the product and the low interest (dividend) yield it produced for policyholders. The ramifications of this conduct spread in several directions. First, consumer pressure built for the true disclosure of the cost of life insurance policies.[8] Also, by the early 1960s a number of companies began to explore the "equities market" and added variable annuities and mutual funds to their product lines.[9] In addition, various insurers began to develop products that would combine into a single plan the fixed insurance elements found in the usual life insurance policy with a variable equity component. But product innovation was also hampered by the extent to which the regulatory framework interpenetrated market processes.

In 1959 the United States Supreme Court had ruled that variable annuities were within the regulatory jurisdiction of the Securities and Exchange Commission.[10] Hence, any equity-based insurance product would, it was believed, be subject to SEC scrutiny at the federal level as well as insurance commission scrutiny at the state level. Given the industry's long-standing aversion to federal regulation, it was not surprising that no groundswell developed among insurers to further submit to overlapping regulation by developing and introducing insurance products with equity features.[d]

Ultimately, most quality related issues involved matters associated with the technical and managerial subsystems of the insurance enterprise. Because these subsystems were already deeply entwined with regulatory activity, the new issues did not, for the most part, create problems outside that framework. It was only as a part of the larger consumerism movement that issues surfaced outside the usual framework of insurer-regulator involvement. Indeed the most outstanding development in this area may have been the activism manifested on behalf of consumers by such maverick insurance commissioners as Denenberg of Pennsylvania.[11]

---

[c]In 1960, for example, a commission on insurance terminology was formed under the aegis of the American Association of University Teachers of Insurance (now known as the American Risk and Insurance Association) to give consistency and understandability to abstruse insurance terminology and to eliminate confusing and unclear terms. The commission was disbanded in 1971 on the grounds that their work was done!

[d]Pure equity products such as mutual funds were also within the SECs regulatory purview and involved disclosure requirements for insurers doing such business. For further discussion see Chapter 8 and the notes cited therein.

Pricing Issues

Many of the problems of insurance availability, and to a lesser extent insurance quality, were resolvable by increasing the price of the insurance product to reflect the expanded scope of coverage. Indeed, as the experience of Lloyd's of London suggests, insurance of virtually any type can be made available to virtually anyone if no price ceiling exists. In practice, of course, the public concern was not only for coverage but for coverage at reasonable prices. Thus the actual demand was for insurance coverages, generally available and affordable, that also met buyers pricing expectations.

The demand for greater availability and price restraint was particularly clear in the area of automobile insurance. The costs of making even minimum liability coverages available to all licensed applicants proved so substantial that a variety of merit rating, compulsory coverage, and assigned risk programs were attempted throughout the 1960s. Yet each plan proved short-lived in its effectiveness and pressures built for further, more systematic change in the insurance delivery mechanism. Ultimately, as will be discussed in Chapter 9, the appearance of the Keeton-O'Connell no-fault proposal as a systematic alternative to the high-cost fault system proved attractive and gathered considerable public support.

Price-related issues affected virtually all lines of the insurance business during the 1960s. In life insurance, where premiums had traditionally been unregulated by insurance commissions, consumer pressure arose for price comparisons among policies and companies. The initial "shopper's guides" to life insurance offered by Commissioner Denenberg's Pennsylvania Department of Insurance provoked great controversy within the industry but were welcomed by the public.[12] As the equity aspects of some insurance products became better known, comparisons of the selling and administrative expenses associated with life insurance sales as opposed to those of other investment vehicles were of increasing public and regulatory concern as well.[13]

In the accident and health insurance area, price concerns involved attempts to increase the minimum proportions of each premium dollar returned as benefits; other pressures were exerted on insurers to utilize their leverage in an effort to force underlying health care costs downward. The pressure for a larger percentage of benefits per premium dollar drew strength from the consumerism movement and created a squeeze on insurer costs and profits. Pressure was placed on insurers to use their leverage to force medical cost controls but created special problems because it disrupted previously stable relations between insurers, hospitals, physicians, and other actors in the health care system.

Public Policy Issues

Inevitably, most of the market issues and trends of the 1960s involved the regulatory system and the joint ability of insurers and regulators to respond to social change. The inability of insurers to respond to the range of market issues described above without the cooperative responses of regulatory agencies underscores a crucial development in the evolving interpenetration between the industry and the public; namely, the inability of insurers to act alone. It is this inability to act alone that characterizes the symbolic joining of the industry to the public interest through administrative regulation.

The cohesion of the industry-regulator relation is strongest when dealing with the technical core of the business. Regulation is most specific and the principles most firmly established in such technical areas as underwriting standards and investment activities. Thus insulation from the effects of social change is greatest when dealing with matters at the technical core of the business. From the companies' point of view, nothing less than drastic social change is likely to prompt any action other than regulatory "fine tuning" to basic underwriting or investment principles.[e] And from the regulator's viewpoint, considerably more than public concern must be evidenced before a need will be felt to reexamine basic principles. The experience of the 1960s suggests that it is only when company concerns escalate because of decreasing sales volume or profitability and are coupled with a major public movement toward reform that the principles, as well as the practices, of insurance underwriting or investment are held up for examination and reevaluation.

In the casualty-property insurance business, automobile insurance and the provision of fire insurance to urban areas stand as major illustrations of this pattern; the cost and availability of health insurance also fits within this category. The failure of life insurance to compete with other financial investments, however, stimulated only insurer concerns during this same period; the absence of a major public movement to make life insurance a more inflation-resistant product had the effect of leaving only the insurers pleading for reform.[14]

When market problems do acquire significant proportions, and when both insurers and the public are pressing for change (albeit in different directions), the public policy process becomes a forum for effecting change. This has been the case with regard to automobile insurance where abandonment of the fault system has generated a major policy debate, with regard to the provision of fire and crime insurance to urban areas where the debate involved federal as well as state governmental processes and institutions, and with respect to health insurance where the very scope of the problem has been progressively redefined as to transcend both state forums and state levels of response.

Nonmarket Issues and Trends

In analyzing the range of market issues and trends one is inevitably forced to recognize the thorough interdependence of the market and public policy

[e]We distinguish between technical *principles* and *practices*. For example, insuring an applicant on the basis of the established "spread" between future premiums and future losses is a principle. Adjustments in the "acceptable" spread, however, amount to an underwriting practice.

processes. This has been a natural outcome of the evolving interpenetration of the insurance industry with American society.[15] Although virtually all market issues during the 1960s were also public policy matters, there existed another set of public policy issues of major consequence that were unrelated to the product market. Perhaps the primary example of the 1960s in this regard involved civil rights and equal employment.

Public policy favoring the extension of civil rights and equal employment opportunities was articulated in federal legislation, notably the Civil Rights Act of 1964; in the development of federal programs, notably EEOC; and in the creation of federal agencies, especially the Office of Economic Opportunity (OEO).[16] The public policy calling for employer action in the elimination of discrimination, the extension of work opportunities to minority groups, and the upgrading of job opportunities were not solely a product of legislation, however. As discussed in Chapter 5, public policy refers to principles guiding action. Before the Civil Rights Act of 1964, before EEOC, OEO, and a host of other Great Society programs, there did exist something approaching social consensus on the question of equal rights for all citizens, irrespective of racial background.[f]

The insurance industry, being a large employer of semiskilled and skilled clerical employees,[17] was called upon to increase employment opportunities for minority groups.[g] In the absence of legislation compelling such action, however, insurer responses varied. What did become clear by the mid-1960s, however, was that insurers that were located in urban areas such as Newark, New York, Hartford, Boston, and Chicago were not going to be able to avoid the problem of, and the public policy that favored, equal employment opportunity.

There were a number of other issues that, like equal employment, were not market matters but that did bear directly on the industry's relations with society through the public policy process. A group of issues including discrimination, urban decay, inadequate slum housing, and chronic unemployment all surfaced as important issues during the 1960s but failed to produce the commitment to improvement that characterized the leading issues on the public policy agenda. The effect was that such issues were not resolved through the public policy process and received limited attention through the early part of the 1970s. Ultimately, inaction contributed still further to these social problems.

The public policy process has structural context, i.e., a framework of institutions and processes within which issues are brought forward to the policy agenda, crystallized, and acted upon. Once an issue is brought to the agenda, some action must be taken, even if it is only to temporarily avoid dealing substantively with the matter. Such was the case during the early 1960s with many urban-related matters.

---

[f]Although fluctuations have occurred, public opinion poll results since the late 1950s suggest that an increasing percentage of the public surveyed has supported the principle of equal opportunity.

[g]This call occurred at local, state, and national levels. A voluntary national plan that enlisted industry cooperation was "Plans for Progress."

Public issues can, of course, be raised again and again in the policy process, and experience has shown that matters that fail to become major agenda items at one point in time may succeed at a later date. The danger is that at some point, partisans with respect to a particular matter may conclude that the policy process is either not open to them or is so dominated by other interests as to effectively prevent any substantive progress regarding an issue. Without a society's confidence in the responsiveness of its problem-resolving processes, the legitimacy of those processes as orderly means of responding to public issues wanes. In retrospect, the urban riots that occurred in the late 1960s were a repudiation of the public policy process as a means of resolving the issues of urban decay, inadequate housing, and chronic unemployment. To be sure, there had been a variety of federal programs and legislative actions taken under the mantle of the Great Society, but at the level of community impact and program implementation there was the frustration and resentment of policy statements without substance.[18]

For the insurance industry as a whole, the nonaffluent urban resident was a newly relevant public in the 1960s. Stories abound of the sort told about Orville Beal, president of Prudential, who was surprised to look out his office window one day and see Newark (Prudential's headquarters city) in flames.[h] Perhaps company presidents had known of the ghetto communities in such headquarters cities as Newark, New York, Hartford, and Chicago, and perhaps there had been an awareness of those companies' importance as holders of wealth and power in such communities. Whatever the level of corporate awareness, it was fairly clear that the ghetto was not perceived as significantly related to insurance companies through the market; and since public policy hadn't compelled any significant insurer involvement in urban matters, it wasn't surprising that insurers had generally adopted low profiles with respect to urban affairs.

As conditions worsened in the cities during the 1960s, insurer cognizance of rising crime rates and civil disorders was translated into calculations about the impact of such factors on urban investments; an awareness grew of the proximity and importance of slums and ghettos to the home offices and commercial districts where insurers were located. And whatever their investment portfolio, insurers and other businessmen recognized the serious extent to which decay in a city spread, progressively destroying more and more of the municipal tax base.

An increasing cognizance of urban ills was a necessary prerequisite to action, but was not, by itself, a commitment to action. The commitments to action that insurers and other businesses made to the improvement of urban conditions seem to have increased significantly following the 1967 riots. At the time of the 1967 riots, the life insurance industry, through a number of its trade associations, announced its intention to commit $1 billion to urban investment through a program of mortgage loans.[19] Two years later a second billion dollars

[h]This story was repeated on a number of occasions by executives of various companies. It has apparently become part of the industry's general lore about urban involvement.

were pledged. Companies established urban affairs units, created minority hiring and training plans, funded community projects, and attempted to rectify, in a flurry of activity, what years of community neglect had produced.

Implications of Interpenetration

The range of issues facing the insurance industry in the early 1970s evolved from social change of considerable magnitude. (See Appendix 7A for some suggestion of the wide range of issues.) Change was manifested in the market, in the public policy process, and in the broad context of general management-society contacts. Throughout the 1960s the industry attempted to mute criticism, deflect issues, and pursue profits through the use of a traditional industry-regulatory agency coalition. But the events of the 1960s demonstrated the inadequacies of that approach. It could not resolve major market issues relating to the availability and price of insurance; it was not effective in insulating the industry from public policy developments unrelated to the market; and it had no legitimacy in the eyes of relevant publics who were being denied insurance coverage, believed themselves exploited by insurer investments, or saw their interests ignored in both the market and public policy processes.

Many forms of social change affected the insurance industry in the 1960s. The market aspects of change saw new forms of organization, new participants in an industry generally dominated by tradition, and sales and underwriting innovations that threatened competitive stability. A residue of important but unresolved market issues were cast into the public policy process for disposition, if not final resolution. And both the public policy process and a broader process of social conflict between the companies and society produced major demands for modified insurer behavior.

Issues were no longer strictly technical, managerial, or institutional in character. At the decade's end, it appeared that every issue had institutional aspects. On the ability of the industry and the public to resolve such crucial issues as reform of automobile insurance, the provision of a significant amount of reasonably priced health insurance, urban redevelopment, equal employment, and inflation-resistant insurance investments, among others, rested the very legitimacy of the private American insurance industry. J. Willard Hurst, the famous legal historian, has remarked that whereas the legitimacy of the business corporation was traditionally based on its utility as a provider of goods and services, it appears that the corporation of the 1970s and beyond will have to meet standards of *responsibility and utility* in order to retain its social legitimacy.[20] In that context, the usefulness of insurers as providers of protection from risk and suppliers of credit has resulted in a broad and significant interpenetration with American society. But as the discussion in this chapter has illustrated, social change during the 1960s made clear that new standards of performance were developing in that society. In the aftermath of the 1960s a major task for insurer managements was to come to terms with the expectations of its relevant publics and to respond to its changing interpenetration with society.

Notes

1. Stewart [152] p. 64.

2. Stewart [152] p. 65. See also Report of the Special Committee on Insurance Holding Companies (1968) in State of New York, *Annual Report of the Superintendent of Insurance*, pp. 149-203.

3. This framework is suggested by Stewart [152]. See Mayerson [103].

4. A typical, though not the only, response to public pressures for greater socialization of risk was voiced by one company president in this manner: "Compulsory social health insurance systems intensify the prurient effects of centralized authority." E.J. Faulkner (President, Woodman Accident and Life Company), "Insurance and Social Policy," *Best's Insurance News* (Life edition) Vol. 61, No. 9 (January 1961), p. 80.

5. Barrett [7].

6. See Wenck [164].

7. Peterson, Rudelius, and Wood [127].

8. See Belth [9].

9. This set of developments is well-reported in the National Underwriter [113].

10. *Securities and Exchange Commission v. Variable Annuity Life Insurance Company of America* [79 S. Ct. 618 (1959)].

11. See Grotta [64].

12. See Belth [9], Orren [121], and Commonwealth of Pennsylvania [34].

13. Stewart [152] p. 63.

14. The experience of the 1960s is a modern version of the problem of the nonnecessity status of life insurance. Since such inflation-resistant products as mutual funds were available to the public from other sources, little public pressure arose to press insurers to develop inflation-proof life insurance. This may also explain the seeming public willingness to allow life insurers to treat premiums as yielding only a 3-4 percent return on investment for dividend purposes, when in fact they earn much more. See Orren [120]. Also see the discussion in Chapter 8.

15. Another aspect of this interpenetration is reflected in Long's analysis of the ethical values that support advanced insurance systems. See Long [97].

16. U.S.C. S 2000c (1964).

17. The fifty largest diversified financial companies had nearly 410,000 employees in 1972; the fifty largest life insurers accounted for 405,000 employees in 1972. See Fortune [51].

18. See Moynihan [109], Levitan [94], Orren [120] and Piven and Cloward [129].

19. See Kolber [88]. A report on the urban investments program is found in Institute of Life Insurance [77].

20. Hurst [74] p. 164.

Appendix 7A

The range and diversity of issues confronting firms in the insurance industry in the 1970s can be illustrated through the building of a simple model.[a] The activities of insurers are categorized as involving operations, investments, human resources, and communications. These activities involve the organization in a number of major relationships, including the marketplace, the economy as a whole, and a variety of governmental agencies. Using this simple matrixlike framework, and using 1972 as a reference date, the major public issues facing the industry are presented in summary form in Table 7A-1.

[a]The actual development of these scanning models is discussed in Post [130], Preston and Post [136] chapter 8, and Post and Epstein [131].

Table 7A-1
Public Issues in the Insurance Industry

Activities	*Price*	*Relationship to Market Availability*	*Quality*	*Relationship to Whole Economy*	*Relationship to Government*
1. Operations					
Life	Methods by which price is determined	Excluded segments of the population?	Policy terms; Adaptation to inflationary pressures	Concentration of assets (antitrust); Competitiveness; Flow of investment funds;	State commission rules in all aspects of the business. Federal consumer protection movement. Federal/State conflicts.
Health	Cost	Right of whole population to adequate health care	Percentage of premiums paid out for claims	Health care as an absolute right; Health care research and development; Use of financial leverage of lower health care costs;	National health care plan–format? Role of states in national health care scheme?
Financial Services	Competitiveness with other suppliers	Service to all market segments?	Credit reporting practices and privacy of the individual	New products–social usefulness? Diversification implications	Who shall regulate such products–e.g., variable life insurance (states or the SEC)?
Casualty/Property					
Personal	Auto: cost (No-Fault)	Auto: discrimination among age, sex, and occupational groups (No-Fault)	Auto: Claims practices, terms, etc. (No-Fault)	General public protection against all types of socially unacceptable risks	Federal no-fault vs. state no-fault plans
Commercial		Crime Insurance		Vehicular safety–R&D	Federal/state conflict in urban redevelopment and appropriate type of insurance plans

2. Investments					
Mortgages	Return on investment–acceptable levels?	Fairness in granting mortgages; redlining; standards for investment	Rates; terms; types of mortgages–e.g., second deed trust mortgages? Dispersion: geographic by racial applicant by age	National housing requirements and the availability of private financing, therefore	Meeting federal and state governmental goals for regional development and urban redevelopment
Securities			Investment of reserves in noninsurance activities of parent corporation	Using ownership and voting leverage to promote the involvement of other institutions in the accomplishment of social goals	Changing federal and state standards for investment–especially regarding "high risk" investments; promoting a loosening of standards to permit investment in socially beneficial projects
3. Human Resources	Wage rates and compensation packages	Training; recruitment programs	Job enrichment; participativeness in decision-making; four-day week Day care services	National full employment goals; effect on aggregate and structural unemployment levels; automation vs. human resource employment	Federal and state equal employment goals; federal affirmative action and job training programs
4. Communications	Shopper's Guides; disclosure of pricing information and cost comparison	Special marketing programs–all segments; information on availability and product choices	Puffing; FTC relations; deceptiveness; mass-merchandising; agency relations vis-à-vis company and customer	Economic role of the insurance industry, present and future; social role of the insurance industry, present and future	Relations with all government agencies–e.g., FTC, FCC, consumer agencies, and insurance commissions
		Consumer information programs of all types.			

8 Mission and Strategy: The Aetna in Historical Context

The Importance of Management History

The agenda of public issues that has confronted private insurers since the mid-1960s has probably threatened to reshape the industry in more fundamental ways than in any period since the Armstrong Commission era. The elements of change differ considerably from that period of scandal, of course, thereby raising the issue for insurers of how to respond. The reader will recall that following the Armstrong investigation disclosures, insurers responded by adopting a pattern of conservative competitive behavior, a moralistic and virtuous public relations stance, and an overall low profile vis-à-vis public issues. Only rarely in the past 50 years have individual insurers become vocal and highly visible proponents on important public issues. In those instances where such a highly visible public posture was required (e.g., Medicare and Medicaid), the tendency was for the industry to speak as a single voice through its various trade associations. In such a way, it could be persuasively argued that good insurance practice called for one or another courses of action without the possibility of contrary public statements by any major insurers.

The agenda of issues confronting private insurers since the mid-1960s forced some rethinking about that pattern of response to change. First, there were many more insurance-related issues on the public agenda than in the past. Secondly, new marketing strategies were segmenting competitors in the industry in a way that undermined the previous bases for trade association coalitions.[a] Thirdly, the perceptions of change possessed by individual managements had differed considerably and led to a serious consideration of new ways of responding to change. Nowhere were these pressures for a new pattern of response to change more evident than at Aetna Life and Casualty, the largest multiple-line insurer in the United States.

Aetna's annual revenues exceeded $4.5 billion in 1973 and its nearly $14 billion of assets made it the largest diversified financial company in the 1974 *Fortune* listing. Its life insurance subsidiary alone was the sixth largest carrier in the industry with 1973 life insurance in force exceeding $84 billion.[1] Aetna's market success and industry prominence have not been phenomena of the

[a]The split between insurers emphasizing group insurance rather than individual policies, for example, was a serious one and led companies emphasizing one or another of these approaches to different conclusions about proposed regulations on advertising and mass marketing.

1970s. The company has been in existence since the 1850s and has been a prominent competitor in insurance markets for over 100 years. Since the early 1900s thc Actna and its affiliated companies have been one of the most influential and trendsetting multiple-line writers of insurance. This history is important and any current assessment of the company is faulted without reference to the traditions and values that have evolved through seven generations of top management.

The importance of tradition and past values must be placed in perspective. Both reflect historical experience and are, therefore, a reference point for management. This experience certainly affects the way in which management perceives and evaluates change in its environment; moreover, tradition and organizational values influence the kinds of decision rules that management will apply to current issues. An understanding of the Aetna's responses to social change during the 1960s and 1970s is bound to be limited without an appreciation of the major themes in the company's historical development. For the most part, these are reflected in the present interests of the technical, managerial, and institutional subsystems of the firm.

The Aetna to 1960[2]

Aetna Life and Casualty is the successor to an affiliated group of companies that have operated under the Aetna name since the mid-1800s. The core company from which the present Aetna Life and Casualty Company evolved was the Aetna Life Insurance Company, formed in 1853 by a group of Hartford, Connecticut merchants.[b] The leader of this group was Eliphalet Adams Bulkeley, a local merchant, lawyer, and judge who served as the company's first president.

Bulkeley's association with life insurance followed from his association as general counsel of the Aetna (Fire) Insurance Company and his previous role as the first president of the Connecticut Mutual Life Insurance Company, a company that he also helped to found in 1846. He had been unseated from the Connecticut Mutual presidency after serving one year when a number of the company's agents solicited proxies from policyholders for the purpose of gaining control of the company. The episode was instrumental in shaping Bulkeley's well-known preference for the stock, rather than mutual, company form.

A provision in the Aetna Fire company's charter that allowed the formation of a life insurance business was initially used to create a life insurance company under the Aetna name (Aetna Annuity Fund), albeit one with a separate

[b]The Aetna (Fire) Insurance Company of Hartford is the earliest antecedent, having been chartered in 1819. The fire company distinguished itself during the nineteenth century by not defaulting on any of its fire policies through the great fires that occurred in New York in 1835, Chicago in 1871, Boston in 1872, and San Francisco in 1906.

capitalization. The company raised its capital through stock subscriptions to fire company stockholders, and in this way, a separate capital base was formed for the purposes of solvency, while the "affiliated company" was able to draw on the good will associated with the Aetna name.

In 1849 New York State declared that fire insurance and life insurance businesses were not to be carried on by the same company. An 1853 revision of the law strengthened the terms of the act and created problems for the Aetna Annuity Fund because of its legal status as a part of the Aetna Fire Insurance Company. Steps were taken to sever the Annuity Fund from the Fire Company (a legislative act was required) and separately incorporate the Annuity Fund as the Aetna Life Insurance Company. In July 1853 the life company was chartered as a separate corporation under the laws of the state of Connecticut. Eliphalet Bulkeley was its first president and headed the company until his death in 1872.

Bulkeley was prominent in Hartford commerce and politics before and during his presidency of the Aetna Life company. His stature in the community constituted an important legitimizing factor vis-à-vis both the Connecticut legislature and the local community. But the Aetna's early growth was not primarily attributable to its political legitimacy. Rather it was the result of aggressive salesmanship and the development of a workable agency system whose architect was Dr. Thomas B. Lacey. Lacey began as a medical examiner for the Annuity Fund but became the "father" of the Aetna Life's agency system by traveling the country, enlisting agents, and spurring sales efforts. The result of these efforts was a life agency system that accounted for Aetna Life's success through the late 1800s.

If Bulkeley was the cornerstone of the company's institutional subsystem, and Lacey the prominent figure in its managerial subsystem, the central figure in the development of the company's technical subsystem was Thomas Ostrom Enders. Enders had come to Aetna as a clerk in 1854, becoming secretary of the company in 1858, and eventually president on Bulkeley's death in 1872. As secretary, he was the chief administrator of the company, making critical underwriting decisions and determining appropriate premium rates. It was Enders who sponsored the formation of a participating (or mutual) life insurance department within the company. The *participating life policy* was the equivalent of the mutual life policy, returning dividends to the policyholder based on investment earnings. It was a highly saleable product and accounted for much of the Aetna Life Insurance Company's growth during the 1860s. Moreover, it enabled the company to successfully compete with such mutual companies as the Equitable. In 1861 when participating insurance was first offered, total income was $78,533 and reported assets were $281,263. In 1867 total income had risen to $5,129,447 and assets to $7,538,612.

Aetna's success attracted the scrutiny of early state regulators and envious competitors alike. Squabbles with such energetic insurance commissioners as

William Barnes of New York were characteristic of the period but were normally resolved in favor of the Aetna through the political skills of Bulkeley and the administrative expertise of Enders. More serious regulatory matters, such as proposals to restrict stock company operations in certain states, were often more threatening to the company, although they were less the result of positive public policy than the efforts of mutual insurers to block stock company growth.[3]

During Ender's presidency (1872-1879), political scrapping gave way to an emphasis on internal administrative matters. The most notable step was the acquisition and development of professionally trained actuaries. This was especially notable because the actuarial staff became the continuing source of new policy forms and devices for tying life insurance to the basic financial protection goals of a growing society. Howell W. St. John, a professional mathematician and Aetna's first trained actuary, was the key figure in this regard. He eventually became a vice president of the company and was also a founder of the Actuarial Society of America. By the end of the 1870s the professional core of the business was well-established within the Aetna and its internal importance was ascending.

Enders was succeeded in 1879 by Morgan Gardner Bulkeley, son of Judge Bulkeley, who served as president for 43 years (1879-1922). A remarkable part of Morgan Bulkeley's impact is attributable to the political career that he simultaneously pursued and that eventually included two terms as Governor of Connecticut, continuous involvement in the Republican Party, and one term as United States Senator from Connecticut; all while Bulkeley was also serving as president of the Aetna Life Insurance Company.[c]

Of the many changes occurring during Morgan Bulkeley's lengthy presidency, the evolution of the affiliated company structure stands out as the most important in shaping the company's growth. Established in 1907 and originally known as the Aetna Accident and Liability Company, the Aetna Casualty and Surety Company had turned an initial capitalization of $500,000 into $2 million by 1922. The Automobile Insurance Company grew even faster, starting with a $300,000 capital stock in 1913 and increasing it to over $2 million by 1922. Aetna Life itself had grown in assets from $25.6 million in 1879 to $207 million by 1922. Annual premium had been multiplied over 22 times to $55.9 million from $2.4 million during the same period; insurance in force increased from $77.7 million in 1879 to $1.3 billion in 1922.[4]

The company's movement toward multiple lines of insurance began in 1891 when the life company created a department to write accident insurance. The Accident Department was operated as separate business, with separate assets and liabilities, staffing, and so forth. Its ties with the Life Company were at the sales level, where agents sold life and accident insurance, and at the top management level, where Bulkeley framed company policy. Health insurance was added in

[c]Morgan Bulkeley was also a founder of the National Baseball League and served as its first president in 1876.

1899; in 1902 liability lines were developed in such areas as employer's liability insurance and workmen's collective insurance. In 1902 the Accident Department became the Accident and Liability Department reflecting its expanding liability lines of business.

Recognizing the potential markets for automobile insurance and other types of property insurance, and also recognizing that most states sought to separate life and property insurance companies, Aetna formed a separate company—the Aetna Accident and Liability Company—in 1907 to write property lines, including auto collision, burglary, plate glass, and other casualty lines. After fidelity and surety bonds were added to the business in 1911, the company changed its name to Aetna Casualty & Surety Company in 1917.

The automobile insurance policy offered by the Company at that time included a fire insurance coverage through a device known as the *consequential loss clause.* When several state insurance commissions objected to a casualty company writing fire insurance, Aetna formed The Automobile Company as a fire insurance affiliate; theft insurance was quickly added and led to the development of such complementary lines as loss of use, explosion, tornado and windstorm, leasehold, and rent. By 1916 the expansion of lines also included ocean marine insurance and in 1920 inland marine insurance. By 1922 the Aetna Affiliated Companies constituted one of the major multiple-line insurance groups and were being referred to in the Hartford insurance press as the largest multiple-line group in the nation.

The Aetna's fourth president (1922-1955) was Morgan Bulkeley Brainard, grandson of Eliphalet Bulkeley and nephew of Morgan Bulkeley. Brainard's career at the Aetna began in 1905. By 1910 he was vice president and an officer of the affiliated companies, thereby gaining direct exposure to the methods and motives of his uncle. As Enders had strengthened the company internally following Judge Bulkeley's presidency, so too did Brainard emphasize organizational development following the expansionist presidency of Morgan Bulkeley.

The Aetna Life Insurance affiliate had become a somnambulent enterprise in the early 1920s, offering little in the way of new insurance coverages and few agency incentives for expanded sales. Brainard's remedy involved a restructuring of the entire home office-agency relationship. Closer home office control over agency field operations was instituted, uniform agency contracts replaced negotiated contracts, procedures for policy service were simplified, the cost of soliciting new business was reduced, and intensive efforts were undertaken to increase life insurance sales. As a result of these efforts, life insurance in force increased from $1.3 billion in 1922 to nearly $3.8 billion in 1929, and assets increased from $207 million to $410 million during the same period.

The affiliated companies suffered from their rapid growth during the mid-1920s, especially The Automobile Company, which was discovered to have seriously understated its liabilities. Brainard's remedy was a severe restriction on underwriting, a concomitant decline of premiums from over $30 million in 1924 to less than $8 million in 1927, and a reestablishment of proper reserves. An increase in paid-in capital was effected to cover liabilities without impairing the capital of the parent Aetna Life Company through an additional stock offering to Aetna shareholders. The Automobile Company's financial solvency was thereby reestablished before the 1929 crash and the company undertook a thorough reexamination of the financial position of all the affiliated companies.

The timing of the reexamination was fortuitous because it enabled the Aetna to withstand the impact of the Depression with relatively minor financial injury. Despite deflated stock prices and increasing mortgage foreclosures, the Aetna companies were able to continue operations, including the payment of policy loans, without interruption during the 1930s. The parent life company had had only 11.7 percent of its assets in common stock at the time of crash and nearly half (5.22 percent) was represented by stock in the affiliated companies. Although stockholder dividends were suspended in July 1932, they were restored by July 1934.

As with other insurers, investments in land became actual land holdings as foreclosures increased during the 1930s. According to company records, Aetna Life owned but one piece of foreclosed farm property in 1920; by 1930 the number was nearly one thousand; by the end of 1934 the number had risen to over three thousand. The value of foreclosed mortgages increased from $7 million in 1930 to $22.6 million in 1934. To manage such holdings, the company appointed field representatives throughout the Midwest to oversee the properties and maintain their productive capacity.

The Depression also highlighted the company's relationship with its employees. Since both life and casualty insurance policies continued to need servicing, employment remained steady throughout most of the period. To the extent declining revenues decreased staffing needs in some departments, the company adopted a policy of not filling vacant positions rather than laying-off or dismissing employees. Similarly, at a time when salary cuts were common, Aetna employees suffered but one 10 percent cut in 1934. By the end of 1935 the company had begun a practice of paying annual bonuses to salaried employees.

In the post-Depression, post-World War II period an especially significant development was the growth of group insurance business, including life, health, and accident insurance. The Aetna had begun writing group insurance before 1920 (1920 group premiums were $3.7 million); by 1930 total group premiums (life, accident, health) had increased to $18.9 million; in 1940 they were $43.7 million. During the Second World War group premiums grew enormously, totaling $107 million in 1945, and by 1953 total group insurance premiums for all group lines had increased to more than $367 million. Group life insurance in force had a face value of over $10 billion in the same year.

Brainard retired as president in 1956, having served for 34 years in that capacity. He was succeeded by Henry S. Beers, a vice-president of the Aetna Life Insurance Company. Unlike Brainard who had been trained as a lawyer, Beers was an actuary by training. Most importantly in terms of the company goals, Beers had been vice president of the group division and was especially well equipped to formulate strategy and policy in that regard. Brainard's administration had successfully weathered the abnormal economic and political conditions of Depression, the New Deal, and World War II. Beers' administration was concerned with the tasks of consolidating the diverse insurance operations and lines of business into which the company had spread and with the development of an organization that was capable of seizing the opportunities foreseen in a period of social and political normalcy.

Beer's most important contribution was the restructuring of the company's executive leadership. Beers reconstituted the Aetna's top management into a triumvirate that included positions of chairman of the board, vice-chairman, and company president. In 1962 Beers became chairman of the board and announced that Olcott D. Smith, a Hartford attorney and member of the board of directors, was named vice chairman; John A. Hill, whose background was insurance sales, became company president. The effect was to create an executive office that included representatives of the technical (Beers, the actuary), managerial (Hill, the salesman), and institutional (Smith, the lawyer) subsystems of the organization.

Henry Beers retired in July 1963 and Olcott Smith became chairman of the board. Hill continued to serve as president, but it was a role clearly subordinate to that of Smith. The vice chairman's position was abandoned. Between 1963 and 1972 it was unquestionably Olcott Smith who was the most influential force in the formation of the Aetna's corporate policy. Smith's prominence did not change the fact that as the company responded to an increasingly turbulent environment, complex bargaining was occurring among the company's technical, managerial, and institutional subsystems, each of which had important interests in the issues of the period. For the Aetna and the insurance industry the critical changes that were occurring were not confined to traditional matters such as sales growth, asset expansion, or insurance in force. Significant changes also had to be described in terms of a new balance between the private and public sectors; in terms of a society that increasingly sought to directly influence the decisions and actions of insurers and regulators; and in terms of the passing away of a period when insurers could limit their social involvement to local communities and narrow product markets.

1963-1972: Strategy and Structure

A strong ideological identification has been a notable characteristic of the insurance business since the mid-1800s. Among its many effects, it has served to reinforce intraindustry differences between life and nonlife companies, between stock and mutual companies, and between agency writers and the direct writers.

For this reason, an important management task in creating a multiple-line insurance company is to overcome the long-standing operating differences between life and nonlife areas that can fracture the organization and make effective policy coordination impossible.

At the Aetna this problem was avoided for many years by operating the company as a group of affiliated companies, each with its own operations, agents, and staff, with profit responsibilities generally resting with the affiliates. During the 1950s, however, a number of factors had caused Aetna's top management to rethink the relationship between Aetna Life and the affiliated companies. In the nonlife insurance business, the recision of New York's Appleton Rule had stimulated the development of many multiple-line companies that were capable of integrating their activities more effectively than an affiliated group.[d] Also specialty insurers such as Allstate, State Farm, and Nationwide had, through the use of exclusive agents and direct marketing techniques, established a prominent position in the automobile and fire insurance businesses. These developments signaled major competitive problems for the Aetna affiliated companies and prompted Aetna's top management to consider means of preserving both the profitability of its casualty business and its market share in individual casualty lines.

The growth of multiple-line insurers, the impact of the direct writers, and the ascendancy of group insurance sales constituted a set of competitive changes that suggested that the affiliated company structure had outlived its competitive usefulness. Structural change seemed to be required since the company faced the twin tasks of maintaining or improving the profitability of individual casualty lines (e.g., fire, auto bodily injury, auto physical damage, burglary and theft) and effecting administrative economies of scale. The multiple-line structure seemed to offer a better means of maintaining this balance between decentralized sales and underwriting operations and centralized administrative operations. Thus one of Olcott Smith's immediate tasks as chairman was to move the Aetna toward multiple-line reorganization.

The reorganization proceeded in several stages. Initially, the capital structure of the affiliated companies had to be consolidated into a single structure, that being the Aetna Life and Casualty Company. This was completed by late 1964. Capital reorganization was followed by internal reorganization. The affiliated companies became subsidiaries of Aetna Life and Casualty, a multiple-line company, and attempts were made to better coordinate sales and underwriting activities among the casualty lines of business. Life and health insurance operations functional apart from the casualty business for the most part.

Aetna's reorganization made it the largest multiple-line insurer in the industry and reestablished the company's competitive presence in the industry. But additional changes were also required. Smith's belief that the international operations of an insurer's corporate clients required a capacity to write insurance

[d]These were discussed at greater length in Chapter 3.

on an international scale led Aetna in 1966 to enter into an operating agreement with Assicurazioni Generali di Trieste e Venezia, an international multiple-line insurer with operations and affiliates in 50 countries. In particular, this affiliation enabled the Aetna to implement group insurance and pension contracts for corporate clients with multinational operations.

Reorganization was taken one step further in the late 1960s when the Aetna petitioned the Connecticut legislature for authority to change its corporate structure to that of a holding company. Such a change was intended to create a parent firm that would own all the stock of the existing Aetna subsidiaries. More importantly, the holding-company structure would enable the Aetna to diversify outside of the insurance business. The prospect of investing the premium income in excess of reserves in the ownership of such profitable businesses as real estate and mutual funds was an attractive one for insurers whose own relative profitability had suffered as a consequence of inflation during the decade. The transition to a holding-company structure was completed in 1967, and the Aetna immediately began an expansion and acquisition program that led it into the mutual fund, real estate, hotel and restaurant, and commercial finance businesses; see Figure 8-1.[5]

The structural changes that the Aetna underwent during the 1960s marked its transformation into a multidivisional organization.[6] As a group of affiliated companies, Aetna was a cluster of semiautonomous, single product line firms, each of which specialized in a single set of insurance coverages. Smith's efforts to create first a multiple-line company, then a holding company were attempts to unify multiple product lines within a single decision-making structure. In fact, most operating decision-making authority was actually placed, and intended to be exercised, at the divisional level. But as the operating environment of the company became increasingly turbulent during the course of the 1960s, new pressures created a greater need within the company to develop means of coordinating and integrating decision-making and organizational action.

In sum, the Aetna began the decade of the 1960s with a need to integrate the activities of its affiliated companies as a response to competitive pressures posed by multiple-line and specialty insurance companies. The structural response was to reorganize the Aetna as a multiple-line insurer. By the mid-1960s the company strategy had shifted in favor of competing with other types of financial institutions for investor dollars. This strategy created the need for an organization structure that would permit mutual fund, real estate, and commercial finance operations. The structural need was for the creation of a holding-company organization, operated on a multidivisional basis.

Overall, the structure of the Aetna during the period 1963 to 1972 was a direct response to economic and competitive change. These were conventional forms of social change and the company had a history of successfully responding thereto. But beyond the structural response lay important questions about the organizational action necessary to effect the Aetna's business strategy.

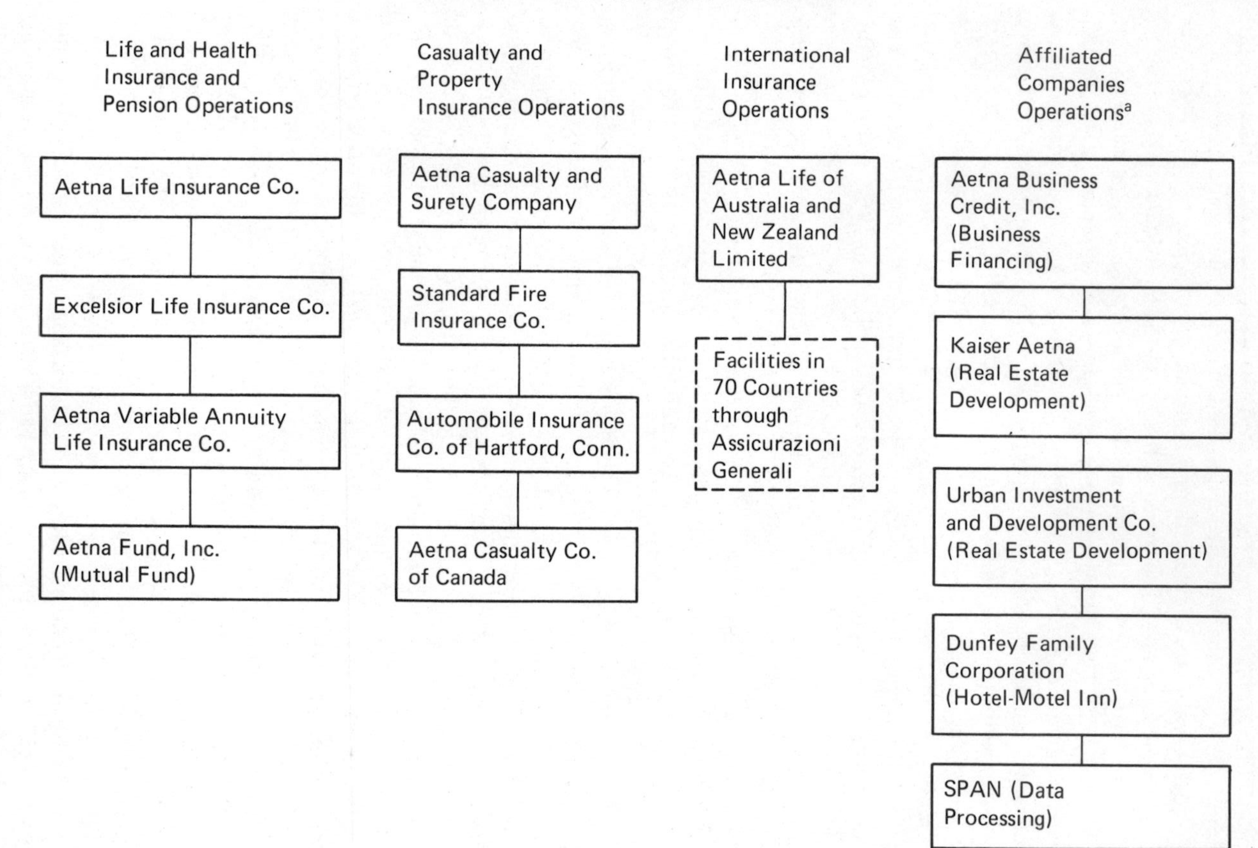

[a]In the 1972 annual report, this is referred to as "Related Corporate Operations."

Figure 8-1. Aetna Life and Casualty Organization Structure (circa 1971-1972).

Insurance Markets, Old and New

The heart of the Aetna's business strategy called for direct competition with financial institutions for investor's dollars and an emphasis on maintaining the profitability of each individual line of business. The implications of this strategy, and the problems associated with its implementation in an environment of considerable social change, are especially evident in two of the Aetna's traditionally important markets: life insurance and fire insurance.

Preserving a Market: The Development of Variable Life Insurance

The broad scope of the Aetna's multiple-line operations does not obscure the continuing importance of the company's life insurance operations. Traditionally, life insurance has been the core of the Aetna Life Company's operations; Aetna Life, in turn, is the hub around which the affiliated companies have been organized. The importance of life insurance to the Aetna during the 1960s is evident. For example, in 1962 total life insurance in force had exceeded $27 billion; annual life, health, and annuity income was nearly $165 million; and investment income from life, health, and annuity funds exceeded $186 million. Moreover, although the premium from life, health, and annuity accounted for 12.2 percent of all premiums received by the affiliated companies, the investment income earned by life, health, and pension operations accounted for more than 87 percent of all investment income earned by the affiliated companies. Thus when Olcott Smith assumed the Aetna chairmanship in 1963 the status of the company's life insurance operations were a matter of continuing concern.

Dimensions of Interpenetration

In 1950 total life insurance in force in the United States exceeded $234 billion. By 1959 that amount had increased to over $542 billion, as both individual life and group life insurance sales increased.[7] Given that history of growth, industry spokesmen were optimistically describing the potential for future life insurance growth during the 1960s. Yet industry optimism was also tempered by a deep concern about the impact of inflation.

Although life insurance is generally promoted and advertised as a basic form of family financial protection rather than as an investment device, there are investment aspects to many types of life insurance policies. *Ordinary life insurance* is usually issued in amounts of $1,000 or more with premiums payable on an annual, semiannual, quarterly, or monthly basis.[8] Ordinary life is the basic form of life insurance in force. It is usually purchased by individuals through agents, and it is the oldest and most widely used form of life insurance coverage. These policies offer more than the protection features normally associated with insurance. All but the term insurance type of ordinary life policy build cash values against which the policyholder can borrow. Ordinary life policies also frequently have a participating feature, which refunds a portion of the premium to policyholders in the form of dividends based on the insurer's annual investment earnings, administrative expenses, and cost experience.[9]

The investment aspects of the life insurance policy operate to place life insurance in competition with other forms of financial investment, especially savings accounts and mutual funds. During periods of inflation, returns on investments such as common stock and mutual funds tend to rise with corporate profits. Fixed return devices, such as savings accounts, may be permitted to increase their interest rates to depositors in an effort to maintain savings levels. Because of restrictions on the size of reserve levels and the permissible types of investment that they can make, life insurers have frequently argued before regulatory agencies in favor of standards that would permit them to more effectively compete for investors' funds. Such a situation existed in the 1960s when life insurers were especially concerned because returns on mutual funds were comparatively high and because banking regulatory authorities had permitted an increase in the interest rates paid to depositors.

The changing role of life insurance as an investment, and the crux of the problem facing life insurers, is reflected in the fact that in 1948 life insurance companies accounted for 47.1 percent of the growth in savings; but in 1967, when institutional savings increased by $64.1 billion, life insurance accounted for only $8.6 billion or 13.4 percent.[10] And although the net rate of interest earned by life insurers on invested funds did increase annually throughout the 1960s (4.11 percent in 1960; 4.61 percent in 1965; 5.12 percent in 1969),[11] the rate was not sufficient to materially change the dividend returns to policyholders.

Patterns of Response

Inflation had been a recognized problem for the industry since the 1950s. The industry was affected in several ways by inflation, and these impacts shaped the responses of member firms. First, inflation obviously affected the quality of the insurance product as an investment. In this regard, it was a matter that affected the technical core of the business. The technical alternatives were to improve the investment return for policyholders by either securing a higher return on invested premiums or by making it possible to treat more of the insurance premium as an investment rather than a purchase of protection. Regulations on permissible sources of insurer investment limited the first alternative; and the fixed return guaranteed by a policy's face value limited the latter. The ability to pursue the first alternative depended on a relaxation of regulatory standards, the second on the development of new products.

A second impact of inflation involved the changes it produced in the flow of investable funds going to insurance companies. If this continued to decrease, in actual dollars or in proportion, the traditional role of life insurers as suppliers of credit, including mortgage funds, would necessarily change. This, in turn, would affect the profitability of an industry that depended upon investment returns, not underwriting, for its overall profit. These concerns primarily touched the managerial subsystem of the insurer; that is, the subsystem that is entrusted with coordinating the flow of resources into the organization and generating the net profit from the provision of final services. Like the technical alternatives, the managerial alternatives were dependent upon a loosening of current restrictions on investment alternatives and on the creation of new products for attracting a continuing flow of premium dollars to the insurance enterprise.

The third impact of inflation was an institutional one. Since the viability of an insurance enterprise is tied to public confidence in the service provided as well as financial integrity of the firm, anything that erodes public confidence in the insurance product has to be a major source of concern. Inflation, of course, had precisely that effect on the life insurance industry. As the investing public became increasingly conscious of the shrinking real dollar value of their life insurance policies, alternatives for protecting one's family were more frequently pursued. The responses available to the industry were limited: campaigns could be undertaken to show the continuing value of life insurance; doubt could be cast on the future solvency of investment alternatives; or the adverse social impact of inflation could be publicized and a call made for a campaign to maintain stable price levels.

At the industry level, the top managements of the leading insurers agreed upon a concerted, industry-sponsored public relations campaign to raise public consciousness of the dangers of continuing inflation. A proposed program of government action to control inflation was publicized, and public support was sought for balanced governmental budgets and wage increases that were limited to actual improvements in worker productivity. The two-year public relations campaign began in 1960 but was abandoned after drawing little significant response from government leaders or the public. As the industry continued to attract proportionately fewer savings dollars, it became apparent to the managements of some companies that alternative strategies for preserving the life insurance market were required.

The strategy selected by a number of companies, including the Aetna, concentrated on the development of new products that could overcome the fixed-return aspects of ordinary life policies. One early product in this regard was the variable annuity. Annuities had been sold in the United States since the 1800s, usually providing that the beneficiary receive a fixed number of payments or a fixed amount of money based on contributions to the annuity fund and estimated investment returns. The variable annuity is based, in whole or in part, on common stock investments or on a cost-of-living index. Part or all of the invested funds are placed in separate accounts to be invested in ways restricted to normal life insurance investments. Because of the long-standing connection between life insurance companies and fixed annuity contracts, state regulatory authorities raised minimal objection to variable annuity programs. By 1968, 317,300 persons were covered by life insurance company variable annuities; in 1969 the number swelled to 426,800, an increase of 109,000 persons.[12]

Variable annuities were not sufficient to compete with the growing popularity of mutual funds however. Thus pressure existed on insurance company managements to develop still other inflation-resistant products. Aetna's basic strategy during the early 1960s had been one of joining new product development and its large life agency force. This would permit the agents to better function as financial consultants, directing a client toward the most advantageous financial package. Since variable annuities could not meet all these needs, Aetna sought to expand its product line still further.

In its 1966 annual report the company announced its intention to expand into the individual annuity contract market by acquisition, rather than by direct business development. The announcement was brief, only stating that to expedite this matter the Aetna was seeking to purchase all of the outstanding shares of the Participating Annuity Life Insurance Company of Little Rock, Arkansas, which had been founded in 1954.[13] Underlying the Aetna's announcement was a story of a decade-long struggle to secure regulatory approval of insurance products with variable components.

During the mid-1950s a number of small insurance companies had attempted to sell to restricted segments of the public insurance products that included a variable component permitting adjustment of the dollar value of the policy under specified conditions (e.g., inflation) and terms (e.g., adjusted premiums). One of the leaders of this movement was John D. Marsh who, after experience with TIAA-CREF, founded the Participating Annuity Life Insurance Company (PALIC) in 1954.

PALIC began its operations by training a group of agents who would be qualified to engage in the sale of variable annuity products. The Securities and Exchange Commission had moved to restrict the sale of such products by unregistered salesmen under the Securities Acts of 1933, 1934, and 1940. Thus the issue was joined as to whether insurance agents would be permitted to sell annuities that had such variable features. A test case was prepared by the various insurers involved, PALIC being one of those that joined in the fight. Eventually the test case was appealed to the United States Supreme Court, and in 1959 the Court ruled that variable annuities might be sold by insurance companies, provided that salesmen also qualify as registered representatives under the Securities Acts.[14]

The case was a victory for the insurance companies, since it established their right to sell annuity products to the public. It was also a victory for Marsh, since he had previously undertaken to train PALICs salesmen for this new business. While the test case had moved through the courts, PALIC had continued to train and register salesmen who were qualified to sell variable annuity products under the SECs registration requirements. Thus, once the Supreme Court established the right of insurers to offer such products, PALIC was prepared to enter the market with a fully trained and registered sales force. Marsh had recognized, however, that large sales of variable products could not be expected without a major advertising effort, including a nationwide system for servicing the accounts. For these reasons, he began to market PALIC to a larger company that was attuned to the variable market and possessed a national marketing system.

The marketing of PALIC took a considerable amount of time. But as the mutual fund business continued to worry insurance executives,[15] the interest in acquiring PALIC began to grow. PALIC had two principle assets: an agency force of more than 6,000 SEC-registered salesmen and the expertise of a management team headed by John Marsh.[16] Relying on the worth of these two sets of assets in an area of the financial services business that was almost entirely unknown to insurance companies, Marsh was prepared to sell PALIC to the highest bidder.

An acquisition of PALIC fit well with the Aetna's strategy of improvement return on investment by moving into more lucrative investment areas than those permitted life insurers under traditional regulation. Moreover, as the Aetna moved broadly into the financial services industry, Marsh's experience could prove increasingly valuable. Eventually, an agreement was reached whereby the Aetna would purchase the total outstanding shares of PALIC with Aetna shares. The actual sale was consummated in March 1967 after the Aetna had itself legally become a holding company.

As an Aetna subsidiary, PALICs immediate task was to embark on a program of training Aetna's national field organization in the variable annuity business and to prepare them for licensing as securities salesmen by the SEC. By late 1967 the Aetna field force had begun selling variable annuities to the public.

Aetna was one of the first large insurers to enter the variable annuity market, and with PALICs expertise and sales force, Aetna's share of the market began to grow rapidly. In 1968 the company reported outstanding first year sales of variable annuities; in 1969 PALICs premium income increased 270 percent to $30.8 million; in 1970 premium income rose an additional 27 percent to $39.1 million at the end of 1970. The field organization's enthusiasm for the variable annuity product was understandable: 25 percent of the first-year premium was paid as commission on each sale. As several sources who were interviewed noted, some field people became millionaires in those first few years and all the field people knew it! Aetna continued to sponsor PALICs growth and market expansion by making a $6 million capital contribution to the subsidiary in 1970.[e]

[e]Technically, Aetna was suffering a loss on the variable annuity business because of a statutory underwriting requirement that stipulated that the entire cost of writing new business must be absorbed in the year of the sale.

A name change transformed PALIC into the Aetna Variable Annuity and Life Insurance Company (VALIC), which continued as a subsidiary of the parent Aetna Life and Casualty Company. By 1972 premium income had grown to $80 million though start-up costs continued to create net losses on the business. The company had also succeeded in expanding its sales force, establishing a substantial premium base, and gaining actuarial and sales experience with variable products. The competence and confidence that the company had acquired with variable products was reflected in the 1972 annual report, when variable annuities were distinguished from other types of variable products that the company was engaged in developing. Among the prospective products then identified was *variable life insurance.*

In contrast with traditional life insurance policies, the variable life insurance contract has a provision whereby death proceeds are contingent upon the actual investment performance of the company.[17] Unlike the normal investment portfolio, which consists primarily of bonds and mortgages, the assets representing variable life contracts are predominantly invested in common stock. The ultimate obligations of the insurer are, therefore, directly related to the investment performance of a specifically designated portfolio of common stock. The Aetna had been engaged in developing a life insurance policy along these general lines.

An important regulatory question arose with regard to variable life insurance: was it to be regulated by the states, as were other forms of life insurance, or, because of its ties to securities, by the SEC? For the Aetna, that decision had to be made by the SEC. Because of its involvement in the variable annuities business, Aetna (VALIC) had become a registered SEC company. Under the terms of the Securities Acts and the rules of the SEC, registered companies cannot sell any product that itself is unregistered. While this presented no problem with regard to variable annuities, it did mean that Aetna had to secure registration of variable life insurance, a step that would thereby bring the product under SEC regulation. Since the state insurance commissions would also regulate the product because of its insurance characteristics, the potential existed for a system of dual regulation.[f] Because of the problems inherent in such a situation, and because of the prospectively inhibiting effect of reduced sales commissions, Aetna applied for an SEC exemption for its variable life insurance contracts.

The SEC responded by granting Aetna an exemption in 1972 that permitted the company to sell variable life insurance as an exempt product, available for sale only with qualified pension plans. The SEC reserved decision on the question of whether individual variable life insurance policies would receive an exemption. The SEC decision thereby allowed sales of variable life insurance on

[f]The effect of SEC regulation was likely to include disclosure requirements, a review of sales literature and techniques, and a limitation on the sales commission that would be substantially lower than the commissions normally paid on life insurance contracts.

an exempt product basis before a final resolution of the question of whether or not variable life would be regulated as a security. In July 1972 Aetna sold the first variable life insurance policy issued in the United States as part of a qualified pension plan.

Receipt of the SEC exemption eliminated one half the regulatory problem. The other half involved securing state insurance commission approval of the variable life insurance contract. The approval of the insurance commissioner of each state in which the company sought to sell the policy had to be secured before any actual sales could take place. The process of securing such approval, at a time when the state commissions themselves were unsure about the SECs course of action, was predictably slow. As of January 1974, only 23 states had passed the necessary enabling legislation allowing such sales and had approved specific variable life insurance contracts for sale within the state. Moreover, as of that date, the large insurance-purchasing states of New York, New Jersey, Pennsylvania, Illinois, and California had neither passed enabling legislation nor had they approved any specific variable life contracts.

The SEC had in January 1973 ruled that individual variable life insurance policies would be exempt from SEC regulation. However, the Commission quickly reconsidered when securities interests objected, thereby further halting any sales of individual variable life insurance policies. As of mid-1974 the Aetna was continuing to lobby with the SEC for an exemption of individual variable life policies. It also continued to sell variable life insurance where permitted as part of qualified corporate pension and profit-sharing plans and continued to pursue state insurance commission approvals of variable life products.

Abandoning a Market: Insuring the Inner City

Unlike life insurance, fire insurance–and its property and casualty coverage offspring–has been considered a social necessity since the 1700s. During the 1960s two severe problems developed in the casualty and property insurance business that directly stemmed from the necessary character of such insurance. The first related to the underwriting pressure on insurers to withdraw from the inner-city market because of increasing hazards to insured property; the second related to the catastrophic losses occasioned by the urban riots and civil disorder that occurred during the summer of 1967. Together they constituted a market problem of such serious consequence to insurers that complete abandonment of the inner city became a frequently discussed form of insurer response.

Dimensions of Interpenetration

Like many other insurance problems of the 1960s, that of providing insurance to the inner city involved a basic dilemma between the availability of insurance coverage and price of such coverage. Fire insurance and crime insurance, in particular, were considered necessities by inner-city property owners and businessmen but were either entirely unavailable from insurers or available only at a price that was not affordable.

Some of the dimensions of the inner-city insurance problems are illustrated by data discovered after the 1967 riots. Following those riots, President Lyndon B. Johnson appointed the National Advisory Commission on Civil Disorders to investigate the origins of the riots and to recommend measures for preventing or containing them in the future. The Commission, in turn, recognized that there were special problems associated with insurance and on August 10, 1967 appointed the National Advisory Panel on Insurance in Riot-Affected Areas. This panel undertook to investigate inner-city insurance needs, industry capacity to meet those needs, and ways to close any gap between them.

As part of its investigation, the Panel surveyed 1500 homeowners and 1500 businessmen in the inner-city areas of Boston, Cleveland, Detroit, Newark, Oakland, and St. Louis. According to the survey results, which were reported in January 1968, over 40 percent of businesses and 30 percent of homeowners had serious property insurance problems.[18] Specifically, 20 percent of businessmen and 6 percent of the homeowners surveyed were without fire insurance coverage, and in Detroit over 12 percent of the homeowners were without it. Of the uninsured, 35 percent of the businessmen and 50 percent of the homeowners said that insurance was simply unavailable; nearly 30 percent of both groups claimed that whatever insurance was available was excessive in cost. In addition, 50 percent of the businessmen surveyed had no burglary and theft insurance; in Boston the figure was 74 percent. Of those without such insurance, 30 percent said it was too costly and 25 percent said it was unavailable at any price.[19]

The problems of availability and cost of coverage were an understood but unquantified matter before the mid-1960s. Insurers had withdrawn from the market on an individual company basis, not en masse, and although the cost for available insurance had been increasing for many years, no concerted effort to remedy the situation had been attempted. The Watts riots in Los Angeles during the summer of 1965 focused public attention on the conditions existing in the inner-city areas of some large cities, however, and some attempts were made to improve availability. But on the whole, public concern was latent and governmental responses limited until the 1967 riots. The number of deaths, the extent of the carnage, and the duration of those disorders riveted public attention on the inner city and convincingly suggested that the long hot summer of 1967 could and might well be repeated in 1968.[20]

As indicated in Chapter 1, the interpenetration between an industry (or firm) and society is likely to vary with scope of the relationship, the salience of the issues, and continuity of the relationship. In the case of fire and other casualty and property insurance coverages, the general need for such coverage by property owners made the scope of the interpenetration between the industry and society quite broad, and the long-standing history of this relationship magnified the continuity problems involved in limiting availability. But it was the salience of the inner-city insurance problem to both inner-city residents and property owners and to the insurers that most precisely identified the interpenetration of the two. Insurers, as well as property owners, had a large stake in resolving the inner-city insurance dilemma.

The stake of the insurers is reflected in several ways. In 1966, for example, the property-liability (nonlife) insurance industry had assets of about $41 billion and annual premium income of $22 billion. Among the relevant property lines of coverage in considering the inner city, fire insurance produced the largest volume of premium ($1.6 billion in 1966) for the industry, which represented 8.69 percent of the stock companies' overall premium income volume and 4.91 percent of the mutual companies' in 1966. Among nearly all relevant coverages involved in the inner-city dilemma, stock insurers' involvement was larger than that of mutual companies.

Testimony presented before the President's Panel indicated that stock insurers were writing over 80 percent of all fire and extended coverage (wind, smoke, riot, vehicle, and hail losses) between 1957 and 1966. Thus during the riots it was the stock companies that stood to suffer the largest numbers and dollar volume of claims. Equally important, however, was the fact that for nearly a decade, stock insurers had been operating with a combined loss and expense ratio in these lines of insurance that was higher than that of the mutual companies.

To combat these high loss ratios, insurers had been imposing special requirements on properties within redlined areas, such as direct underwriting inspections, coverage restrictions, and a variety of surcharge, deductible, and coinsurance clauses. On an underwriting basis alone, abandonment of the inner-city market was becoming a rational economic response. The stock companies were being tempted, in effect, to follow the lead of the mutual companies and lower their loss ratios by insuring only the most preferred urban properties.

According to the Advisory Panel, the constricted market for fire and property insurance for inner-city markets was attributable to standard insurer underwriting practices. Basically, insurance companies generally regarded any business in the urban core as relatively unprofitable. According to the Panel, rather than basing decisions to insure solely on the merits of individual properties, many companies assessed the application of an inner-city homeowner or businessman on the basis of the neighborhood where the property was located.[21] The result had been the development of a variety of technical devices for limiting the receipt of such applications through underwriting standards and the identification of "redline" districts within which business ought not be written by agents. Such a course of behavior was, of course, quite consistent with the standard approach of seeking to create an underwriting profit on each piece of insured property.[22] Yet, even this course of action had generally been failing for insurers before 1967.

Into the bleak underwriting picture of the inner city, the riots injected a second major element: the catastrophic loss. For insurance companies, especially stock insurers, the prospect of continued civil disorder was especially disturbing. In the aftermath of the 1967 riots over $75 million of claims had been filed.[g] Although the companies had the capacity to sustain another loss of such magnitude, the pertinent question was whether the inability to estimate probabilities of further disorders would lead companies to prudently withdraw all coverage from the inner city as a means of minimizing future losses. Such a course of action would operate to place the burden of any losses squarely with the public, either directly on property owners or indirectly through some government-sponsored program.

Patterns of Response

There were three major facets of the inner-city insurance problem for the individual companies involved. First, there was an organizational aspect to the problem. The technical and managerial subsystems within the insurers had the information and factual basis to support a course of action that would lead to no further writing of insurance on inner-city property, and indeed, for canceling that which was already in force. In many firms this coalition was sufficient to sway the institutional subsystem into approving such a market withdrawal. For firms that had not withdrawn, the 1967 riots provided further evidence of the absence of a feasible market strategy other than abandonment.

The organizational dynamics resulted from the second, or economic, aspects of the problem. If risks were judged on an individual property basis, the premium charged an insured had to be commensurate with the probability of the risk of loss. Underwriters argued that the estimated probability of a loss depended, only in part, on the insured property itself. Another element in the equation had to be the nature of the nearby properties and the general neighborhood. As an area deteriorated, even an exceptionally well-preserved property in the area acquired a higher probability of loss. If one judged risks on a neighborhood or community standards basis, rather than an individual basis, whole districts were evaluated for insurability on the basis of aggregate characteristics. During the early 1960s various insurers used combinations of the individual property and community standards rating schemes to appraise the insurability of properties. Irrespective of the rating system, however, by the mid-1960s the inner-city areas of many metropolitan communities were unac-

[g]This was considerably less than the $715 million loss sustained by insurers from hurricane Betsy in 1965 but did amount to about 13 percent of the entire industry's 1966 underwriting profit.

ceptable risks. The economics of insuring the inner city had simply become too unattractive to insurers.

The third facet of the inner-city insurance dilemma for the firms was political in nature. Great concern was manifested in industry councils about the effect of a complete withdrawal of insurance coverage. Urban areas, and the inner city in particular, had become politically volatile topics at both the state and federal levels of government during the mid-1960s. Whatever the rationale presented by the technical and managerial subsystems of the insurers in favor of abandonment, that course of action was deemed certain to provoke serious public consequences. Whatever the arguments favoring a strategy of abandonment, the issue of private insurer legitimacy would surely be raised, should a major movement develop among the companies (especially the stock companies) to withdraw from the inner city.

The alternatives to withdrawal were limited in number, but some had received industry attention during the early part of the 1960s. In some cities, the industry had voluntarily established urban area plans that were designed to induce greater insuring of urban-core properties. The critical feature of these plans was that the insurers agreed that they would not refuse to insure a piece of property without first taking into account the inspection report prepared by a designated private or government agency. In this way, all properties in a red-lined district, for example, received an individual and independent evaluation of their insurability.

Another response that received considerable attention during the mid-1960s involved development of a pool of insurer resources that were used to underwrite risks otherwise unacceptable to individual insurers. Although the industry had historically not favored pooling arrangements for risks that could not be individually written, the arrangement received much publicity when such a program was established in California in 1965 to provide insurance to businessmen in the Watts area of Los Angeles. Although the Watts pool was voluntary in nature, insurers were leery of the legislative temptation to make such pooling compulsory.[23] Indeed, during the spring of 1967, several months before the riots, a number of cities and states had begun to implement various combinations of voluntary and involuntary pooling arrangements.

The tendency of state legislatures to think in terms of compelling insurers to accept virtually all properties was not viewed with enthusiasm by the industry. Nonlife companies had experience with pools in the automobile insurance area and had found them to be costly. Moreover, pools for providing insurance to the inner city were designed to cover normal fire and casualty losses. The catastrophic losses caused by the riots were a dimension of the inner-city problem for which existing pools provided no answer.

As indicated above, insurer losses from the 1967 riots amounted to about $75 million, an amount that the President's Advisory Panel concluded the industry was well able to sustain. Nevertheless, the climate of public opinion and the formalization of a presidential inquiry into the causes of civil disorder, as well as the establishment of a special presidential panel to examine the relevant insurance questions, provided a unique opportunity for the industry to cast its underwriting and profit problems directly into the public policy process for resolution. As the transcript of the hearings conducted by the Advisory Panel makes clear, the insurance industry sought to achieve through public policy what it could not do through the market—safeguard the primacy of the private insurance mechanism while receiving a guarantee that insurers would not be unduly injured by catastrophic losses arising as a result of the riots.

The basic device sought by the industry was a back-up arrangement whereby either the states and/or the federal government would guarantee that private insurers would not have to bear the full cost of a catastrophic loss. Given such an arrangement, the insurers then seemed prepared to discuss alternative means of guaranteeing a market for necessary fire and casualty coverages, including Urban Area Plans and voluntary, as well as involuntary, pooling arrangements. As Michigan's Commissioner of Insurance, David J. Dykhouse, pointed out, the basic policy issues flowed from the underlying assumptions being made by regulators and insurers alike. The assumptions were that, first, property insurance on a continuously available basis was a social necessity; second, that the basic coverage was basic fire and extended coverage; and third, that the private insurance industry should be the fundamental provider of this insurance. Based on these assumptions, the two critical issues were, first, who would determine what property was eligible for basic insurance coverage? Second, if eligibility were to remain solely an industry decision, should some form of financial subsidy be provided the industry by government?[24]

As to the first question, testimony from industry representatives indicated a preference for a system involving only the insurers or an insurer-dominated rating bureau. As to the second, it was either discreetly avoided or claimed that since riots were a sociological phenomenon, society as a whole ought to bear the consequences.[25]

The manner in which industry representative testified before the Panel on the compelling need for a governmental back-up arrangement suggested unanimity of thinking, if not a more explicit agreement. Others perceived a note of industry coercion on the matter. The Insurance Commissioner of California, Richard Roddis, commented that while the public sought only a resolution of the coverage problem, the insurers were engaged in a process of political brinksmanship. Roddis charged that the insurers knew 1968 was an election year, that the summer could be a powderkeg, and that if insurers began to withdraw from urban markets, the states would be forced into uneconomical compulsory pooling plans.[26] In this environment what the insurers were demanding was a back-up, a system of governmental guarantees that would ensure that the insurers would not suffer unduly if they helped insure the inner city.

Commissioner Dykhouse also took note of the political aspects of the insurer's call for government participation. In his testimony Dykhouse specifically noted that the stock insurers had been most strongly pressing for a federally subsidized reinsurance plan for riot and crime connected losses. As Dykhouse saw it, such a plan, in the absence of increased exposure in the urban areas, could actually result in a better financial and underwriting result for the companies.[27] Moreover, according to Dykhouse, however useful such reinsurance proposals might be for the insurers, such a plan would not solve the basic problem of actually providing insurance to the inner city. Reinsurance is the sale of a part of a given risk to another company. According to the Commissioner, there was no reason to believe that just because the insurers could purchase reinsurance from the government they would deliberately go into the inner city and write additional amounts of coverage. The primary insurers would still have to assume some portion of the risk associated with the inner-city property and reinsurance would not change that.

The stock insurance companies, including the Aetna, were united by organizational, economic, and political interests. They were the foremost suppliers of fire insurance coverage to the inner city, they had suffered the largest losses, and they had a large stake in whatever plans resulted. Because of these common interests, stock insurers had long been active in supporting the existence and efforts of the American Insurance Association (AIA), a stock insurer trade association. During the 1967 hearings, the AIA was the primary stock insurer spokesman.

The Aetna was a major supporter of the AIA and the position taken by the AIA was, for nearly all purposes, the position of the Aetna. The company had ranked fourth in the industry in the provision of fire insurance in 1960, with a 3.7 percent market share. By 1965 the Aetna had moved to first in ranking, with a 5.8 percent market share. The profitability of the business had so diminished thereafter, however, that by 1970 Aetna's market share diminished to 2.9 percent, ranking it tenth in the industry. More importantly, the company had shifted its underwriting emphasis toward more profitable pieces of business, net premiums written being $30 million less in 1970 than they were in 1965.[28]

The program developed by the stock companies and presented by the AIA at the hearings consisted of five main points:

1. That a government reinsurance program was an essential ingredient of any plan and that this reinsurance might initially be funded by the federal government, thereafter by the states.
2. That an urban areas inspection plan would include mercantile and residential properties.
3. That a pool, if required at all, be voluntary in nature and administered on a national basis.
4. That such a pool reinsure fire and extended coverage risks not written under

the urban areas inspection plan, and, in addition, that burglary risks also be eligible for pooling.

5. That all riot and civil disorder losses, wherever located, would be reinsured by the government above a certain percentage of earned premiums.[29]

The various points of the program were expanded upon, in greater detail, by representatives of AIA member companies. William O. Bailey, vice president of Aetna Life and Casualty and in charge of the property and casualty underwriting department, emphasized the mechanics of a federal back-up system in his presentation.[h] Bailey's testimony related the company's prior participation in urban area plans, in the Watts pool, and the Aetna's preparedness to support the extension of the urban area plan concept to other geographic areas and to commercial properties as soon as necessary catastrophic protection against the riot peril was provided.[30] It also touched on the other industry goals of a voluntary pool arrangement, the primacy of individual insurer judgment about insurability, and the need for a bureau-operated inspection service. Bailey concluded by noting that while the Aetna did not favor pooling as a means of spreading coverage among insurance companies in general, they would support the concept of a voluntary pool to provide fire and extended coverage protection for those insurable properties that could not find an individual insurer because of acute environmental factors that could not be removed or that were beyond the control of the insured. Such a pool should operate solely as a reinsurance facility for the subscribing companies and be available only after the urban areas inspection procedures were applied.[31]

In short, convincing federal and state governmental authorities of the need for a governmental supported back-up system was an intensely political act. Aetna management, recognizing this and also its identity of interest with other stock insurers, pursued a common strategy of political action through the AIA.

In January 1968 the President's National Advisory Panel on Insurance in Riot-Affected Areas submitted its report and called for the establishment of a voluntary participation plan whereby insurers would assure every property owner an individual inspection of the property, written notice of improvement necessary to make it insurable, and guaranteed insurance if the property were maintained according to reasonable insurance standards. These were the so-called FAIR Plans, an acronym for "fair access to insurance requirements." The FAIR Plans were to be supplemented by state pools that would guarantee insurance to qualified property even when the property was subject to an environmental hazard. Lastly, the Panel recommended creation of a National Insurance Development Corporation to provide reinsurance to member companies who participated in the FAIR Plans.

[h]Seymour E. Smith, senior vice president of the Travelers Insurance Companies, emphasized the need for a federal back-up system; he was followed by Bailey; H. Clay Johnson, president of the Royal-Globe Insurance Companies, described the role of pools in the program; Louis W. Niggerman, president of Fireman's Fund American Insurance Companies, concentrated on the importance and implications of insurer solvency.

Within the year, Congress enacted legislation to implement the Panel's recommendations. The federal government agreed to serve as the back-up or reinsurer for the state insurance pools in which insurers could voluntarily participate. In brief, federal participation constituted the "carrot" of riot reinsurance protection; in return for it, participating insurers promised to meet the inner city's insurance needs either directly, or, most likely, through the state pools. State legislatures had to implement the FAIR Plan legislation by creating the pools, either directly or through their state insurance commission. By mid-1969 twenty-seven states had done so; these states represented 75 percent of the property insurance premiums collected in the United States.[32] Yet at the same time, riot-occasioned losses in the first half of 1969 had declined to $15 million, a decrease that some feared might reduce the attractiveness of the federal reinsurance coverage and lead insurers to withdraw from FAIR Plan participation.[33] Since then, the FAIR Plans have continued to function but have regularly faced the twin problems of insurer "dumping" (i.e., placing most inner-city risks in the pools) and the threatened withdrawal of companies from the underwriting pools.

Summary: Conventional Modes of Response

The American insurance industry and, more specifically, the Aetna Life and Casualty Company have successfully responded to a variety of new risk situations throughout their history. In Chapter 3 we described how the industry developed as insurers reacted to continuously changing conditions of opportunity and risk. In the first part of this chapter the Aetna's own evolution was described in terms of organizational needs in light of perceived opportunities and risks.

Because organizations are learning mechanisms, successful responses to either opportunity or risk are likely to be used again in similar situations. That, indeed, is the nature of the conventional response, whether it involves organizational reaction to change (adaptation) or organizational efforts to create change (manipulation).

The two cases described in this chapter represent conventional kinds of risk situations for insurance companies. Both matters were at the core of the business, one involving possible forfeiture of a major position in the life insurance business, the other threatening to lock the company into a fire insurance market that offered no prospect of achieving breakeven economics. Inaction in either case involved risks that were unacceptable to Aetna's management. Thus the chosen course of action in each instance was one offering the best prospect for achievement of what Perrow called the operative goals of the enterprise. The fact that conventional patterns of response were followed in these cases ought not to be surprising; the problems bore some resemblance to problems of the past. But as will be seen in Chapter 9, not all current issues bear such a resemblance. In such cases, old responses may fail or may not be used at all. Under such conditions there may develop significant new kinds of organizational response to social change.

Notes

1. Data derived from Aetna annual reports and *Fortune* [52].

2. The material for this section was drawn from Hooker [72], Aetna annual reports, and other materials on file at the Aetna home office library.

3. A discussion of this type of manipulative behavior is found in Kimball's analysis of the Wisconsin records [84].

4. All figures are from Hooker [72] p. 100.

5. The structural changes that occurred at the Aetna during the 1960s signified its passage from what Bruce Scott [143] has called a Stage II organization to a Stage III form of enterprise. According to Scott, a Stage I organization is characterized by a single product or line of products, little or no formal management structure, and relatively small size. The Stage II enterprise typically has a single product line, but its management is characterized by functional specialization (i.e., finance, marketing, production) and its structure is designed to effectively manage a business that is larger in scale than that of the Stage I entity. A Stage III firm differs greatly from the Stage II entity; this results from the fact that the Stage III enterprise has multiple product lines, which are frequently operated as separate businesses. Management in such an organization is also different from that encountered in the Stage II firm: specialization is based on product market relationships, with functional management being a subsidiary form of activity. The multidivisional structure is the characteristic Stage III form, with divisions based on product lines and functional managers reporting to divisional officers. See Scott [143] and Fouraker and Stopford [53].

6. Chandler's [25] discussion of DuPont's transition to a multidivisional organization in the 1920s provides a rich example of the implications of centralized decision-making authority and information networks in an organization whose competitive environment has undergone significant change.

7. Institute of Life Insurance [76] p. 24.

8. Institute of Life Insurance [76] p. 120.

9. Institute of Life Insurance [76] p. 26. In 1970 participating life insurance accounted for 61 percent of all life insurance in force with U.S. life companies. Thirty-nine percent was of the nonparticipating type, which generally has lower premium rates.

10. Olson and Winklevoss [119]; Goldsmith [60].

11. Institute of Life Insurance [76] p. 55.

12. Institute of Life Insurance [76] p. 55.

13. Letter to Shareholders, *1966 Annual Report*, Aetna Life and Casualty.

14. *Securities and Exchange Commission v. Variable Annuity Life Insurance Company of America* [79 S. Ct. 618 (1959)].

15. As mentioned earlier, by the mid-1960s a number of insurance companies had reorganized as holding companies in order that they might thereby control subsidiaries that could sell equity products, especially mutual funds.

16. PALIC had been managed by a triumvirate composed of Marsh, Charles Baughman, an actuary, and Arthur Blakeslee, III, a lawyer with extensive SEC experience.

17. For a basic discussion of the principles underlying variable life insurance see Olson and Winklevoss [119].

18. President's National Advisory Panel on Insurance in Riot-Affected Areas [133] p. 2.

19. All data are from President's National Advisory Panel on Insurance in Riot-Affected Areas [133] pp. 115-160, 203.

20. See National Advisory Commission on Civil Disorders [111].

21. President's National Advisory Panel on Insurance in Riot-Affected Areas [133] pp. 5-6.

22. Seymour E. Smith, an executive vice president of the Travelers Insurance Companies, characterized the matter in this manner during the Advisory Panel's 1967 hearings: "We are basically sales oriented. We want to write every risk we can on which we think we can make a profit. We are geared to viewing those risks, to the hazards inherent within the risk itself. It is the external environmental hazard that we are not able to cope with nor to control, and the only one that seriously concerns us is this riot potential." President's National Advisory Panel on Insurance in Riot-Affected Areas [132] p. 223.

23. A full discussion of these alternatives is presented in Chapter 3 of the Panel's final report [133] pp. 55-85.

24. President's National Advisory Panel on Insurance in Riot-Affected Areas [132] p. 67.

25. The testimony [132] p. 222 of the executive vice president of the Travelers Insurance Companies is illustrative. "I find it irresistable, sir, if I may, . . . to respond to the question that you asked the previous witness as to the differentiation between catastrophes from natural rather than those resulting from social change.

"While the precise timing and location of hurricanes and other acts of God or aberrations of nature are not precisely predictable, there is a body of knowledge that is available. We have access to meteorological studies, predictable patterns. In addition, there is a large premium base to support these aberrations.

"We do not have as an industry any depth of technical knowledge as to sociology.

"Furthermore, I doubt if there is any individual in this room that really knows or has a strong ability to completely predict what is going to happen in the nature of social change. It is the completely unknown that is staggering our industry.

"The magnitude of what has happened in the past is not what we are talking about. It is what conceivably could happen, and as long as this cloud hangs over us, of completely unknown dimensions, in which we have no expertise, we have no background of knowledge, no reasonable degrees of protection or predictability, that we find ourselves in this position."

26. Richard Roddis' testimony [132] p. 59.
27. David Dykhouse's testimony [132] p. 72.
28. Data derived from Best [14].
29. Statement of T. Lawrence Jones, President of AIA [132] pp. 185-194.
30. William O. Bailey's testimony [132] p. 226.
31. William O. Bailey's testimony [132] p. 227.
32. See Best [14] 1970 and Bernstein [12].
33. See Bernstein [12].

9 The Aetna and Social Change

Conventional Patterns of Response

The Aetna's responses to the problems of a changing market for life insurance and an increasingly undesirable urban market for fire and crime insurance are not merely interesting vignettes about insurance problems in the past decade. They are symbolic of the everchanging relationship between private insurers and the American public and illustrative of the conventional ways of responding to change (Table 9-1).

As we have argued before, critical analysis of an organization's actions always involves, either explicitly or implicitly, certain assumptions about the relationship between the organization and the society in which it operates. One can speculate about the interpretations others might give to the cases described in the preceding chapter, but it is still more important that we clarify our own. Throughout this study it has been emphasized that the relationship between any firm or industry and society is one involving social systems, each influencing and being influenced by the other. Hence the appropriate first step in analyzing a particular issue or organizational response is to assess the dimensions of the interpenetration between the firm and society. In the case of the changing market for life insurance, the complexity of the relationship was described in terms of the scope of life insurance ownership, the effect of inflation on insurance investment, and the attractiveness of substitute investment forms. In the case of the inner-city insurance needs, the crucial dimensions involved the necessitous character of fire insurance, the high loss ratios involved in carrying insurance on urban-core area properties, and the crucial need for a mutually satisfactory resolution of the dilemma.

Once the dimensions of interpenetration are understood, it is legitimate to focus on the issue of the pattern of organizational response that emerges as aspects of the interpenetration change. It is at this juncture that the adaptive and manipulative models prove useful, emphasizing as they do the organization's (or industry's) reaction to change after it has occurred in the environment or its attempt to promote and encourage that form of environmental change that serves the industry's purposes.

The Aetna's efforts to preserve the market for insurance products is an almost classic example of an adaptive response to change. Beginning with a significant market change in the form of an increasing public demand for inflation-resistant investments, the Aetna's response involved a pattern of

Table 9-1
Patterns of Response to Change

Variable Life Insurance: An Adaptive Response

a. Market change
b. Industry's institutional response
c. Aetna's response
   1. Technical subsystem: development of variable life insurance
   2. Managerial subsystem: acquisition of PALIC
   3. Institutional subsystem: holding-company structure
d. Societal response: public policy in the form of federal securities (SEC) and state insurance regulations (commission) to be met

Insuring the Inner City: A Manipulative Response

a. Preexisting market conditions
b. Industry losses and market responses
c. 1967 riots and public hearings
d. Industry response:
   1. Technical: environmental hazards limit insurability
   2. Managerial: inner-city areas are large loss elements in industry profit picture; and riots create an unpredictable catastrophic loss element
   3. Institutional: industry will cooperate in a public sector/private sector venture to insure the inner city.
e. Societal response:
   public policy in the form of FAIR Plan legislation and programs.

product innovation designed to permit it to maintain its market prominence. Internally, the technical subsystem was charged with developing annuity products and, in time, with creating a variable life insurance policy. The managerial subsystem, concerned about premium flows and overall profitability of operation, recognized the limited success of the variable annuity product and actively pursued the acquisition of PALIC. The institutional subsystem initially responded to changing social conditions by cooperating in the industry's antiinflation public relations campaign. When that failed, it became primarily engaged in lobbying at the state level for legislative approval of the holding-company structure; still later, it was involved in lobbying with the SEC and the states for their respective approval of the Aetna variable life insurance product.

In one respect the Aetna's attempt to write variable life insurance was a straight-forward reaction to a changing market. Yet the example is complicated by the fact that at a previous point in time society had acted to regulate those individuals and organizations who would engage in the sale of securities and investments. The public policy expressed in the Securities Acts, and implemented through the activities of the Securities and Exchange Commission, made the Aetna's attempt to adapt to change more complicated. In an unregulated industry a firm might acquire another organization and market a new product in a relatively unfettered manner. But in an industry where society has, through public policy, expressed its desire to rely on prior approval of such activities, the actions of the competitive firm are constrained. At the least, Aetna's experience with variable life insurance shows that adaptation to change takes longer to effect in a regulatory climate because of the need to comply with more precisely articulated standards of socially permissible organizational behavior.

The insurance industry's actions in coping with the inner-city insurance dilemma form a sharply contrasting pattern of response. In 1968 the industry's arguments prevailed and Congress enacted a federal reinsurance program for riot-occasioned losses. That legislation stands as a monument to the concentrated efforts of the industry, and the stock companies in particular, to remove the obstinate insurance problems of the inner-city market to the public policy process for disposition. That transfer was accomplished at a time when the industry's bargaining leverage was considerable. The riots had provided an occasion for the stock insurers, through the AIA, to press federal and state governments for relief from a market problem that the companies alone had been unable to resolve in their operating environment. Raising rates and/or reducing available coverage were traditional market responses; both were limited alternatives for insurers because of public pressures. A government sponsored reinsurance plan surfaced as an alternative that would preserve both insurer profitability and insurer legitimacy by providing subsidized coverage to the inner city at affordable rates. Not surprisingly, the new plan was described as a fine example of private sector-public cooperation in the public interest.

In retrospect, the 1967 riots appear to have not been the social change that prompted the insurers to respond, so much as the occasion that allowed the stock companies to promote a restructuring of the competitive environment in their own best interest. In this regard, the action of the stock insurers in support of a federal reinsurance plan was more manipulative than adaptive in character.

During the Panel's hearings, California Insurance Commissioner Roddis had observed that the business responsibilities of the insurance underwriter and the cry of the ghetto for succor and social justice could not be readily reconciled.[1] The insurance needs of the inner city, however, were *in fact* a matter that the industry—and the stock insurers especially—could not ignore. The interpenetration between the insurance industry and society made the provision of fire insurance a matter of high salience to insurers and to the inner city alike. The problem was the inability of one process of interaction, the market, to resolve the problem to the satisfaction of both the industry and the relevant publics. By removing the issue to an alternative process of management-society interaction—namely, the public policy process—the industry attempted to both resolve the issue and stabilize its operating environment.

In summary, the two cases involving variable life insurance and the provisions of fire insurance to the inner city serve to highlight the critical elements in each of the conventional models of organizational behavior and also emphasize the multiple processes through which a firm and society continue to interact. In the case of variable life insurance the Aetna was attempting to adapt to changes in the competitive (market process) environment. The firm's ability to adapt, however, was constrained by the political (public policy process) environment. It was the prior decision of the American public to regulate securities investment through the Securities Exchange Commission that constrained the Aetna's efforts to innovate in the development of an inflation-resistant insurance product by joining a securities component with an insurance policy. Ultimately, it is the resulting pattern of dual regulation (SEC and the insurance commissions) that has limited the product's market success.

In the case of providing insurance to the inner city, the relationship between the market process and public policy process differed. There it was the coalition of insurers who sought to manipulate the prevailing political environment in such a way as to create congressional acceptance of the concept of a federal reinsurance mechanism. This manipulative action in the public policy process, which was not in any way an illegal course of conduct, was an attempt to restructure the competitive (market process) environment in which the insurers would sell fire and crime insurance.

New Patterns of Response

The adaptive and manipulative models highlight the critical elements of two extreme forms of organizational behavior. They do not, however, exhaust the range of possible patterns of response. Certainly, a single firm may exhibit elements of both kinds of behavior in dealing with a single issue over time. It may also attempt to anticipate and act in advance of external change, while not attempting to inhibit or modify that change through its action. Or, it may even attempt to promote small, incremental changes in the environment (e.g., create a coalition of organizations) in anticipation of a significant and important external change. These possibilities, plus many others, suggest that while the adaptive and manipulative models are useful abstractions, their capacity to explain all organizational responses to social change has some limits.

As the reader will note, the considerations that led the Aetna to respond to changing markets for life insurance by developing the variable life insurance policy and to cooperate in an industry attempt to influence the creation of a government-sponsored plan to meet the insurance needs of the inner city each produced limited, incremental solutions to critical industry problems. Both kinds of action reflect traditional patterns of response to change, yet neither course of action produced a response that effectively stabilized the environment for more than a brief period. This suggests that either the analysis of the problems, the choice of a strategy of response, or the implementation of that strategy failed. At the Aetna the consideration of these questions produced a notable alternative pattern of action on the matter of no-fault auto insurance.

Transforming a Market: No-Fault Automobile Insurance

Automobile insurance has been an important line of business for the Aetna since the 1920s. The company is a major competitor in the auto insurance business, as reflected by its market rank in the various bodily injury and physical damage liability lines. (See Table 9-2.) Its principal competitors during the 1950s and early 1960s were the direct writers, such as Allstate and State Farm, who had steadily increased their market shares and, more importantly, set competitive trends in pricing and marketing. In this context, the sale of automobile insurance coverages, like the sale of life insurance and fire insurance, was a basic and important aspect of the Aetna's relation with society.

The sale of auto insurance is an activity with important secondary consequences for the insurance industry in the aggregate, and for individual casualty insurers. At the aggregate level, automobile liability insurance had become as much a public necessity as the automobile itself by the early 1960s. With increasing automobile usage, however, accidents also increased and, in turn, injuries to persons and property. The need for security from the effects of liability to others for injuries caused by automobile use and the presumption that a prudent person would be insured against such liability contributed to a deepening interpenetration between the industry and the public. In fact, this interpenetration meant that insurers were pressured to correct problems in the system but only in ways that would not impair the availability of liability insurance.

For the individual casualty insurer, the problems associated with the prevailing automobile reparations system directly affected the activities and interests of the technical, managerial, and institutional subsystems. Since the issue impacted on all three, rather than funneling through the institutional subsystem alone, an important question arose about the relative influence of each of the subsystems in shaping the organization's response. In the variable life insurance case discussed in Chapter 8, the managerial and technical subsystems formed a coalition that the institutional subsystem supported; in the case of inner-city insurance coverage, the institutional subsystem vetoed the action proposed by the technical and managerial subsystems and moved the issue to the public policy process for disposition. In the case of the Aetna's response to the no-fault issue, still a third pattern of interaction emerged.

Dimensions of Interpenetration

The extent to which the automobile has become a vital part of American society tends to obscure the fact that its entire history is less than 100 years in duration. In less than that time, automobile insurance has passed from a tentative new

Table 9-2
Aetna Life and Casualty, Net Premiums, Selected Automobile Lines
(000's Omitted)

	1960	*1966*	*1970*	*1974*
Automobile Bodily Injury Liability				
Net premium written				
(a) Aetna	97,540	161,246	230,515	371,539
(b) Industry	2,563,913	2,286,223	5,494,148	8,513,997
(c) Aetna as % of industry	3.8%	7.0%	4.2%	4.4%
Net premium earned				
(a) Aetna	93,477	154,293	228,246	370,849
(b) Industry	2,461,878	2,194,065	5,326,450	8,450,651
(c) Aetna as % of industry	3.8%	7.0%	4.3%	4.4%
Profits				
(a) Aetna	−9,079	−13,617	−21,516	26,765
(b) Industry	−141,239	−195,252	−151,047	−46,227
Aetna rank	#3	#4	#4	#3
Miscellaneous Bodily Injury Liability				
Net premium written				
(a) Aetna	43,729	43,497	81,882	163,849
(b) Industry	701,877	878,855	1,322,967	2,701,318
(c) Aetna as % of industry	6.2%	4.9%	6.1%	6.1%
Net premium earned				
(a) Aetna	41,839	41,418	78,212	164,588
(b) Industry	663,304	880,461	1,244,142	2,644,513
(c) Aetna as % of industry	6.3%	4.7%	6.3 6.3%	6.1%

Profits				
(a) Aetna	−1,145	5,567	−24,510	−18,292
(b) Industry	21,243	59,373	−71,749	−442,666
Aetna rank	#1	#2	#1	#2
Automobile Physical Damage Liability				
Net premium written				
(a) Aetna	40,418	64,349	100,646	205,182
(b) Industry	1,117,796	1,553,131	2,371,865	5,341,603
(c) Aetna as % of industry	3.6%	4.1%	4.2%	3.9%
Net premium earned				
(a) Aetna	39,505	60,987	98,730	201,453
(b) Industry	1,084,296	1,481,173	2,282,055	5,213,389
(c) Aetna as % of industry	3.6%	4.1%	4.3%	3.9%
Profits				
(a) Aetna	950	−7,312	−14,354	−10,451
(b) Industry	23,812	−106,609	−271,408	220,687
Aetna rank	#4	#4	#3	#3
Automobile Collision				
Net premium written				
(a) Aetna	30,794	58,277	97,706	205,182
(b) Industry	1,284,980	1,848,533	2,805,147	3,500,530
(c) Aetna as % of industry	2.3%	3.0%	3.5%	5.9%
Net premium earned				
(a) Aetna	30,760	58,277	97,706	201,453
(b) Industry	1,255,800	1,739,804	2,700,817	3,401,545
(c) Aetna as % of industry	2.4%	3.0%	3.5%	5.9%

Table 9-2 (cont.)

	1960	*1966*	*1970*	*1974*
Profits				
(a) Aetna	2,451	−3,620	−4,063	−10,451
(b) Industry	118,842	−40,469	−179,883	57,864
Aetna rank	#8	#5	#4	#3
Auto, Fire, Theft, Comprehensive				
Net premium written				
(a) Aetna	17,006	31,395	44,447	–[a]
(b) Industry	670,216	1,011,746	1,391,715	–
(c) Aetna as % of industry	2.5%	3.1%	3.2%	–
Net premium earned				
(a) Aetna	16,706	29,423	43,760	–
(b) Industry	640,358	959,129	1,329,661	–[a]
(c) Aetna as % of industry	2.6%	3.0%	3.3%	–[a]
Profits				
(a) Aetna	1,605	1,245	−3,443	–
(b) Industry	44,094	64,042	−25,236	–
Aetna rank	#6	#5	#3	–

[a]Comparable information not available.

Source: Compiled from data in *Best's Aggregates and Averages*, 1960, 1966, 1970, 1974.

kind of coverage to a major line of business for many nonlife insurers; at the same time, it has been transformed from a regulated market matter to a major social problem. No issue in any line of the insurance business appears to have so deeply involved the interests of such a broad segment of the public and the industry as reform of the automobile insurance system did in the late 1960s and early 1970s.

Early automobile insurance policies provided coverage against the threat of fire, collision, and other physical hazards. Such policies provided that the policyholder (first party) was to be reimbursed in event of loss. But since third parties were also injured by the operation of automobiles, there was an obvious need for liability protection as well. Under tort law, an automobile owner could be held liable for injuries to third parties and/or their property if he were at fault—that is, if his conduct fell below that of a reasonable man in the same or similar circumstances. This fault system depended, however, on the ability of the liable owner to actually pay the injured third party. The courts could enforce the judgment only to the extent the liable party had economic resources that could be used to satisfy the judgment.

As early as the 1920s the enormity of the automobile's impact in terms of death, injury, and property loss served to focus policy debate on the need for a system that would encourage the purchase of liability insurance. The outcome of this debate was the emergence of *financial responsibility laws.* These laws, with the exception of the 1927 Massachusetts act that made automobile liability insurance compulsory, sought to encourage the public to voluntarily purchase such insurance. The situation worsened through the 1930s, however, and interest in compulsory laws grew throughout the 1940s and 1950s and led to a gradual strengthening of existing laws. By 1971 every state had a financial responsibility law, ranging from outright compulsion to security deposit laws that required the equivalent of a bond in lieu of a liability insurance policy.[2] The consequence of this movement was, as expected, that increasing numbers of liability insurance policies were being sold and that a public need was growing for some guaranteed access to liability insurance coverage. As indicated in Chapter 7, availability of insurance coverage was a problem in a number of insurance lines, including automobile liability insurance. The financial responsibility laws reflected a public consensus that all drivers have liability coverage but did not answer the question of who would insure the worst risks in the driving population. Standard underwriting practices favored insuring those drivers with the fewest accidents and best claims experience. In other lines of insurance, especially, high risks can be covered if the insured agrees to limit certain activities, correct special problems, or share in some part of any loss (*coinsurance*). Since those were options that were generally not viable in the auto insurance area, however, a coverage and cost dilemma arose. As long as insurers could not require high-risk drivers to pay an appropriately high premium sufficient to meet underwriting requirements, the challenge was to cover such risks at acceptable cost levels. The attempts to meet these dual objectives ranged from sophisticated merit rating plans to assigned risk pool arrangements.[3] Still, the problems worsened.

As the problems of the price and availability of automobile insurance mounted, pressure for reform intensified. Beginning in the mid-1950s and continuing throughout the 1960s and early 1970s, a variety of technical underwriting solutions were developed including merit rating plans, safe driver training programs, assigned risk pools, and a surcharge or penalty system for especially hazardous risks.

Each technical solution seemed to generate its own new set of pressures as segments of the driving public bore the impact of such changes. Although criticisms were numerous, it is likely that such technical tinkering with underwriting practices would have continued to characterize the industry's response but for the fact that large losses were being shown by insurers on their automobile business. Loss ratios rose through much of the 1960s, and pressures arose within the managerial subsystems of the firms for corrective action.[4] An obvious managerial solution was to raise premium rates, and that was a course that was followed throughout the 1960s. Since rate increases were tempered by the need for prior regulatory approval in many states, a scenario developed whereby insurers announced proposed rate increases, relevant publics objected, the state insurance departments investigated, and a compromise rate increase was approved. If the knee-jerk response of the technical subsystem was more restrictive underwriting arrangements, the knee-jerk response of the managerial subsystem was to increase auto insurance premiums.

Patterns of Response: Social Reform

Reliance on fault as a basis for distinguishing between those who will and will not collect the proceeds of an insurance policy is something of an anomaly in twentieth-century insurance practice. Normally, one can claim the proceeds of a policy when a stated event occurs. Life insurance, fire insurance, accident insurance, and many other forms of coverage operate on some version of this principle. Automobile liability insurance, however, has traditionally relied on a third-party system, under which the insurer asks a potential claimant: "Were you at fault?" If so, recovery is barred.

In theory, the tort liability system serves the purposes of resolving social disputes in favor of the innocent party, enabling all to comprehend and anticipate the consequences of their actions, while also educating the public to the behavior that is publicy acceptable and unacceptable.[5] Given a public sentiment that supports the view that the innocent victim of another's negligence ought to recover damages for injuries incurred, the tort system does fulfill the three social functions just mentioned. When the public sentiment supporting the system wanes or when the system fails to fulfill the social functions mentioned above, however, a breakdown of the system occurs. As applied to automobile insurance reparations, both public sentiment and the system's ability to fulfill its social functions diminished by the 1960s. The result was a public atmosphere in which proposals for radical modification of the system could receive a serious hearing.

Attempts to modify the tort liability system as it applied to automobile reparations had been made from time to time since the 1930s. A pioneering proposal with regard to a no-fault system of automobile compensation was the Columbia University Committee Plan, developed in 1932.[6] The proposal figured prominently in a no-fault plan adopted by the Canadian province of Saskatchewan in 1946. In the 1950s the issue received some renewed interest in the United States, though no major legislative activity occurred before the mid-1960s.

The catalyst for major public debate of a no-fault insurance plan in the 1960s was the Keeton-O'Connell proposal for a "Basic Protection Plan," originally presented in 1965.[7] The proposal suggested major changes in the law affecting victims of automobile accidents and attracted great attention throughout the latter half of the decade.

There were two main features to the proposal: (1) development of a new form of automobile insurance, called *Basic Protection insurance*; and (2) a change in the law that would eliminate claims based on negligence, within specified limitations. Basic Protection insurance was a combination of coverages already in existence and closely resembled medical payment insurance.[8] It envisioned a two-party claims system in which the insured or anyone else injured as a result of the ownership, maintenance, or use of the insured's vehicle would be compensated under the insured's policy. Two exceptions were those who were intentionally injured and those who were parties in other vehicles (who would be covered under the policies of the owners of those vehicles). To effect such a system, the plan would have to be compulsory, applying to all registered motor vehicles.[a]

The plan applied only to bodily injuries, property damage continuing to be adjusting on a fault basis. This provision reflected Keeton and O'Connell's view that the abuses of the negligence system were most serious in compensating the accident victim.[b] Most importantly, Basic Protection was intended to be an excess coverage—that is, there would be no payments made for losses reimbursed from other sources, such as health or medical payment insurance.

The Keeton-O'Connell plan sought to preserve one aspect of the fault

[a]A special problem involved out-of-state autos entering a no-fault state and autos covered under a no-fault system that traveled to states with fault systems.

[b]The existence and widespread use of collision insurance is, in effect, a two-party system for property damage to the automobile. The insured collects from his own insurance company irrespective of who caused the damage. If the third party was at fault, the insured's insurer may proceed against him on a liability basis, in which case the third party's liability insurance would come into play.

system with regard to personal injuries. A motorists' exemption from legal liability for negligence would be limited to $5000 and for other injuries to $10,000. Where injuries caused expenses in excess of $10,000 for economic loss and $5000 for pain and suffering, the Basic Protection plan would revert back to the negligence system.

The impact of the Keeton-O'Connell proposal was felt at two different levels. As an input into the public policy process, the plan was well publicized, in part because the authors were successful in publishing a large number of articles in the popular press, and in part because the proposal became a natural focal point in the discussion of all types of auto insurance reform. In a second and more technical context, the proposal served to stimulate the development of alternative proposals for major reform from both within and outside of the industry. By 1968 a number of alternative no-fault proposals had been offered by such companies as INA and such groups as the American Mutual Insurance Alliance (originators of the "Illinois Experiment in Guaranteed Benefits") and the American Insurance Association ("The Complete Personal Protection Automobile Insurance Plan"). Further proposals were made by various segments of the industry between 1968 and 1970.[9]

The public concern with the availability, price, and quality of automobile insurance had generally been diffused before Keeton-O'Connell. Their proposal served to focus diverse criticisms of the industry and weld discussions of the problems into a coherent attack on the system of fault reparations rather than peripheral attacks on availability, price, or quality matters. The greatest value of the proposal initiated by Keeton and O'Connell may have been the systematic reform of the automobile insurance business that would otherwise have been years away. Experiments of the no-fault variety began to be implemented in public policy programs. Puerto Rico became the first U.S. jurisdiction to adopt a compensation plan for automobile victims when it enacted a "Social Protection Plan for Victims of Automobile Accidents" in 1968, to be effective in 1970. Massachusetts enacted the first state no-fault insurance plan in 1970, and by 1971 similar proposals had been introduced in a number of state legislatures.

Patterns of Response: The Aetna

The Aetna's response to the development of no-fault proposals occurred in three stages. The first stage involved the company's direct response to the Keeton-O'Connell proposal and led to a decision to undertake an internal analysis of the effects of a no-fault system on a sample of its own previously settled automobile accident cases. The second stage involved the company's disclosure of the results of its study and its cooperation with a federally sponsored study of the prevailing automobile insurance system. A third stage followed when the Aetna, at its own initiative, became the first major automobile insurer to actively promote the passage and implementation of no-fault automobile insurance legislation.

Before the mid-1960s the Aetna had tended to support the type of technical responses favored by the industry as a means of correcting pricing and availability problems. The Keeton-O'Connell proposal and the discussion it generated prompted the company to reexamine its position, however, and the management of the Casualty and Surety Division undertook an analysis of the new reform proposals. An internal divisional study was conducted under the supervision of William O. Bailey, then head of the underwriting department within the Casualty and Surety Division. The format that Bailey adopted was designed to concentrate on evaluating the impact of the Keeton-O'Connell plan on a sample of cases drawn from the Division's automobile claims settlement files. Each was reexamined with a view toward answering the central question of what effect a no-fault system would have had on the settlement of the case. The conclusion reached by Bailey and his staff was that had a system like that proposed by Keeton and O'Connell been in effect, average claims payments would have decreased in amount and a substantial rate reduction could have been passed on to policyholders. According to one of the staff members who participated in the study and subsequent discussions, the analysis was convincing to even the most skeptical among the Casualty and Surety Division staff.

The staff report became a catalyst within the division for a rethinking of the company's position about automobile insurance reform. As indicated elsewhere, an insurance company's managerial subsystem is typically concerned with premium flows (sales), on the one hand, and settlement flows (claims), on the other. In the case of automobile insurance, the narrowing between premium inflows and claims outflows was a major management concern throughout the 1960s. Recognizing the practical difficulties involved in the continuing escalation of premium rates, the Aetna's no-fault study was of importance as technical support for a course of action supporting reform. The net effect was that by late 1967 considerable support existed within the company for publicly advocating the no-fault concept in what seemed certain to be a major public policy debate.

The second stage of the Aetna's response occurred when the company made public its position on no-fault by cooperating with the Department of Transportation's 1968 study of automobile insurance[10] and at the same time spurred the American Insurance Association's research into the merits of the Keeton-O'Connell plan. The result of the latter was that by October 1968 the AIA announced that it had developed its own no-fault proposal; it thereafter moved for legislative enactment of such a no-fault plan by state legislatures. The result was that long before the DOT study was concluded in 1970, the Aetna was on record as being in full support of the no-fault approach to automobile insurance reform.

The Aetna's public endorsement of a specific no-fault proposal presaged the development of a third stage wherein the company took positive action to promote no-fault legislation. In 1969 no-fault legislation was considered in 10 states. In each the Aetna actively supported, through press releases and lobbying, those proposals that substantively approximated the AIA plan. The company was one of only a few insurers to support the no-fault legislation enacted in Massachusetts in 1970, and the company's affirmative posture has continued since then, involving lobbying on behalf of genuine no-fault proposals and against counterfeit no-fault plans that would impose limitations or restrictions on a first-party indemnification system. A further step was taken in 1974 when the company announced its support for a federal no-fault legislative package that would establish a national no-fault automobile insurance system for those states that failed to enact no-fault legislation or for those whose legislation failed to meet minimum federal standards. This action further set apart the Aetna from the rest of the industry on the no-fault issue but was actually a continuation of the basic policy formulated in 1968.[c]

Policy formation involves two distinct dynamics, one of which is internal to the organization, the other external to it. The internal dynamic involves the interaction of the technical, managerial, and institutional subsystems and the manner in which the company's posture develops as part of the terms of trade among the organization's components. The external dynamic involves the relationship between the organization and the relevant public with whom its interacts overlap, interface, or even interfere. A perceptive management will recognize the relevant publics with which the organization does have issues in common and will attempt to calculate the impact of its own actions on those publics.

The formulation of a policy in support of no-fault reform primarily involved the Aetna's technical and managerial subsystems. Since the initiative for the no-fault study came from the managerial subsystem, support for a policy favoring no-fault reform depended on negating the objections of those relevant publics related to the managerial subsystem. In particular, account had to be taken of the impact of a no-fault system on the agents upon whom the company relied for its automobile business. Some fears existed among independent agents that a first-party indemnity system might enable the insurers to bypass the agents and deal directly with the public.[11] The Aetna sought to assuage such fears by publicizing its own intention to place greater reliance on the agents as client representatives in dealing with claims as well as sales matters.

As equally knotty concern within the managerial subsystem was the effect of an AIA-like no-fault plan on the Aetna's other lines of insurance. A special concern existed that a no-fault system for bodily injury indemnification would duplicate applicable health insurance coverages. That raised the question of

[c]Recognition of the necessity for eventually having to support federal legislation was manifested as early as March 1971, when William O. Bailey, senior vice president of the Casualty and Surety Division wrote to Olcott D. Smith, chairman, that the company would seek legislation at the state level wherever it offered a reasonable chance of success, even though federal action or federal sanctions might be necessary to bring about a rational reparations system for motor vehicle accident victims throughout the United States.

whether the public might not perceive a diminished need for medical insurance coverage that was sold as part of many automobile policies. (This is included under the Miscellaneous Bodily Injury Liability heading in Table 9-2.) After study, the company concluded that such a plan would allow coordination of benefits and would eliminate unnecessary duplication of coverage; as a whole, it would not result in any significant loss of revenue to other lines of business. The most significant impact would involve a substantial revenue loss for bodily injury liability insurance coverage. But since that had been an unprofitable line of business throughout most of the 1960s, a revenue loss was tolerable if a break-even or underwriting profit point could be achieved.

The coalition of technical and managerial interests supporting the no-fault policy within the company might not have prevailed had serious objections been raised by the institutional subsystem as it had with a similar coalition's suggestion to abandon the inner-city fire insurance market. In fact, however, such a policy was readily endorsed at the institutional level. The plan was responsive to public demands for reform and had the potential of stimulating development of a system that could both serve the public's needs and utilize the capacities of the private-carrier industry.

Whatever the intraorganizational dynamics involved in the formulation of new policy, the impact of action on relevant publics determines the ultimate effectiveness of a chosen management policy. Recognition of this fact can lead an astute management to anticipate or estimate the impact of various policy alternatives on the organization's relevant publics before finalizing a policy choice. This was the case when the Aetna's management considered the effect of the AIA no-fault plan on the independent agents who represented Aetna policyholders. Similar consideration was given to the impact on other relevant publics, such as the Aetna's competitors (stock companies, mutuals, and direct writers forming three distinct groups), industry trade associations, state insurance departments, and state and federal legislators. With respect to each, Aetna's management attempted to anticipate the reaction to the company's endorsement of a no-fault plan, a calculation that was made more difficult since no other insurers had made similar policy commitments.

Formulation of a policy position also generates a set of issues relating to the implementation of policy. For the Aetna the decision to support the AIA plan involved decisions about the extent to which the company would actively promote legislation and lobby on behalf of the plan. A more important consideration in practice was the point at which the Aetna would compromise in order to secure the passage of no-fault legislation. As experience was gained in the promotion of no-fault legislation during the 1969 and 1970 legislative sessions, it became apparent that opponents of no-fault legislation would seek to "defang" the legislation by forcing compromise on the threshold limit beyond which an injured party could resort to the tort liability system. In 1967, for example, the Massachusetts State Senate defeated a Keeton-O'Connell Basic

Insurance Protection Bill that would have established a $10,000 threshold and deducted all collateral source recovery. The Personal Injury Protection plan that was finally enacted in 1970 set a $2000 threshold for tort suits and deducted only wage continuation payments. Moreover, where the 1967 plan eliminated pain and suffering suits under $5000, the 1970 law permitted such suits where a medical loss exceeded $500. The position that the Aetna finally adopted was that any compromise that would result in a de facto retention of the tort system would be unacceptable. Thus only an extremely high threshold figure (one as high as the financial responsibility law itself imposed) would be an acceptable compromise. This position, and the passage of a number of "counterfeit" no-fault plans that actually retained the tort liability system, ultimately led the company to publicly support the establishment of federal no-fault standards.

Responding to Public Policy

The Aetna's approach to the issue of automobile insurance reform illustrates a number of important points about managerial responses to social change. First, response to change is itself a process involving continuous management perceptions of the environment, action taken in light of such change, and the evaluation of effects. The Aetna's own market losses in the auto insurance reform contributed to management awareness of the seriousness of the matter. The Keeton-O'Connell proposal may have been the high point in this stage for Aetna's management because it seemed to galvanize the casualty and surety division into making the internal study of a no-fault system's impact on loss settlements. That study was also the transition from a cognizance or awareness stage to an action stage. It was during this second stage that the Aetna's response to no-fault differed from the conventional responses it pursued in the case of variable life insurance and fire insurance protection for the inner city. In the case of no-fault the internal study served to seriously raise the question of the secondary involvement aspects of the matter within the division and to raise the possibility of new kinds of alternatives. This openness to an examination of the merits of no-fault proposals had the effect of allowing the public's reform demands to become internalized within the managerial subsystem of the casualty division. The results of the study then supported the proposal from the technical subsystem's perspective; lastly, the coalition of the managerial and technical subsystems secured institutional support for the chosen course of action: public support of no-fault legislation. At that point, the institutional subsystem prompted development of the AIA plan. Eventually, the company even broke away from the AIA per se and stood alone as a spokesman for federal no-fault standards. This transition to a positive, initiative-taking posture signified the movement into a third stage of response, a stage that was not reached in either the life insurance or inner city insurance instances.[12]

The no-fault auto insurance case also highlights the process by which certain by-products of the market process have important consequences on society and become important public concerns. The Aetna's response involved both an awareness of this involvement and several forms of action designed to positively interact with society to resolve the dilemma. To be sure, the company had a real interest in resolving what for it was an important market problem. It had incurred underwriting losses despite rate increases and selective underwriting while public pressure itself was mounting to limit both of these managerial and technical subsystem responses. But the important point is that the Aetna not only reacted to change but attempted to integrate prevailing public values into its own decision-making—it chose a course of action that would not simply react to, or manipulate, the environment but would positively interact with the developing public goals. It had, in effect, internalized the public values for reform.

Unlike the inner-city situation where the company supported a market course of action (withdrawal) until public pressure helped cast the entire matter into the public policy process, the Aetna's decision to actively support a public policy transformation of the rules of the game by which the auto insurance system would be administered was neither a reaction to environmental change nor an attempt to manipulate the situation and effect a change in the environment for its own purposes. In those states where no-fault auto legislation was enacted, liability rates for drivers were reduced as much as 15 to 20 percent in the first year. The 1974 data presented in Table 9-2 indicate the continuing problems facing the Aetna—and the industry—in the physical damage lines where no-fault had not been applied. Yet, indication that no-fault has been improving the settlement of bodily injury claims from auto accidents is clear, if not overwhelming.[13] These results have prompted the Aetna to continue its support and active encouragement of genuine state no-fault plans and federal no-fault standards.

Notes

1. Richard Roddis' testimony [132] p. 49.

2. See Rokes [140] pp. 26-27. Security deposit laws require that a motorist involved in an automobile accident and unable to establish evidence of liability insurance must deposit security sufficient to cover the amount of any claim or suit against him or lose his driving privileges and registration.

3. The courts also served to articulate the public policy aspects of financial responsibility legislation, especially a fundamental concern for accident victims. The California Supreme Court ruled, for example, that the financial responsibility law in that state had to be interpreted in a way that would foster the primary objective of giving monetary protection to the large, and ever-

changing, group of persons who suffer injury because of the negligence of others while using the highways. See *Interinsurance Exchange Automobile Club of Southern California v. Ohio Casualty Insurance Co.* [58 Cal. 2d 142, 373 P.2d 640]. This policy of protecting innocent victims was extended to prevent insurers from avoiding payment because of minor breaches of such policy conditions as notice of loss or a failure to cooperate. A New York appellate court ruled in 1969 that serious injury or prejudice to the insurer must be shown in order to allow the insurer to forfeit coverage. In the absence of such prejudice, forfeiture of coverage would be a public disservice because insurance is an instrument of social policy calling for victims of negligence to be compensated. *Allstate Insurance Co. v. Grillon* [251 A2d. 256]. The court's view echoes Cardozo who argued that the final purpose of law is the welfare of society and that a rule that misses its aim cannot permanently justify its existence [23], p. 66.

4. *Loss ratios* refer to the amount paid out in satisfaction of claims in comparison to premium dollars received. In 1970, for example, loss ratios in the automobile insurance industry reached 64.7 percent. National Underwriter [113] p. 16.

5. See Berman and Greiner [11] chapter 1.

6. For a discussion see Rokes [140] pp. 51-52. Rokes also suggests that the earliest proposals involved the application of a workmen's compensation approach and were presented as early as 1919 [140] p. 18.

7. See Keeton and O'Connell [81].

8. See Rokes [140] p. 55.

9. A discussion and point-by-point comparison of these and other proposals can be found in Rokes [140].

10. See Department of Transportation [42].

11. This concern persisted throughout the period of the 1971 hearings before the House of Representatives Subcommittee on Commerce and Finance. An important part of the testimony presented by the National Association of Mutual Insurance Agents, for example, related to the role of the independent agent in the marketing of automobile insurance. U.S. House of Representatives [161] pp. 271-273. The development of programs for the mass marketing of insurance coverages reinforced the agents' fears.

12. Preston and Post [136] chapter 4 have described this multistage process as being one of "organizational socialization."

13. A review can be found in *Barron's*, "No-Fault Insurance: The Evidence Is Mixed, but the Drive Is On," August 25, 1975, pp. 3ff.

Part IV
The Insurance State

10 Private Insurers and the Insurance State

New Dimensions of Interpenetration

The changes to which the Aetna and other private insurance carriers have been forced to respond since the mid-1960s have profoundly affected the industry and the behavior of individual companies. As discussed in Chapter 7, the social changes touching the industry have only, in part, been market related. Many nonmarket matters have also come to the foreground as public issues that neither the industry nor individual firms could ignore. The prominence of equal employment opportunity as a major public policy matter, for example, made it impossible for insurers to ignore the issue. Urban affairs, including dealing with conflicting community groups and being involved in efforts to rebuild core areas, also emerged as a significant area of public concern that demanded a corporate response. That these matters were not, or could not be, translated into direct market matters did not obviate the necessity of the insurers to cope with the problems.

The salience of nonmarket issues to companies such as the Aetna emphasizes the proposition advanced throughout this study that the involvement of an organization with society is not mediated through the market alone. There are other kinds of involvements and interactions and they are of direct importance to society, and perforce, the enterprise. The interpenetrating systems concept emphasizes this multidimensional interaction and the resultant consequences for the firm and society alike.

Equal employment and the impact of a company on a local community are but two examples of matters, not directly mediated by the market, that are nevertheless linked to other aspects of the firm's operations. A company, such as the Aetna, for example, engages in a set of core activities, including insurance sales and investment of premiums, that constitute its *primary involvement* with society. This set of core activities, as well as other allied activities, has a set of by-products and consequences that constitute the firm's *secondary involvement* with society.[1] A manufacturer's secondary involvements might include such by-products as the air and water pollution occasioned by manufacturing operations. For an insurance company the impact of its hiring practices on a community are a secondary involvement effect, as is the impact of supporting some civic groups but not others. Primary involvement activities, such as selling fire insurance, have secondary involvement consequences when, for example, that insurance is systematically withheld from certain market segments, as in the case of the inner city. Similarly, the failure of an insurer to invest any mortgage funds in inner-city properties has a consequence of contributing to further deterioration in those neighborhoods. The point is that it is not the market alone that determines the salience of an issue for the firm. Since the relationship between a firm and society is interpenetrating, and each can affect the other, the organization cannot ignore the impacts of its core of business activities, simply because they are not directly manifested in the market. Since these consequences—or secondary involvements—affect society (i.e., relevant publics) and are of concern to it, they are necessarily matters of importance to the organization as well.

The fact that matters such as equal employment and urban affairs became matters of great importance to insurers, no less in their significance than the problems of automobile insurance or fire insurance in inner-city markets, suggests that the scope of public issues (and hence, the scope of the interpenetration) about which the organization must act has transcended the marketplace. Moreover, the range of relevant social expectations with which the firm must be concerned is not only tied to the market but also to the evolving public policy agenda. Society, of course, cares about matters that do not relate to the insurance industry in any direct way as, for example, national defense. Arguably, such matters are outside the scope of primary and secondary involvements and, hence, do not require an insurer response. For matters that are within that scope of primary and secondary involvements, however, insurers must respond and can do so by looking to developing public policy trends. Such a pattern of response characterized Aetna's action with regard to no-fault automobile insurance, a pattern that differed significantly from the conventional adaptive and manipulative patterns. Similarly, the development of affirmative action programs to hire minorities and women before they were required by law is more responsive in nature than merely reacting to the legal change or manuevering to prevent change.

To many observors of corporate behavior, equal employment and urban affair matters are issues of social responsibility that implicitly suggest they are only to be seriously considered if they do not affect profits. But as this study has shown, such a notion is clearly absurd! Changing public expectations are a fundamental fact of life for the management of any organization in any industry. Rephrased, the point is that every organization that exists for any but the briefest period of time will be faced with the necessity of responding to a changing society. For the management of some organizations this reality is quite difficult to accept, and a tendency emerges toward action calculated to inhibit some changes and promote others, all in service of the entity's operative goals. For others, however, an awareness of the permanence of social change develops and a willingness to be responsive to everchanging societal expectations is translated into action.

It would be both grandiose and unwarranted to suggest that the insurance industry as a whole, or even significant numbers of insurers, had developed a responsive posture to all public expectations and at all times. Nevertheless, the concept of social responsibility and the permanence of social change seem to have become permanent parts of the management ideology in the insurance industry. Under the aegis of the Institute of Life Insurance, a leading trade association, the industry has established a Clearinghouse on Corporate Social Responsibility, which gathers, disseminates, and publicizes the socially responsive actions of member firms.[a] The Clearinghouse has also undertaken an annual survey of member firm responses in such areas as equal employment opportunity for minorities and women, charitable contributions, environmental impact, and investments.[2] The Institute of Life Insurance has also initiated a research program into the analysis of social trends and developments. This *trend analysis program*, as it is called, has resulted in recent reports to member firms on such diverse social trends as transportation, cultural transformation and societal ethics, information science technology, and technological advances in science and health.[3] More than academic background studies, these reports are designed to focus on potential public policy directions in each area and on the implications, direct and indirect, for insurers. This work is a recognition of the importance of change, on the one hand, and an effort to make possible more responsive actions by insurers, on the other. Not a panacea in themselves, such programs only suggest that the industry, through the mechanism of the trade association and its alliances with the institutional subsystems of member firms, has recognized the necessity for continuously positioning itself in such a way as to retain its societal legitimacy.

Three Transformations

The efforts of the American insurance industry to respond to the implications and issues arising out of its growing interpenetration with American society, and the ideological acceptance of change as a factor in that relationship, does not imply that the industry's viability and prosperity is itself insured. Indeed from the perspective of the present it appears that even more profound changes are affecting the industry than those that occurred between 1963 and 1973. What has been occurring for several decades, and what has become starkly apparent in the past few years, is that the relationship between the insurance industry and American society is undergoing another major transformation. It is a transformation in which the insurance ethic is becoming a fundamental part of societal ideology.

The American insurance industry has undergone two great transformations

[a]The principle vehicle for disseminating this information is a publication entitled, *Response*, a bimonthly newsletter sent to member firms and interested readers both within and outside the industry.

in its history, transformations that have resulted in a major restructuring and realignment of the industry and its relévant publics. One involved the transformation of the insurance business from a series of selective markets dominated by individual clients to one composed of mass markets wherein the clients are primarily groups of individuals. The other transformation has involved the emerging and burgeoning regulation of both insurance enterprise and the behavior of insurers. As the discussion in Chapters 5 and 6 indicated, the industry has long been affected with the public interest, a condition that has made it a subject for regulation. The last major shift in regulation probably occurred about 70 years ago when the Armstrong investigation produced substantial and widespread regulation of insurer behavior. Together these market and regulatory transformations have shaped the modern American insurance industry and provided the basic context for understanding the industry and its member's actions.

Since the 1960s there has been a basic change occurring in America with respect to the social treatment of risk. Before the twentieth century, insurance was treated as a private good, a service to be secured by individuals in the marketplace. In the twentieth century there has been a continuing trend toward providing risk protection to all citizens. Among the risks for which such guarantees have been attempted are unemployment, workmen's injury, old age, and poor health. For each, public insurance or government programs founded on insurance concepts have been provided as public goods.[4] Although the private carriers have participated in many of these programs, the existence of the plans has clearly been public in character and has significantly affected the private market for insurance protection. At the least, an expectation of positive government action to protect the public against intolerable risks has been cultivated.

Since the late 1960s public policy has repeatedly expanded the list of risks for which broad social protection is afforded. In less than a decade the list has come to include the risks of defective products; personal health; pollution of air, water, and work environment; personal liability; professional liability; nuclear hazards; earthquakes, floods, and hurricanes; and riots and crime. The agenda of risk areas for which public insurance proposals have been enacted or submitted has grown rapidly and, in some instances, private insurance carriers have been directly or indirectly forced to participate in programs that strained conventional underwriting and actuarial principles. Historian William Letwin has written that the result of this rapid expansion has been the emergence of an *insurance state*, a society in which public policy is increasingly used to safeguard a growing set of public interests.[5] It is a society in which the state increasingly seeks to protect its citizens against the hazards of societal existence by shifting risk from those few who might normally expect to be injured to the whole population. It is a transformation as profound as the market and regulatory transformations that preceded it.

Emergence of the Insurance State

Risk is an inherent part of modern life, and the desire to minimize or protect against risk has compelled men to devise a multitude of cooperative arrangements. Indeed the story of the effort to create devices for protecting against risk, or for minimizing its adverse consequences, is the organic underpinning of the history of the American insurance industry. It is an industry that has been continuously characterized by creative actions in response to the problems of risk.

Throughout much of American history, risk-avoidance and risk mitigation have been accomplished through the collective action of individuals pursuing personal interests. The American insurance industry, including stock and mutual companies, agency writers and direct writers, local insurers and national companies, has evolved as a succession of innovative organizational devices each designed to overcome its predecessors' shortcomings. Whenever existing insurers have failed to provide coverage for a new kind of risk, a new geographic area or a particular group of risk-bearers, new companies or devices have been created.

But the changing societal expectation of governmental action to meet new public needs has changed this heretofore predictable pattern of risk and response. The trend toward looking at governmental or public programs as alternatives to private insurance programs has accelerated sharply in the past two decades. It is a change that is not confined to the insurance industry but bespeaks a 20-year trend toward an expanding role for government.

The broadened role of government is not the central element of the insurance state. Rather, the role of government is merely a means to the attainment of an important public end that is perhaps best described as relief from the normal risks of living in this society.

The substance that underlies such a characterization is quite broad, but the critical points can be emphasized by reference to a few selected situations. An inspection of the agenda of leading public issues, including employment, inflation, health, safety, and education, discloses the frontiers of the insurance state. In each of these areas, the principle of insurance offers a major policy alternative. In employment, for example, the risk that one will lose a job and be left without work can be mitigated by unemployment insurance. Regular contributions from all who are working can create a fund from which those who are without work may draw financial remuneration. When they return to work, they too will contribute to the fund from which still others will draw. To the extent that only employees contribute to the fund, it operates as a mutual insurance plan. For many years, the labor unions and guilds have operated plans on such a mutual assistance basis.

When the restricted unemployment funds have more demands that can be sustained by contributions, a crisis arises. Each recipient could receive proportionately less; each contributor could contribute proportionately more; fewer total recipients could be paid; or more contributors could be solicited and induced to pay into the fund. While each of the alternatives has its limitations, the fourth—getting more contributors—offers the best prospects for satisfying existing claimants and building a base for the future. But such a course of action requires either special inducements to attract the new contributors or some means of compelling new parties to participate in the plan. Historically, of course, the telling argument has generally been that unemployment payments are publicly desirable and necessary, and hence, all workers should be compelled to contribute to the fund. Whatever the cogency of the argument, it has had the effect of making unemployment compensation a public good, not a private good.

The current public debate about whether people have a right to a job offers an extension of the unemployment compensation argument. Here the insurance principle is being pressed to an extreme where what is being advocated is protection against loss of a job, not the income from such a job. To insure that all will have actual jobs, an employer of last-resort mechanism must be created. Several possibilities exist. One is to make it illegal for employers to discharge employees for cyclical economic reasons. Also the government itself can become an employer of last resort. Or government may subsidize employers so as to maintain maximum employment levels, even when product demand falls off.

Each scheme has its costs, but each also serves to transfer the risk of unemployment from the relatively few who would normally be without a job to the whole population who must pay for the deficit or subsidy necessary to implement the guarantee. Whatever the approach, the role of the public sector is certain to be enlarged, and the cost of the public insurance will be borne by the many, not the few.

The insurance principle can be extended to virtually any area of social risk. William Letwin, for example, has described its extension to such matters as pollution and consumer product safety in his paper on the insurance state.[6] The risks of polluted air and water or defective products can be effectively transferred from the few who would normally bear them to all those who can be required to pay an insurance fee that guarantees they will either not suffer from the risk or will be compensated if they are injured. In each case, a societal decision is required in the public policy process that favors socializing the risk rather than leaving it privatized.

Richard Titmuss, in his analysis of modern social policy, argued that social costs and social insecurities are the product of a changing society and changing values.[7] If these personal disservices are not to be borne solely by the individuals upon whom they fall, then some form of redress must be made available. The law may offer redress through the awarding of damages, as in the case of the wrongful death caused by neligence. An alternative is for the individuals to insure against the risk, as through the purchase of an insurance policy. And lastly, there may be social services provided to some or all of the population so affected.[8] When he analyzed these alternatives less than a decade ago, Titmuss concluded that the United States was more prone to rely on legal redress, Great Britain on private insurance, and the Scandanavian countries on direct social services. What we are asserting with regard to the insurance state is that as legal redress has increasingly failed, guarantees of rights to services are being made in public policy, while the cost of those guarantees is spread across the whole population. It is an extension of the insurance ethic to the mitigation and avoidance of all risks associated with social change itself.

Limits of the Insurance State

The limits of the insurance state are unknown, but it is increasingly clear that there are substantial social costs associated with the large-scale transference of social risk. Criticisms of the welfare state frequently focus on the expense of administering a social system of transfer payments in a society that is increasingly dependent upon them. Direct dollar costs are only the most obvious costs in an insurance state, however. Of more serious consequence are the indirect costs of guaranteeing protection against a growing list of broadly defined risks (e.g., poor health, pollution) without a concomitant understanding of the secondary consequences that such protection may involve. The case was clearly drawn in the public health area during the recent crisis in medical malpractice insurance.

The Medical Malpractice Crisis, 1974-1976[b]

In terms we have used throughout this study, the problems associated with medical malpractice insurance are problems of availability and pricing. Beneath the surface issues, however, it is clear that the malpractice crisis is more than an insurance crisis alone; it is a complex of problems involving the practice of medicine, underlying social changes, and the entire system of social insurance. More importantly, the availability and pricing problems associated with malpractice insurance seem directly attributable to the expansion of the insurance state in the area of health care. In this it is illustrative of the problems involved in extending the insurance state and symptomatic of the types of difficulties that are occurring, or may reasonably be expected to occur, in other areas.

Manifestations of the Crisis

In early 1974 Mutual Insurance of Wausau (Wisconsin), the company that had carried malpractice insurance for physicians in New York State since 1949,

[b] I am indebted to Suzanne Mahler, a graduate of the Boston University MBA program in health care management, for research assistance on this matter.

announced an intention to withdraw coverage as of July 1, 1974, the end of their contract with the Medical Society of the State of New York. At the time MIW covered 27,000 of the 32,000 insured physicians in New York. The reasons for the withdrawal were quite simple: the company was incurring higher liability in the greater numbers of malpractice cases being brought to trial. Clyde Schleueter, president of the company, announced that even the higher premiums that the State Insurance Department had authorized would not be sufficient to cover the increased size of settlements; hence, the company had no option but to withdraw.

The State Medical Society had difficulty finding an insurer willing to write the requisite coverages. As the July 1 deadline approached, and no substitute insurer was named, word was leaking throughout the medical community about the astronomical rate increases being demanded as the *quid pro quo* for underwriting. A crisis atmosphere began to build, and it was not much relieved by the announcement that the Argonaut Insurance Company of Menlo Park, California had agreed to write a group policy on the 28,000 members of the Medical Society at a premium increase of 93.5 percent. The new average rate for most specialities rose to about $3500 per year.

The crisis did not abate and took a dramatic turn when in December 1974, barely 6 months into the new contract, Argonaut requested a 196.8 percent increase in premiums to be effective January 10, 1975. The company had lost $56 million in 1974 and indicated that if the request were denied by the insurance superintendent, Argonaut would be forced to discontinue coverage at the end of the contract period. The proposed increase would affect all medical specialities and the new average premium rate would escalate to nearly $10,000.[9]

On January 6, 1975, only a few days after the company had announced that it would also seek a 185 percent increase in hospital malpractice rates, an agreement was announced between the State Insurance Superintendent and Argonaut whereby the rate requests were withdrawn with the proviso that the company would terminate all physician and hospital malpractice coverage in July 1975. Insurers, insureds, and regulators alike knew that a major crisis was looming.

On January 28, 1975 the New York State Senate responded by passing a measure that required all insurers who underwrote personal injury liability policies to participate in an insurance pool to underwrite medical malpractice coverage. The insurers objected vigorously and lobbied against the bill. Nevertheless, pressures from physicians, hospitals, and the public swayed the legislators into creating the Medical Malpractice Insurance Association, a joint underwriting association of insurers. Under the legislation, the MMIA was required to write malpractice insurance for a period of 6 years and to issue policies to any physicians or hospital that applied; discounts were to be provided to new physicians and those with limited practices, and rates were to be established by specialty groups.

In June 1975 the MMIA filed a rate request for a 100 percent increase over Argonaut's rates for physicians and a 194.6 percent increase for hospitals. The State Insurance Department eventually disapproved the request, granting only a 20 percent increase in rates. At the same time, the governor and legislature agreed on the necessity of a special panel to review the entire malpractice problem and to report to the governor on possible courses of action. The governor received the report in early January 1976.

New York was only one of a number of states facing a malpractice insurance crisis. Indeed, by late 1975 thirty-five states had created special panels and commissions to review the malpractice crisis. The U.S. Department of Health, Education, and Welfare (HEW) was conducting a national study and congressional committees in both the United States Senate and House of Representatives initiated hearings into the matter. Medical malpractice and the medical malpractice insurance crisis had become major items on the public policy agenda.

Dimensions of Interpenetration

Simplification of the causes and reasons for the malpractice insurance crisis are dangerous or foolish, or both. Indeed, a review of the factors contributing to the crisis suggests that there are either no devils in this matter or that we are all devils! Rather than purport to offer a definitive explanation of the many factors contributing to the problem, we shall simply identify some of the more fundamental elements contributing to this complex interpenetration of actors and influences.

Perhaps the central phenomenon of medical practice since World War II has been the emergence of the medical specialties as the principal area of physicians' employment. Indeed, so dramatic has this trend become that an availability crisis has developed with respect to general and family practitioners. Specialization has resulted in two important effects. First, a technologic imperative, as Victor Fuchs called it, has emerged within the medical profession that recommends that any procedure of possible value to the patient be done.[10] Hence certain practices have become normative quite apart from their value in any cost-benefit context. The transition from a state of medical practice where such procedures are used only in cases of clear need to a state in which they are customary and more broadly dispensed served to reinforce the specialty trends. Inevitably, medical frontiers are pushed forward and scientific advancement, rather than patient cost or comfort, becomes the prime mover in producing change in medical care.

The importance of medical specialization is accented when one considers that the transition in providing such services from *need only* to *standard practice* basis has been accompanied by a broadening of public access to health care services. Access has increased in two distinct ways. First, direct access has been facilitated by programs designed to make medical care available to new segments of the population. The wide range of public health programs at the state and local level has served to generate more diagnosis, and inevitably, more demand for the treatment of diagnosed illness. But the most dramatic change in recent decades has occurred at the federal level, where the Medicaid and Medicare programs have greatly expanded the population entitled to receive medical diagnosis and treatment. Secondly, indirect access to the health care system has long been facilitated by the existence and spread of third-party compensation arrangements. Private-carrier health insurance plans and programs such as Blue Cross/Blue Shield have done much to create a greater demand for health care services within the existing institutional framework.

The second great effect of specialization arises from the combined impact of heightened demand for health care and the ethic of maximum medical care for each patient. In the absence of a proportionately expanding supply of physicians to service the new demand, the existing institutional system becomes overloaded. This has meant heavier patient loads for private physicians. In turn this has also led to an increasing role for hospital emergency rooms, clinics, and out-patient services. Moreover, it has generated new service institutions in the medical system, such as Health Maintenance Organizations, and new contractual arrangements for the operation of emergency rooms and such specialized services as surgery by groups of physicians. These new institutions, in turn, have become devices for distributing the fund of available specialized services.

The growth of medical specialization and the spread of such services to larger segments of the population has produced dramatic changes in public expectations about the quality of care that a patient can expect in the health care system. As patient awareness of specialty practice grows, the anticipation is that a physician's or a hospital's actual performance will approach the level of the best possible care. That one cannot personally afford to pay for such care is no deterrent to this expectation when it is also understood that either a third-party carrier (insurer) or government will insure the payment for such service. It is the highpoint of the insurance state, for the patient is insured against less than maximum medical care by a public guarantee to medical care providers that they will receive payment. The system is costly, of course, but public opinion polls have continued to demonstrate public support for a health care system that guarantees each person the right to medical care.

Whatever the support for maximum therapeutic patient care, it has also produced rising expectations about the quality of diagnostic medical services. It is one thing to argue that an individual with a particular illness is entitled to the best care medical science can provide, yet quite another to argue that the best diagnostic service also be given to each patient. In many areas of medical practice, the lines between generic disease and psychological disease are difficult to delineate and may be made only by long-term diagnostic observation. In other cases, only the most sophisticated (and expensive) diagnostic testing can detect a disease in its earliest stages.[11] Should this too be required in the case of all patients, whatever their ability to pay? There is at least some legal precedent for such an extension of the insurance state principles. In a landmark case, *Helling v. Carey,*[12] the Washington Supreme Court overturned a jury verdict in favor of two ophthalmologists who failed to perform a glaucoma pressure test on a woman under 40 years of age. Under the prevailing professional standards in the community, the test was not ordinarily performed on persons in this age group. But the court found that the failure to perform this test resulted in severe damage to the woman's visual field and concluded that the physicians were guilty of negligence. The glaucoma test was relatively inexpensive to administer and it was a consideration that influenced the court. More importantly, however, is the fact that the physicians were held to a standard of care notably beyond prevailing community standards, a standard that suggests that even in diagnosis, the prudent level of medical service is that which approaches the maximum level of service. If one ignores the cost issue temporarily, it is logical to believe that the sophisticated body-scanning technology that now exists and is in limited use will soon be a normal part of the diagnostic routine, not the exceptional test that it is now considered to be.[13] The issue of cost, of course, cannot be ignored, but that is where the principle of the insurance state becomes operative. How much better, some will argue, to spread the cost of the scanning technology over the whole population—thereby requiring each to pay only an incremental amount—rather than leaving the great cost burden to only the few who can afford the test? It is the heart of the insurance state argument—that the risk that falls on a few can be eliminated by spreading the cost over the population—extended to the diagnostic and preventive, as well as the therapeutic aspects of health care.

Against this background of a more sophisticated medical science, a broadened distribution of foremost therapeutic care, and a growing tendency to require similar standards in diagnosis and prevention, one must add the consideration of changing social relationships. Primary among these is the passing away of the traditional patient-physician association. As patients deal with specialists about whom they know little and who know little about them beyond their medical profile, the human glue of trust and personal confidence that marked the traditional family physician-patient relation becomes ever less binding. What results is a more abstract and sterile relationship, one that calls for new types of mediating influences. Hence, institutional ombudsmen replace the congenial family physician; legalistic "bills of rights" for hospital patients supplant the counsel of the family doctor, the neighborliness of a nursing staff, and the humanism of the community hospital.[14]

Another manifestation, of course, is the increasing tendency of patients to file malpractice suits against the specialists. It has been estimated that malpractice suits are increasing at the rate of 10 percent annually,[15] a number that threatens the courts, the medical community, and the insurance industry. At a time when the quality of medical care is probably better (practice at the frontier again!) and more broadly distributed, the growing volume of malpractice suits is a peculiar anomaly of the insurance state. The argument has long been made by trial lawyers and aggrieved plaintiffs that the burden of the lawsuits is not really placed on the physicians or hospital because they have third-party protection in the form of malpractice coverage. But as the events in New York, California, and elsewhere have proven, it really does hurt the physician, the hospital, and ultimately, the patient. First, an availability crisis occurs; then a rate crisis follows; eventually both occur simultaneously. At that point, as the experience in California has shown, a crisis in medical care itself develops. In San Francisco physicians who could either not get malpractice coverage or who could obtain it only at astronomical rates refused to practice. A physicians' strike occurred in Los Angeles.[16] Even the American Medical Association House of Delegates officially approved the use of slowdowns.[17] Across the country physicians responded to the existing incentives. Many closed offices and retired; others moved to localities where malpractice insurance was guaranteed or where rates were substantially less. In the end, the insurance state had produced a system wherein the intended beneficiaries became the ultimate victims. To paraphrase Alice in Wonderland, the world became increasingly curious.

Resolving the Malpractice Crisis

Despite the implication above, the medical malpractice insurance crisis does not appear close to resolution. The systemic relations that have emerged under the aegis of the insurance state themselves seem to obstruct creative solutions to the problems.

Variations of the joint underwriting associations suggested by the New York Medical Malpractice Insurance Association have been developed in a number of states as a device for providing malpractice coverage, although like New York, increased rates have been the price of such availability. More importantly, where such associations are not able to require all purchasers of malpractice coverage to secure it through the association, better risks—e.g., those who can secure coverage elsewhere at lower rates—will leave the association. In Massachusetts, for example, 11 hospitals that claimed they had been assessed only $250,000 in claims and awards in the past 5 years yet were required to pay $8 million in premiums to a state-sponsored joint underwriting association chose to establish their own insurance company in the Caribbean for the purpose of insuring themselves at considerable savings. While the state's insurance commissioner fulminated that such action was within the letter, but clearly against the spirit of the (joint underwriting) law, the hospitals argued that their preferred risk status made it reasonable for them to separate themselves from the poorer risks.[18] The effect of such preferred risk withdrawals, of course, is to inevitably raise the rates of those poorer risks that are forced to stay in the joint underwriting association.

An alternative that is often discussed is the transformation of the entire malpractice system into a no-fault insurance arrangement.[19] Most acknowledge that such a system will be considerably more expensive to operate, but if it guarantees top quality medical care in diagnosis and treatment and insures physicians against malpractice problems, is it not worth the cost? Once again, the reasoning of the insurance state's proponents is alluring.

Standardization of professional practice standards is still another route advocated as a means of resolving the problems underlying the malpractice issue. The establishment of Professional Standards Review Organizations (PSROs) on a local, regional, or even national basis is seriously discussed as a means by which levels of medical practice can be stabilized and improved. The great number of problems in developing meaningful standards for an almost unlimited number of complex care and diagnostic situations suggest that much effort is being expended to develop guidelines that must necessarily remain somewhat vague. At best, existence of the standards and the conformity they encourage may provide a better defense in malpractice cases than currently exists. Indeed, in many state legislatures the price that the medical profession has been forced to pay for a state-supported malpractice insurance plan is acceptance of a professional standards mechanism.

Whatever course is selected to resolve the malpractice insurance dilemma—joint associations, a no-fault system, or PSROs—the prospects for success are limited. The systematic relationship between physicians, hospitals, insurers, and patients that is known as the malpractice system is only a part of the much larger health care system. Generic factors in that larger system have produced the disequilibrium in the malpractice subsystem, and for that reason, it is unlikely that tinkering with the malpractice mechanism alone will permanently resolve the crisis. Rather, each bit of tinkering increases the need to require that all physicians, or all hospitals, or all insurers, or all patients participate in a compulsory scheme designed to stabilize the system. Ultimately, the insurance state must ensure that disequilibrium in one part of the health care system will not jeopardize the whole system. If the only way of guaranteeing the working of the whole system is to compel some relevant public or set of actors to do what they would prefer not to do, the tendency will be to force all to bear the burden of making the system work. The insurance state can only survive as an ideal if the public wishes it to survive; it can only survive as a reality if the agenda of guarantees is expanded.

Private Insurers and the Insurance State

The emergence of the insurance state has served the interests of private insurance carriers in many respects, including the expansion of new markets, the guarantee of a right of participation in developing areas of social insurance, and by providing strong ideological support for the insurance ethic. But further extension of the insurance state poses serious problems for private insurers. New risks exist for the private insurance industry and the responses of insurance managers to them will foretell the future of the private-carrier business.

The insurance state has created several direct and specific threats to the private carriers. First, as such areas as health, product safety, and employment have become affected with the public interest, there has been a tendency to argue in favor of public rights to health care, safe products, or jobs. This, in turn, has supported the argument that the health of a nation's citizens, protection against unsafe products, or guaranteed jobs are really public goods whose supply should appropriately be guaranteed by government. To the extent that this argument gains public support, the case in favor of government programs to ensure the existence of these public goods grows. If, as in the case of health insurance or product safety insurance, private carriers cannot or will not supply all of the coverage demanded, an incentive exists for establishment of a public insurance plan. When this occurs, the primacy of the private insurance system is itself called into question.[c]

The risk to private carriers from more public insurance programs is both ideological and financial in nature. Ideologically, the populus becomes increasingly attuned to the existence of government as an insurer. Moreover, each new public program encourages comparison and debate about the desirability of using government programs as a supplement to the private system or formulating comprehensive public insurance programs. The financial aspects of public programs constitute a second major threat to the private carriers, this involving a demand that preferred risks, as well as poor risks, be included in the public plan. The deficits that government-sponsored insurance programs frequently run has led budget-conscious administrators of those programs to argue that either more funds must be given to underwrite the deficit or that more good risks be included in the plan to offset the losses of the bad risks.[20] These good risks, of course, can come only at the expense of the private insurers who would thereby lose both premium volume and actual clients.

The very ideology of the insurance state also constitutes a specific threat to the private carriers because it is an ideology that supports the idea of compulsory participation. As this principle of many contributing so that an injured few will not bear the full burden of loss is extended to various areas of social activity, it becomes clear that it is sometimes necessary to compel the unwilling to participate, for if they do not, the insurance scheme must fail. The example of the joint malpractice underwriting association in which insurers must participate symbolizes precisely such a threat for the insurance companies. Forced participation in order to make insurance available to the public may be unacceptable on principle to some insurance executives; but it is absolutely intolerable when compulsory participation is coupled with restricted rates. Yet

[c]This is exactly the case with regard to national health insurance where some argue for building on the private carrier system while others favor a government operated plan.

that is what occurred in the malpractice case in New York and, most recently, in attempts to establish an underwriting association to guarantee product liability insurance to small manufacturers in Massachusetts.[21] When insurance becomes a public good, it can no longer be priced as a private good. For the unwilling insurers who must provide that public good, that is an increasingly unsatisfactory state of affairs.

Still another threat posed by the insurance state is the ironic emergence of self insurance as an ever more important facet of American insurance practice. Risk management, as the profession has become known in the past decade, involves a professional assessment of which of a number of alternative courses of action offer an individual or organization the best opportunity for securing insurance protection at a minimum price. At one time, this involved the relatively simple process of comparing the services and prices of competing insurers. Since then it has involved comparison with government program alternatives, and most recently, it has involved the analysis of how to self-insure (i.e., establish reserves) against risk. For good risks in particular, self insurance is an increasingly popular device for risk management. Ultimately, such developments further serve to erode the markets available to the private carriers.

Today, the private-carrier insurance industry finds itself in a situation where it must chart a strategy between the growing presence of public insurance plans on the one hand and the increasing willingness of buyers to explore self-insurance possibilities on the other. So complete has the interpenetration between the industry and society become that growing public acceptance of the insurance ethic has ironically produced an insurance state that now threatens the long-term outlook for the industry. This is a new kind of risk, one that the industry has never before faced, and it is surely one to which the conventional adaptive and manipulative patterns of response are unsuited. Whether the industry as a whole, and private insurers individually, can respond in an appropriate manner remains an unanswered and vital question.

Notes

1. The distinction between an organization's primary and secondary involvements with society is made in Preston and Post [136]. The thesis is that a firm is responsible to society for the primary and secondary involvement consequences of its activities but not for matters otherwise unrelated to it.

2. See, for example, 1975 *Social Reporting Program of the Life and Health Insurance Business* (New York: Clearinghouse on Corporate Social Responsibility, 1975). This reporting program has expanded over the course of the past 5 years.

3. See Institute of Life Insurance, *TAP Reports*, Numbers 10-13 in particular, published since 1975.

4. A concise discussion of the difference between public and private goods is found in Buchanan [19].

5. Letwin [93].

6. See Letwin [93].

7. Titmuss [158].

8. Titmuss [158] p. 76.

9. See *New York Times*, December 23, 1974, p. 1.

10. Fuchs [56].

11. See *New York Times*, "Popular New X-Ray Unit Could Raise Cost of Care," May 8, 1976, p. 1.

12. [83 Wash.2d 514, 419 P2d 981 (1974)] reversing [8 Wash. App. 1005 (1972)].

13. *New York Times*, "Popular New X-Ray Unit Could Raise Cost of Care," May 8, 1976, p. 1.

14. See Annas [4] and Annas and Healey [5].

15. See Brook, Brutoco, and Williams [18] p. 1197.

16. Brook, Brutoco, and Williams [18] p. 1214.

17. See Altman, "A.M.A. Backs Doctors Curbing Service," *New York Times*, June 18, 1975, p. 81.

18. L. McLaughlin, "Eleven Hospitals Set Up Insurance Firm," *Boston Globe*, March 14, 1976. Also *Boston Globe* editorial entitled "Malpractice Innovators," March 21, 1976, p. A6. The hospitals involved, all affiliates of Harvard University, pledged that the savings achieved through the plan would be passed on to patients in the form of lower costs.

19. See the discussion in Annas, Katz, and Trakimas [6] and Havighurst [67].

20. Federal Insurance Administrator, J. Robert Hunter, for example, recommended that the federal crime insurance program be terminated by Congress because the structure of the program has proven unduly narrow. See *New York Times*, January 5, 1976, p. 1. Also, Edmund Gravely, Jr., "U.S. Crime Insurance: It Seemed Like a Good Idea," Sunday *New York Times*, March 14, 1976, "Week in Review," p. 4.

21. R.S. Kindleberger, "Small Firms Say Lack of Insurance May Be Fatal," *Boston Globe*, January 13, 1976, p. 1. Also R.S. Kindleberger, "Mass. Manufacturers Seek Aid on Liability," *Boston Globe*, January 14, 1976, p. 59. The most recent academic argument on extension of the no-fault concept to product liability is found in O'Connell [117].

Bibliography

Bibliography

1. Ackerman, Robert W. "How Companies Respond to Social Demands." *Harvard Business Review* (July-August, 1973): pp. 88-98.
2. American Conservation Company, comp. "The Bible of Life Insurance." *Reports and Biography of Elizur Wright*, Chicago: American Conservation Company, 1932.
3. Andrews, Kenneth R. *The Concept of Corporate Strategy.* Homewood, Illinois: Dow Jones-Irwin, Inc., 1971.
4. Annas, George. *The Rights of Hospital Patients.* New York: Avon Books Inc., 1975.
5. Annas, George, and T. Healey. "The Patient Rights Advocate: Redefining The Doctor-Patient Relationship in the Hospital Context." *Vanderbilt Law Review* 27 (1974): 243.
6. Annas, George, Barbara Katz, and Robert Trakimas. "Medical Malpractice Litigation under National Health Insurance: Essential or Expendable?" *Duke Law Journal* (1975): 1335.
7. Barrett, Francis D. Jr. "Congress v. The Insurance Industry," *The Annals of the Society of CPCU* Vol. 25, no. 1 (March 1972): pp. 63-73.
8. Bell, Daniel. *The Coming of Post-Industrial Society.* New York: Basic Books, Inc., 1973.
9. Belth, Joseph M. *Life Insurance: A Consumer's Handbook.* Bloomington, Indiana: Indiana University Press, 1973.
10. Bendix, Rheinhard. *Work and Authority in Industry*, New York: John Wiley, Inc., 1956.
11. Berman, Harold J., and William R. Greiner. *The Nature and Functions of Law*, 3d edition, Mineola, Foundation Press, 1974.
12. Bernstein, George. "The Federal Riot Reinsurance and Flood Insurance Programs," an address by Mr. Bernstein, Federal Insurance Administrator, to the state national directors of the National Association of Insurance Agents, 1969.
13. Bernstein, Marver. *Regulating Business by Independent Commission.* Princeton, N.J.: Princeton University Press, 1955.
14. Best, Alfred M., Inc., *Best's Aggregates and Averages.* Annual Editions, 1959-1973.
15. Bickelhaupt, David L. *Transition to Multiple-Line Insurance Companies.* Homewood, Illinois: Richard D. Irwin, Inc., 1961.
16. Boorstin, Daniel J. *The Americans: The Democratic Experience.* New York: Random House, Inc., 1973.

17. Brandeis, Louis D. *Other People's Money*. New York: Harper and Row, 1967.

18. Brook, Robert H., Rudolf L. Brutoco, and Kathleen N. Williams. "The Relationship between Medical Malpractice and Quality of Care." *Duke Law Journal* (1975): 1197.

19. Buchanan, James. *Bases for Collective Action.*Morristown, N.J.: General Learning Press, 1970.

20. Buckley, Walter. *Sociology and Modern Systems Theory*. Englewood Cliffs, New Jersey: Prentice-Hall, Inc., 1967.

21. Buley, R. Carlyle. *The American Life Convention, 1906-1952*, Vols. 1 and 2, New York: Appleton Century Crofts, 1953.

22. Buley, R. Carlyle. *The Equitable Life Assurance Society of the United States, 1859-1964*, Vols. 1 and 2, New York: Appleton Century Crofts, 1967.

23. Cardozo, Benjamin, *The Nature of the Judicial Process.*

24. Chamberlain, Neil W. *The Limits of Corporate Responsibility*. New York: Basic Books, Inc., 1973.

25. Chandler, Alfred D., Jr. *Strategy and Structure*. Cambridge, Mass.: M.I.T. Press, 1962.

26. Chatov, Robert. "The Role of Ideology in the American Corporation," in Dow Votaw and S. Prakash Sethi. *The Corporate Dilemma.* Englewood Cliffs, New Jersey: Prentice-Hall, Inc., 1973, pp. 50-73.

27. Chatov, Robert. *Corporate Financial Reporting: Public or Private Control?* Riverside, New Jersey: Free Press, 1975.

28. Christensen, C.R., Kenneth R. Andrews, and Joseph L. Bower. *Business Policy*, 3d edition, Homewood, Illinois: Richard D. Irwin, Inc., 1973.

29. Clough, Shepard B. *A Century of American Life Insurance: A History of the Mutual Life Insurance Company of New York, 1843-1943.* New York: Columbia University Press, 1946.

30. Cochran, Thomas C. *Business in American Life: A History*. New York: McGraw-Hill Book Co., 1972.

31. Cochran, Thomas C. *Social Change in America: The Twentieth Century*. New York: Harper & Row, Inc., 1972.

32. Cohen, Kalman J. and Richard M. Cyert. "Strategy: Formulation, Implementation, and Monitoring." *The Journal of Business*, XLVI, no. 3 (1973).

33. Collins, John W. and Chris G. Ganotis. "Managerial Attitudes toward Corporate Social Responsibility." In *The Unstable Ground*, S. Prakash Sethi, ed., Los Angeles: Melville, 1973, pp. 303-320.

34. Commonwealth of Pennsylvania, Insurance Department. *A Shoppers Guide to Life Insurance*, and supplements thereto. April 1972.

35. Crowe, Robert, and Ronald C. Horn. "The Meaning of Risk." *The Journal of Risk and Insurance* (September, 1967): pp. 459-474.

36. Cyert, Richard M. and James G. March. *A Behavioral Theory of the Firm.* Englewood Cliffs, New Jersey: Prentice-Hall, Inc., 1963.

37. Dacey, Norman. *What's Wrong with Your Life Insurance.* New York: Crowell-Collier Press, 1962.

38. Davidson, Kenneth M. "Government Role in the Economy: Implications for the Relief of Poverty." *Journal of Urban Law*, 43, no. 1 (1970): pp. 1-88.

39. Davis, Keith, and Robert L. Blomstrom. *Business, Society, and Environment: Social Power and Social Response*, 2d edition. New York: McGraw-Hill Book Co., 1971.

40. Denenberg, Herbert S. "The 1970s–The Decade of No-Fault and the Year of the Dog." *Best's Review.* March 1971.

41. Denenberg, Herbert, et al. *Risk and Insurance.* Englewood Cliffs, New Jersey: Prentice-Hall, Inc., 1964.

42. Department of Transportation. *Automobile Insurance and Compensation Study: Public Attitudes toward Auto Insurance.* A Report of the Survey Research Center, Institute for Social Research, The University of Michigan to the Department of Transportation. March 1970.

43. Douglass, Elish P. *The Coming of Age of American Business: Three Centuries of Enterprise, 1600-1900.* Chapel Hill, N.C.: University of North Carolina Press, 1971.

44. Edelman, Murray. *The Symbolic Uses of Politics.* Urbana, Ill.: University of Illinois Press, 1964.

45. Emery, F.E., and E.L. Trist. "The Causal Texture of Organizational Environments." *Human Relations*, 18 (1965): pp. 21-32.

46. Epstein, Edwin M. "Dimensions of Corporate Power, Part 1." *California Management Review*, XVI, no. 2 (Winter 1973).

47. Epstein, Edwin M. "Dimensions of Corporate Power, Part 2." *California Management Review* XVI, no. 4 (Summer 1974): pp. 32-47.

48. Equitable Life Assurance Society of the United States. *Henry Baldwin Hyde: A Biographical Sketch.* New York: Equitable Life Assurance Society of the United States, 1901.

49. Etzioni, Amitai. *Modern Organizations.* Englewood Cliffs, New Jersey: Prentice-Hall, Inc., 1964.

50. Ezeel, John. *Fortune's Merry Wheel.* Cambridge: Harvard University Press, 1960.

51. Fortune, "The Fortune Directory." *Fortune* (July 1973): pp. 120-127.

52. Fortune, "The Fortune Ratings." *Fortune* (July 1974).

53. Fouraker, Lawrence E., and John M. Stopford. "Organizational Structure and Multinational Strategy." *Administrative Science Quarterly*, 13 (1968): pp. 47-64.

54. Friedman, Lawrence M. *A History of American Law*. New York: Simon and Schuster, 1973.

55. Friedman, Milton. *Capitalism and Freedom*. Chicago: University of Chicago Press, 1963.

56. Fuchs, Victor, "The Growing Demand for Medical Care." 279 *New England Journal of Medicine* 190, 1968.

57. Galbraith, John Kenneth. *The New Industrial State*. Boston: Houghton Mifflin Co., 1967.

58. Galbraith, John Kenneth. *Economics and the Public Purpose*. Boston: Houghton Mifflin Co., 1973.

59. Golding, C.E., and D. King-Page. *Lloyd's*. New York: McGraw-Hill Book Co., 1952.

60. Goldsmith, Raymond W. *Financial Intermediaries in the American Economy since 1900*. National Bureau of Economic Research Study, Princeton, N.J.: Princeton University Press, 1958.

61. Greene, Mark R. *Risk and Insurance*. Cincinnati: Southwestern Publishing Company, 1962.

62. Greene, Mark R. *Risk Aversion, Insurance, and The Future*. Bloomington, Indiana: Graduate School of Business, Division of Research, Indiana University, 1971.

63. Gross, Bertram, M. "Social Systems Accounting." In Raymond A. Bauer, ed., *Social Indicators*. Cambridge, Mass.: M.I.T. Press, 1966.

64. Grotta, Daniel. "The Ralph Nader of Insurance." *Saturday Review* (July 1, 1972): pp. 34-41.

65. Gusfield, Joseph L. "Social Structure and Moral Reform: A Case Study of Women's Christian Temperance Union." *American Journal of Sociology* 61 (1955): pp. 221-232.

66. Hall, Richard H. *Organizations: Structure and Process*. Englewood Cliffs, N.J.: Prentice-Hall, Inc., 1972.

67. Havighurst, Clark. "Medical Adversity Insurance–Has Its Time Come?" *Duke Law Journal* (1975): 1233.

68. Hayek, Frederick. *The Road to Serfdom*. Chicago: University of Chicago Press, 1944.

69. Hayek, Frederick. "The Corporation in a Democratic Society." In *Management and Corporations, 1985*, Melvin Anshen and George Bach, eds., New York: McGraw-Hill Book Company, 1960.

70. Hellriegel, Don, and John W. Slocum, Jr. *Management: A Contingency Approach*. Reading, Mass.: Addison-Wesley Publishing Co., 1974.

71. Hensley, Roy J. *Competition, Regulation, and the Public Interest in Nonlife Insurance.* Berkeley and Los Angeles: University of California Press, 1962.

72. Hooker, Richard. *Aetna Life Insurance Company: Its First Hundred Years.* Hartford, Connecticut: Aetna Life Insurance Company, 1956.

73. Houston, David B. "Risk, Insurance, and Sampling." *The Journal of Risk and Insurance* (December 1964): pp. 511-538.

74. Hurst, James Willard. *The Legitimacy of the Business Corporation in the Law of the United States, 1780-1970.* Charlottesville: The University Press of Virginia, 1970.

75. Institute of Life Insurance. *1959 Annual Meeting and Staff Reports.* New York: Institute of Life Insurance, 1960.

76. Institute of Life Insurance. *1971 Life Insurance Fact Book.* New York: Institute of Life Insurance, 1971.

77. Institute of Life Insurance, Clearinghouse on Corporate Social Responsibility. *A Report on the $2 Billion Urban Investment Program of the Life Insurance Business.* New York: Institute of Life Insurance, 1973.

78. James, Marquis. *Biography of a Business, 1792-1942.* Insurance Company of North America, Indianapolis: Bobbs-Merrill Co., 1942.

79. James, Marquis. *The Metropolitan Life.* New York: The Viking Press, 1947.

80. Joskow, Paul L. "Cartels, Competition, and Regulation in the Property-Liability Insurance Industry." *The Bell Journal of Economics and Management Science*, 4, no. 3 (Autumn 1973): pp. 375-427.

81. Keeton, Robert E., and Jeffrey O'Connell. *Basic Protection for the Traffic Victim: A Blueprint for Reforming Automobile Insurance.* Boston: Little, Brown and Company, 1965.

82. Keller, Morton. *The Life Insurance Enterprise 1885-1910: A Study in the Limits of Corporate Power.* Cambridge, Mass.: Belknap Press and Harvard University Press, 1963.

83. Kenney, Roger. *Fundamentals of Fire and Casualty Insurance.* Dedham, Mass.: Kenney Insurance Studies, 1949.

84. Kimball, Spencer. *Insurance and Public Policy: A Study in the Legal Implementation of Social and Economic Public Policy, Based on Wisconsin Records, 1834-1959.* Madison, Wisconsin: University of Wisconsin Press, 1960.

85. Kimball, Spencer, and Herbert S. Denenberg, eds. *Insurance, Government, and Social Policy.* Homewood, Illinois: Richard D. Irwin, Inc., 1969.

86. Knight, Frank H. *Risk, Uncertainty, and Profit.* Boston: Houghton Mifflin Co., 1921.

87. Kohlmeier, Louis M., Jr. *The Regulators: Watchdog Agencies and the Public Interest.* New York: Harper and Row, Inc., 1969.

88. Kolber, Jay. "Life Insurers and Social Responsibility." *Best's Review* (Life/Health edition) March 1972.

89. Krooss, Herman E., and Martin R. Blyn. *A History of Financial Intermediaries.* New York: Random House, Inc., 1971.

90. Lauer, Robert H. *Perspectives on Social Change.* Boston: Allyn and Bacon, Inc., 1973.

91. Lawrence, Paul R., and Jay W. Lorsch. *Organization and Environment.* Cambridge, Mass.: Harvard University Press, 1967.

92. Lawrence, Paul R., and Jay W. Lorsch. *Developing Organizations: Diagnosis and Action.* Reading, Mass.: Addison-Wesley Publishing Co., 1969.

93. Letwin, William. "Social Responsibility of Business in an Insurance State." Paper presented at the conference on "Business and Society: State of the Art and Program for the Future," held at University of California at Berkeley, March 24-26, 1975.

94. Levitan, Sar. *The Great Society's Poor Law, A New Approach to Poverty.* Baltimore: The Johns Hopkins Press, 1964.

95. Livermore, Shaw. *Early American Land Companies.* New York: The Commonwealth Fund, 1939.

96. Lodge, George C. "Business and the Changing Society." *Harvard Business Review* (March-April 1974): pp. 59-72.

97. Long, John D. *Ethics, Morality, and Insurance: A Long Range Outlook.* Bloomington, Indiana: Bureau of Business Research, Graduate School of Business, Indiana University, 1971.

98. Long, John D. "The Ethical Pillars of Insurance." *CLU Journal* 26, no. 1 (January 1972): pp. 61-67.

99. Lowi, Theodore J. *The End of Liberalism.* New York: W.W. Norton and Co., 1969.

100. Mangum, Garth L. *The Emergence of Manpower Policy.* New York: Holt, Rinehart and Winston, Inc., 1969.

101. Maurer, John G., ed. *Readings in Organization Theory: Open System Approaches.* New York: Random House, Inc., 1971.

102. May, Earl C., and Will Ousler. *The Prudential.* Garden City, N.Y.: Doubleday and Company, Inc., 1950.

103. Mayerson, Allen L. "An Inside Look at Insurance Regulation." *Journal of Risk and Insurance* 32, no. 1 (March 1965): pp. 51-75.

104. McConnell, Grant. *Private Power and American Democracy.* New York: Alfred A. Knopf, Inc., 1966.

105. McGill, Dan M. *Life Insurance.* Rev. ed., Homewood, Illinois: Richard D. Irwin, Inc., 1966.

106. Michelbacher, G.F., and Nestor R. Roos. *Multiple-Line Insurers: Their*

Nature and Operation, 2d edition. New York: McGraw-Hill Book Co., 1970.

107. Michels, Robert. *Political Parties.* New York: The Free Press, 1962.

108. Milgram, Stanley. *Obedience to Authority: An Experimental View.* New York: Harper and Row, Inc., 1974.

109. Moynihan, Daniel P. *Maximum Feasible Misunderstanding.* New York: The Free Press, 1969.

110. Muir, William K. *Prayer in the Public Schools: Law and Attitude Change.* Chicago: University of Chicago Press, 1967.

111. National Advisory Commission on Civil Disorders. *Report of the National Advisory Commission on Civil Disorders* (aka the "Kerner Commission Report"). Washington, D.C.: U.S. Government Printing Office, 1968.

112. National Association of Insurance Commissioners. *Annual Reports.*

113. National Underwriter. *Appraisal 75*, Property and Casualty edition, sec. II. National Underwriter, Inc., 1972.

114. New York State. *Testimony taken before the Joint Committee of the Senate and Assembly of the State of New York.* (To investigate and examine into the business and affairs of life insurance companies doing business in the State of New York) Vols. 1-10. Albany, N.Y.: Brandow Printing Co., State Printers, 1905.

115. Oates, James F., Jr. *Business and Social Change: Life Insurance Looks to the Future.* New York: McGraw-Hill Book Co., 1968.

116. O'Connell, Jeffrey. "Living with Life Insurance." *The New York Times Magazine*, May 19, 1974, pp. 34ff.

117. O'Connell, Jeffrey. *Ending Insult to Injury.* Urbana, Illinois: University of Illinois Press, 1975.

118. O'Donnell, Terence, comp. *History of Life Insurance in its Formative Years.* Chicago: American Conservation Company, 1936.

119. Olson, Douglas G., and Howard E. Winklevoss. "Equity Based Variable Life Insurance." *Wharton Quarterly* (Summer 1971): pp. 26-40. Reprinted in Mark R. Greene and Paul Swadener, eds., *Insurance Insights.* Cincinnati: South-Western Publishing Co., 1974, pp. 305-319.

120. Orren, Karen. *Corporate Power and Social Change: The Politics of the Life Insurance Industry*. Baltimore: Johns Hopkins University Press, 1974.

121. Orren, Karen. "The Insurance Industry and The 'Other' Consumer." Mimeographed paper, 1974.

122. Parsons, Talcott. "An Approach to Psychological Theory in Terms of the Theory of Action." In *Psychology: A Study of Science.* Vol. 3, Sigmund Koch, ed., New York: McGraw-Hill Book Co., 1959, pp. 612-711.

123. Parsons, Talcott. *Structure and Process in Modern Societies.* New York: The Free Press, 1960.

124. Patterson, Edwin W. *The Insurance Commissioner in the United States.* Cambridge: Harvard University Press, 1927.

125. Perrow, Charles. "The Analysis of Goals in Complex Organizations." *American Sociological Review* 26, no. 6 (Dec. 1961).

126. Perrow, Charles. *Complex Organizations.* Glenview, Illinois: Scott-Foresman and Co., 1972.

127. Peterson, Robert A., William Rudelius, and Glenn L. Wood. "Spread of Marketing Innovations in a Service Industry." *The Journal of Business* 45, no. 4 (October 1972): pp. 435-496.

128. Pfeffer, Jeffrey. "Administrative Regulation and Licensing: Social Problem or Solution? *Social Problems* 21, no. 4 (April 1974): pp. 468-479.

129. Piven, Frances Fox, and Richard A. Cloward. *Regulating the Poor: The Functions of Public Welfare.* New York: Random House Inc., Vintage Books, 1971.

130. Post, James E. "Scanning the Environment–A Working Model." *Proceedings of the Academy of Management, 1973:* pp. 619-625.

131. Post, James E., and Marc Epstein. "Information Systems for Social Reporting." *Academy of Management Review*, forthcoming in 1977.

132. President's National Advisory Panel on Insurance in Riot-Affected Areas. *Hearings before the President's National Advisory Panel on Insurance in Riot-Affected Areas.* Washington, D.C.: U.S. Government Printing Office, 1968.

133. President's National Advisory Panel on Insurance in Riot-Affected Areas. *Meeting the Insurance Crisis of Our Cities.* Washington, D.C.: U.S. Government Printing Office, 1968.

134. Preston, Lee E. "Corporation and Society: The Search for a Paradigm." *Journal of Economic Literature* XLL, no. 2 (June 1975): pp. 434-453.

135. Preston, Lee E., and James E. Post. "The Third Managerial Revolution." *Academy of Management Journal.* (September 1974): pp. 476-486.

136. Preston, Lee E., and James E. Post. *Private Management and Public Policy.* Englewood Cliffs, New Jersey: Prentice-Hall, Inc., 1975.

137. Puth, Robert C. "Supreme Life: The History of a Negro Life Insurance Company, 1919-1962." *Business History Review* (Spring 1969): pp. 1-20.

138. Reich, Charles. "The New Property." *Yale Law Journal* 73 (1964): pp. 733-787.

139. Robinson, Richard D. "The Developing Countries, Development, and the Multinational Corporation." *The Annals* 403 (September 1972): pp. 67-79.

140. Rokes, Willis P. *No-Fault Insurance.* Santa Monica, California: Insurers Press, Inc., 1971.

141. Schein, Edgar II. *Organizational Psychology.* Englewood Cliffs, New Jersey: Prentice-Hall, Inc., 1965.

142. Schlusberg, Malcolm. "The Political Character of Business in an Organizational Regime." Mimeographed, 1974.

143. Scott, Bruce. "The Industrial State: Old Myths and New Realities." *Harvard Business Review* (March/April 1973): pp. 133-148.

144. Scott, Robert A. "The Factory as a Social Service Organization: Goal Displacement in Workshops for the Blind." *Social Problems* 15, no. 2 (Fall 1967): pp. 160-175.

145. Selznick, Philip. *T.V.A. and the Grass Roots.* Berkeley and Los Angeles: University of California Press, 1949.

146. Selznick, Philip. *Leadership in Administration.* New York: Harper and Row, Inc., 1957.

147. Sills, David L. *The Volunteers.* New York: The Free Press, 1957.

148. Smelser, Neil. *The Sociology of Economic Life.* Englewood Cliffs, New Jersey: Prentice-Hall, Inc., 1963.

149. Sobel, Robert. *The Big Board: A History of the New York Stock Market.* New York: The Free Press, 1965.

150. Sobel, Robert. *AMEX, A History of the American Stock Exchange, 1921-1971.* New York: Weybright and Talley, 1972.

151. Stalson, J. Owen. *Marketing Life Insurance: Its History in America.* Bryn Mawr, PA: McCahan Foundation, 1969. Originally published by Harvard University, 1942.

152. Stewart, Richard D. "Insurance Regulation: Current Issues and Problems." *The Annals* 400 (March 1972): pp. 59-68.

153. Stone, Mildred. *Since 1845: A History of the Mutual Benefit Life Insurance Company.* New Brunswick, N.J.: Rutgers University Press, 1957.

154. Swadener, Paul. "Gambling and Insurance Distinguished." *The Journal of Risk and Insurance* (September 1964): pp. 463-468.

155. Terreberry, Shirley. "The Evolution of Organizational Environments." *Administrative Science Quarterly* 12 (1968): pp. 590-613.

156. Thompson, James D. *Organizations in Action.* New York: McGraw-Hill Book Co., 1967.

157. Thompson, James D., and William J. McEwen. "Organizational Goals and Environment: Goal Setting as an Interaction Process." *Administrative Science Quarterly* 23 (February 1958).

158. Titmuss, Richard M. *Social Policy.* London: George Allen and Unwin, 1974; U.S. distribution by Pantheon Books.

159. Trennery, C.F. *The Origin and Early History of Insurance.* London: 1926.

160. Turnbull, John G., C. Arthur Williams, Jr., and Earl F. Cheit. *Economic and Social Security*, 3d edition. New York: Ronald Press Co., 1968.

161. U.S. House of Representatives. *Hearings before the Subcommittee on Commerce and Finance on Bills Relating to No-Fault Motor Vehicle*

Insurance, 92nd Congress, April 1971. Vols. 1-4. Washington, D.C.: U.S. Government Printing Office, 1971.

162. Vinovskis, Maris A. "The 1789 Life Table of Edward Wigglesworth." *Journal of Economic History* 31, no. 3 (September 1971): pp. 570-590.

163. Votaw, Dow, and S. Prakash Sethi. *The Corporate Dilemma.* Englewood Cliffs, New Jersey: Prentice-Hall, Inc., 1973.

164. Wenck, Thomas L. "The Historical Development of Standard Policies." *The Journal of Risk and Insurance* 35, no. 4 (December 1968): pp. 537-550.

165. Williams, C. Arthur, and Richard M. Heins. *Risk Management and Insurance.* New York: McGraw-Hill Book Co., 1964.

166. Williamson, Harold F., and Orange A. Smalley. *Northwestern Mutual Life: A Century of Trusteeship.* Evanston, Illinois: Northwestern University Press, 1957.

167. Woodward, Joan. *Industrial Organization: Theory and Practice.* London: Oxford University Press, 1965.

168. Worsley, Frank, and Glyn Griffith. *The Romance of Lloyd's.* New York: Hilman-Curl, Inc., 1936.

169. Wright, Kenneth M. "Social Concerns, Public Policy, and Life Insurance Investments." *CLU Journal* 26, no. 1 (January 1972): pp. 32-39.

Index

Index

About the Author

James E. Post is Assistant Professor of Management Policy, Boston University. A holder of degrees in economics, law, and management, he has engaged in extensive research into the nature and implications of changing management-society relationships. With Lee E. Preston, Professor Post is co-author of *Private Management and Public Policy* (Prentice-Hall, 1975); he has also authored and co-authored articles in academic and professional management journals.